D0521843

East Anglia

A
Literary
Pilgrimage

Peter Tolhurst

Foreword by
Elspeth Barker

Black Dog Books

First published in England 1996
by Black Dog Books
4 St John's Road, Bungay, Suffolk, NR35 1DJ

Reprinted 1997

Text and Illustrations Copyright ©1996 Peter Tolhurst
(unless otherwise acknowledged)
Foreword Copyright ©1996 Elspeth Barker

All rights reserved. No part of this publication may be reproduced, stored in a retrieval system, or transmitted in any form or by any means, electronic, mechanical, photocopying, recording or otherwise, without the prior permission of the Copyright holders.

A CIP record of this book is available from the British Library.

ISBN 0 - 9528839 - 0 - 2

Typeset in 10 point Times

Printed in Great Britain
by St Edmundsbury Press, Bury St Edmunds, Suffolk
Bound by WBC Bookbinders Ltd, Mid Glamorgan

To
The Memory
of
Harry Mountford

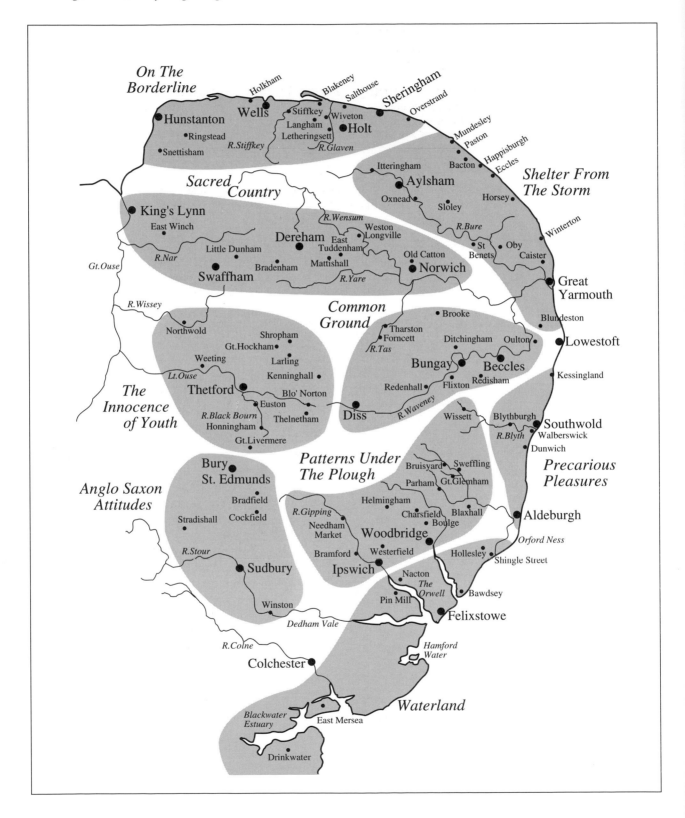

*On The
Borderline*

Holkham

Blakeney
Salthouse

Sheringham

Overstrand

Hunstanton   Wells
•Stiffkey   Wiveton   Mundesley
•Ringstead   Langham   Holt   Paston
Letheringsett   Happisburgh
•Snettisham   *R.Stiffkey*   Eccles
R.Glaven
Bacton

Sacred   Itteringham   *Shelter From
Country*   Aylsham   *The Storm*

King's Lynn   Oxnead   Horsey
East Winch   *R.Wensum*   Sloley   Winterton
Weston
Dereham   Longville   *R.Bure*   St
East   Benets   Oby
Little Dunham   Tuddenham   Caister
R.Nar   Old Catton
Gt.Ouse   Bradenham   Mattishall   Norwich   Great
Swaffham   Yarmouth
R.Yare
R.Wissey
Blundeston
Common
Ground   Brooke
Northwold   Tharston   Lowestoft
Shropham   Forncett   Ditchingham   Oulton
Gt.Hockham   *R.Tas*
Weeting   Larling   Bungay   Beccles   Kessingland
Lt.Ouse   Kenninghall   Redenhall   Redisham
The   Flixton
Innocence   Thetford   Blo' Norton   *R.Waveney*   Blythburgh
of Youth   •Euston   Diss   Wissett   Southwold
R.Black Bourn   Thelnetham   Walberswick
Honningham   Dunwich
Gt.Livermere
Bruisyard   Sweffling   *Precarious*
Bury   *Patterns Under*   *Pleasures*
St. Edmunds   *The Plough*   Parham   Gt.Glenham
Anglo Saxon   Bradfield   Helmingham   Charsfield   Blaxhall
Attitudes   Cockfield   *R.Gipping*   Boulge   Aldeburgh
Stradishall   Needham   Woodbridge   *Orford Ness*
Market
R.Stour   Bramford   Westerfield   Hollesley   Shingle Street
Sudbury   Ipswich   Nacton   *The*   Bawdsey
Pin Mill   *Orwell*
Winston   Felixstowe
Dedham Vale
Hamford
R.Colne   *Water*
Colchester   *Waterland*

*Blackwater
Estuary*   East Mersea

Drinkwater

Acknowledgements

I would like to thank the many individuals and organisations who dealt so patiently with my requests for information, especially those people who welcomed me into their homes and took such an interest in my work. Unless otherwise stated, properties mentioned in the text are not open to the public.

I owe a particular debt to the following for their personal recollections and generous help and for drawing my attention to some of the more obscure references: Elspeth Barker, Christopher Barker, Sebastian Barker, John Batten and Griffin Beale of The Powys Society, Commander Mark Cheyne, Caroline Davison, David Gentleman, Lady Harrod, Nicky Hodgkinson, Richard Mabey, Andrew Plumridge of The Folly Fellowship, Lady Spender, Anthony Thwaite, Enid Stevenson of The Hungate Bookshop, Arnold Wesker and Anne Williamson of The Henry Williamson Literary Estate. I must also thank the staff of the National Portrait Gallery, Norfolk Local Studies Library and the Suffolk Records Office.

My warmest thanks go to the following for helping nurse the book through to completion: to Bernice Owen of Diss Library whose efforts on my behalf made the research such a pleasure; to Rebecca Goff who transformed my handwritten manuscript into something legible; to my co-editors Sally Hirons and Marilyn Tolhurst for their advice and constant encouragement; and above all to Magdalen Bear for her unfailing generosity and invaluable help with the design. There remains a small group of friends who have sustained me throughout my wanderings in East Anglia. Without their support I would have got bogged down in a ploughed field long ago.

*   *   *   *   *

Every effort has been made to identify the owners of copyright material and obtain the necessary permissions, but the author would be grateful if any inadvertent errors or omissions could be brought to his attention.

The author would like to thank all those for permission to reproduce the following illustrations: Lady Harrod, 13, 52a, 65; John Murray Ltd, 14; Commander Cheyne, 15, 138, 146; Adrian Wright, 16, 91; The National Trust, 85, 210b, 214; Norfolk Library & Information Service, 22, 33a, 33b, 53, 75, 101, 143, 144, 169b, 186; Norfolk Museums Service, 35, 50; Arnold Wesker, 36b, 132, 134; Elspeth Barker, 41a; Christopher Barker, 41b, 45, 136; Susanna Pinney, 43; The National Portrait Gallery, 47, 64, 67, 70a, 77b, 99, 117, 147, 160a, 162, 176a, 181, 204, 207b, 223, 227, 231a, 236, 240; Ancient House Museum Thetford, 57, 105, 160b, 248; Peter Brooks, 68; Richard Mabey, 73; the Seago Estate, 77b; David Fox, 78; RSPB, 82b; Roger Tidman, 84; Norfolk County Council, 89; The Hulton Getty Picture Collection, 90, 120, 178; David Osborne, 109; Diana Hyde, 115b; The Powys Society, 111, 188a; David Gentleman, 123, 124, 190a, 190b 198, 200a; Eastern Counties Newspapers, 141a, 233; Dunwich Museum, 161, 167b, Robin Guthrie, 165a; Dorset County Museum, 175, Linda Cooper, 184a; Ronald Blythe, 198; John Baxter, 200b, Ipswich Borough Council, 205; Suffolk Record Office, 206a, 219; Jeremy Burgess, 216; Jennie Marshal, 241; Paul Joyce, 244.

The author would also like to thank the following for permission to quote from copyright material: for *The Cloak That I Left* by Lilias Rider Haggard, *The Farmer's Year* & *The Private Diaries of Sir Henry Rider Haggard*, Commander Cheyne; for *The Hills and The Sea*, the estate of Hilaire Belloc; for *All Done From Memory*, Osbert Lancaster & John Murray Ltd; for *The Go Between by L P Hartley*, Hamish Hamilton; for *As Much As I Dare* & *Roots*, Arnold Wesker; for *Collected Poems* by John Betjeman, John Murray Ltd; for the works of George Barker, Elspeth Barker; for the works of Sylvia Townsend Warner & Valentine Ackland, William Maxwell & Susanna Pinney; for *Poems From Oby* by George Macbeth, Secker & Warburg; for *Poems 1953-88, The Dust of the World* & *The Mill House*, Anthony Thwaite; for *Devices and Desires* & *Unnatural Causes* by PD James, Faber & Faber Ltd; for the works of Virginia Woolf, Random House UK Ltd; for *World Within World* & *Collected Poems 1928-85* by Stephen Spender, Lady Spender & Faber & Faber Ltd; for WH Auden's essay in *The Old School*, Curtis Brown Group Ltd; for *Home and Away* by John Pudney, Michael Joseph; for *The Collected Poems of Stevie Smith*, Penguin Books & James MacGibbon; for *The Eagle Has Landed*, Jack Higgins; for *Food For Free* & *Home Country*, Richard Mabey; for *The Story of a Norfolk Farm*, the Henry Williamson Literary Estate, for *Performing Flea* & *Jeeves and the Impending Doom* by PG Wodehouse, Random House UK Ltd; for the *Eustace and Hilda* trilogy, The Society of Authors & the estate of LP Hartley; for *A Change of Climate*, Hilary Mantel; for *The Collected Ghost Stories of MR James*, Nick James; for *A History of Thetford*, Alan Crosby; for the works of John Cowper Powys, the estate of John Cowper Powys; for the unpublished Foreword to *The Fields of Dulditch* by Mary Mann, Diana Hyde; for the works of Ronald Blythe, Ronald Blythe; for the works of George Ewart Evans, Faber & Faber Ltd; for the *Journals of Elizabeth Smart*, Sebastian Barker; for *Corduroy* & *Men of the Fields* by Adrian Bell, Martin Bell; for *The Clegyman's Daughter* & the *Letters of George Orwell*, the estate of the late Sonia Orwell & Martin Secker & Warburg Ltd; for *Collected Poems*, Peter Porter & Oxford University Press; for *The Letters of Edward Thomas to Gordon Bottomley*, Myfanwy Thomas; for *George Crabbe-The Poet and the Man*, by E M Forster, The Society of Authors & Kings College Cambridge; for *Aldeburgh:The Vision and the Reality* & *The Albatross*, Susan Hill; for *Lytton Strachey By Himself*, The Society of Authors & The Strachey Trust; for *Joseph and his Brethren* by HW Freeman, H Massey; for the Introduction to *Mehalah* by John Fowles, John Fowles; for *The Collected Works of Alun Lewis*, Seren Books; for *Borstal Boy* by Brendan Behan, Random House UK Ltd; for *Ordinary Families* by E Arnot Robertson, Jonathan Cape; for *We Didnt Mean To Go To Sea* & *Secret Waters*, the Arthur Ransome estate; for *The Snow Goose* (1941), Paul Gallico; for *Sylvia Townsend Warner:A Biography*, Claire Harman; for *The Wild Garden*, the estate of Angus Wilson; for *A Child in Time* by Ian McEwan, Jonathan Cape.

Foreword

The fusion of literature and landscape offers peculiar joys, great and small. Who could look unmoved upon the links at Cromer where Arthur Conan Doyle, inspired by his golfing partner's tale of Black Shuck, conceived the notion of 'The Hound of The Baskervilles'? In a certain Norfolk cliff-top cafe one may encounter Miss Havisham dispensing tea and cake with a remote and icy dignity appropriate to one who has unaccountably wandered out of 'Great Expectations' and into 'David Copperfield'. There is a brand of metal corkscrew with lifting arms which never fails to conjure up for me that terrifying, spectral figure which comes bobbing over the groynes in M R James' 'Whistle And I'll Come To You My Lad'. Such correspondences bring delight to the daily round. On a wider scale one's whole life is enriched by the knowledge of those who have gone before us, who have recorded our landscape through their own unique sensibilities.

East Anglia has a long and proud tradition of tolerance and Non-Conformism which has extended to the motley throng of writers who have lived here, a lineage so various that their only common denominator is their sense of place. Some, like Anna Sewell or George Crabbe were born to this landscape and grew up with a sense not only of its beauty but of the inexorably desolate lives of its impoverished inhabitants: *There pigs and chickens quarrel for a meal / There dropsied infants wail without redress / And all is want and woe and wretchedness.* Others came on holidays, or to visit friends or relatives and returned again and again. The great houses, parklands, sprawling rectories and shadowy rook-haunted trees entranced the childhood imaginations of L P Hartley, M R James and Osbert Lancaster. Conversely, for the adolescent Brendan Behan East Anglia was a borstal on the Suffolk coast; for Arnold Wesker it was the kitchen sink of the Bell Hotel in Norwich. Over a drink or two Captain Marryat swapped his London house for one in Langham, where he wrote 'Children of the New Forest'.

Other writers came to research, to escape from London, or simply by chance. Some were drawn by literary obsession; Benjamin Britten by Crabbe, W H Hudson by Bloomfield. Once here, not everyone wished to stay. Sabine Baring-Gould, redoubtable author of 'Onward Christian Soldiers', found Essex a litter of warped minds and sealed fates overcast by a miasma of sewage and sprats and mosquitoes. At the seaside Virginia Woolf predictably displayed her talent for snobbery, while Henry Williamson struggled miserably with his unyielding land. Of the dissenters here, most poignant is the poet Cowper, melancholic and ill at Mundesley, brooding on a solitary pillar of rock at the highwater mark: *I have visited it twice and found it an emblem to myself. Torn from my natural connections, I stand alone and expect the storm that shall displace me.* Most comical is George Orwell, resentfully writing 'Down and Out in Paris and London' amid the bourgeois comforts of genteel Southwold.

A writer's landscape is both factual and imaginary, cast and then rearranged in the mind's eye. The desolation which overwhelmed Cowper was a thrilling delight to Sylvia Townsend Warner: *The east wind sobs and whimpers like a Bronte in the kitchen.* The fluctuations of those coastal, marginal lands, transient and treacherous, 'ambiguous territory', have brought solace to unquiet spirits. The solitary, anxious, self-questioning task of the writer may assume perspective amid such constant metamorphosis, a literal rendering of Villon's *Autant en emporte le vent.* Where there is loss and displacement there is also freedom.

Not everyone is bound by wind and water. Inland affords its own pleasures. Lytton Strachey found transcendence in the Suffolk grasslands; Angus Wilson's garden, cleared from the wild wood, became for him a practical realisation of *the symbols underlying my novels.* Ronald Blythe remarked on the invisibility of farm workers *slipping back into the earth they had toiled for thousands of years*, but it was George Ewart Evans who, in his unsentimental oral histories, gave their recollections a voice and a lasting validity. A surprising number of writers here have also farmed their land. How curious it is to learn that Sir Rider Haggard, author of some sixty novels, was knighted for his work on agriculture and smallholdings.

While East Anglia is famous for its painters, it has been poorly served by compilers of Literary Companions. Peter Tolhurst's wonderful book, a true labour of love, is a timely avenger. The diversity of the landscape is mirrored by those who celebrate or disparage it. No one is indifferent. It is impossible not to be profoundly moved and exhilarated by these fragments of other lives. Here are two estuarine experiences. For Richard Mabey *the mud slid out of the ebbing water with the moist shine of a new-born animal.* Sylvia Townsend Warner meanwhile, and elsewhere, is simply *socketed into the universe, passionately quiescent.* This is a book which urges the reader on to authors unvisited, unknown even. If some of their landscapes have been altered or destroyed, we may recreate them, pass there ourselves like ghosts, knowing them with an older familiarity.

Much has not changed. The lime tree avenue where Dorothy and William Wordsworth walked still stands. Rider Haggard noted road rage long since, tormented by coveys of bicycling clergymen: *Thrice have I nearly fallen victim to their rage!* And Edward Fitzgerald, translator of Omar Khayam and one of my very favourite people here, - by his own modest declaration *a very lazy person who do nothing* - 140 years ago was lamenting that *the petty race of squires who have succeeded only use the earth for an investment.* Turning away from felled trees and levelled violet banks he found content on the water *where friends are not buried nor parkways stopt up; but all is as the poets say, as Creation's Dawn beheld.*

To read this book is to attend an impossibly perfect millennial party. Radicals, dissenters, monks, mystics, farmers, fascists, free-lovers, poets and novelists mingle and time is suspended. Outside, forgotten, the equinoctial gales wail in off the marshes, and a great black dog pads silently along the cliff path.

Elspeth Barker

Preface

For the last two centuries writers and poets have been engaged in a passionate love affair with the English landscape. The scenic possibilities of scale and vista, of atmosphere and the historic sense, have been so celebrated that we seem to appreciate landscape through the eyes of those who have gone before and seen more clearly. The countryside continues to be a glorious inspiration but with the destruction of so many cherished scenes, the imaginative response alone remains inviolate.

Do some places retain what John Cowper Powys called the 'psychic echo' of a more sacred age, audible only to the sensitive ear? Or is it simply the working of some poetic fallacy by which we project our own internal landscapes onto the external geography of hills and rivers? Perhaps both are true, but what is certain is that places immortalised in literature become transformed. Any work of fiction has its own reality but for many, our enjoyment is increased by experiencing the places themselves.

This may seem perverse when so many places have changed beyond all recognition. Dickens' Yarmouth exists now only in the pages of 'David Copperfield' and Hunstanton is no longer the Edwardian resort of L P Hartley's 'The Shrimp and The Anemone', but visit the town, identify the landmarks in the novel and you begin to re-enter the world of Eustace's childhood. Cycle the country lanes around Blo' Norton and you become aware of that same *'strange, dreaming, philosophising and remembering land'* that Virginia Woolf found so enchanting, or sit among the gravestones and read George Barker's 'At Thurgarton Church', and the poem takes on fresh meaning.

Elements of the East Anglian landscape have come to exert a powerful influence on the region's literature. Through the 'inscape' of Crabbe's 'Peter Grimes' the desolate mudflats of the Alde estuary shape the character of his murderous anti-hero, while for Angus Wilson the wild garden at Bradfield St George came to assume an importance in his writing that he only recognised years later. At the turn of the century the ruined church perched precariously on the clifftop at Dunwich came to symbolise the destruction of a whole town and a sense of loss that has inspired generations of poets and writers. Here it is the very absense of place that stirs the imagination.

Childhood memories, often brought into sharp focus during long periods of exile, are a recurring theme in the literary landscape of the region. Robert Bloomfield wrote his hugely successful poem 'The Farmer's Boy', recalling his youth in the Black Bourne valley, while living in a London garret, and images of the river Wissey resurfaced years later in the opening chapters of John Cowper Powys' novel 'A Glastonbury Romance' during his time in America. For some though the experiences of childhood proved more traumatic. Stephen Spender endured years of unhappiness at Greshams and whatever L P Hartley witnessed in the outbuildings at Bradenham Hall left emotional scars that even his finest novel failed to erase. In 'Norfolk', recalling the pleasure of holidays on the Broads with his father, John Betjeman laments his own lost innocence:

Time bring back / The rapturous ignorance of long ago, / The peace before the dreadful daylight starts, / Of unkept promises and broken hearts.

I realise now that this, my own literary pilgrimage, is rooted in the tribal confines of my Kentish boyhood. There in the Stour valley, roaming along the river bank, fishing in the millpond, tracking through the fields to secret hideaways deep in the bluebell woods, we marked our territory and I began to assimilate my mother's delight in the countryside. Brought up in a cottage on the downs near Canterbury, she found herself between two very different worlds. Behind were the grounds of the mental hospital where, as master tailor, my grandfather made straightjackets for the more violent inmates. In front the land dropped away steeply; exhilarating views of woods and hop fields stretched away, a liberating prospect full of hope, full of promise.

This sense of being on the edge is also part of my inheritance, a way of seeing that I took with me when, years later my wife and I came to live in Norfolk. At Forncett in the Tas valley we learnt that Dorothy Wordsworth had set up a village school in the rectory. We discovered this from Miss Armstrong, a kind and gentle spinster who had herself been head teacher and church organist for many years, at a time when the ancient meadows below the rectory were threatened. Saved by a campaign we helped to organise it was only later while reading Dorothy's letters that I found she had often walked through those same fields and dreamt of a cottage there where she would be reunited with her beloved William. The meadows, a profusion of rare and beautiful fowers each spring, are a memorial to her and the spirit of Mary Armstrong who died so tragically. Here in another sheltered valley I rediscovered a sense of place and a literary landscape that set me on a journey. This book is a record of that journey.

Peter Tolhurst

1

Sacred Country

King's Lynn
to Norwich

Bradenham Woods was doomed and nearly all the magnificent oaks for which the estate was famous and which had been the pride of his father's heart, would suffer the same fate. The hall and its contents were gone, the land was gone, the trees were going - he could no longer bear to see the place thus stripped of everything that had made it beautiful to his eyes. The curtain had rung down for the last time on the scenes of his childhood, leaving only an empty house, an overgrown garden and some graves in the little churchyard.

From *The Cloak That I Left* by **Lilias Rider Haggard**

King's Lynn

This thriving seaport town has been well used to foreigners since the middle ages. The magnificent Flemish brasses in St Margaret's church and the Hansiatic warehouse (1428) are reminders of the long and productive trade links with northern Europe. For centuries Dutch merchants and Norwegian seamen mingled on the quayside with local fishermen home from whaling trips to Greenland. At about the same time (1485) the curious brick octagon known as Red Mount Chapel was completed as an overnight stop for pilgrims on their way to Walsingham.

Brought up in this atmosphere of religious piety and cosmopolitan travel, **Margery Kempe's** arduous journeys to Rome and the Holy Land were in those days still a remarkable achievement for a merchant's daughter married with 14 children. Her ardent prayer and unrestrained weeping on the floor of St Margaret's church were believed by many to have invoked the snowstorm that saved Lynn from a disastrous fire in 1421. Others regarded her mystical reputation to be nothing more than witchcraft but, despite several arrests for heresy, she escaped conviction. Unlike her contemporary, Julian of Norwich (see p28), Margery shunned the contemplative life, preferring to search for God on the road to Jerusalem and Compostella. Returning eventually to her home town, this extraordinary woman dictated *The Book of Margery Kempe* (1501), an account of experiences that took her to most of the known medieval world and a record of her own spiritual journey. Published some years after her death, it remains the first known autobiography in the English language and one of the earliest travel books.

Foreign trade and the rich agricultural estates of west Norfolk ensured the town's continued prosperity, a prosperity symbolised by Henry Bell's stately Custom House (1683), the Georgian-fronted merchants houses in King Street and the Corn Exchange (1884), *'jolly and vulgar'*, in the Tuesday Market Place. In 1725 Defoe enthused *'here are more gentry, and consequently is more gaiety in this town than in Yarmouth, or even in Norwich itself; the place abounding in very good company.'* But unlike Norwich it had no intellectual life worth speaking of and few prospects for an ambitious young composer like Charles Burney, organist at St Margarets. Born in 1752 his daughter, **Fanny Burney**, began writing the diary for which she is perhaps best remembered, in a little summer house near the river where the *'annoying oaths of the watermen'* and the damp air sometimes drove her indoors. She was still very young when her father took the family to live in London and although she returned to spend holidays with her stepmother, Fanny soon found the society of London's blue stocking circle more congenial. There she wrote three novels that bought instant success but today her literary reputation rests more firmly on the journals and letters that offer such a vivid account of Georgian society.

By far the best way to approach Lynn today is by road across the Fens or along the west bank of the Ouse, the route taken by **Hilaire Belloc** at the turn of the century near the end of an arduous hike round the shores of the Wash. Whatever your mode of transport the twin towers of St Margaret's church rising above a cluster of medieval warehouses along the waterfront, form an impressive skyline; a foretaste of the architectural delights that awaited Belloc:

King's Lynn waterfront, the view that greeted Hilaire Belloc and more recently Paul Theroux at the end of exhausting walks round the Wash.

You can see the past effect of ownership and individuality in Lynn as clearly as you can catch affection or menace in a human voice. The outward expression is most manifest and to pass in and out along the lanes in front of the old houses inspires in one precisely those emotions which are aroused by a human crowd .... and in between ran these oldest bits of Lynn, somnalescent and refreshing - permanent.

Since Belloc the town has continued to receive ecstatic reviews from a succession of eminent visitors. In a letter to Llewelyn Powys in 1933 the novelist Sylvia Townsend Warner, described Lynn as a *'most beautiful town, stately and prim, with seagulls crying through it.'* James Lees-Milne, voice of the National Trust, declared it had *'the finest old streets anywhere in England'* and *'more worth seeing than any other town of equal size'* was the verdict of Lady Harrod in 1957. A few years later Nikolaus Pevsner found Lynn was still *'a delightful little town'*, but by then the chorus of praise had acquired a predictable ring.

It was another twenty years before the American travel writer, **Paul Theroux**, cast a more sober eye over the place. Arriving in 1982 on his journey round the coastline of Britain, he was in dismissive mood having just squelched round the Wash in Belloc's somewhat indistinct footsteps. *'Dignified and dull, its stately centre so finely preserved it looked embalmed'* was all he could manage. He did grudgingly concede that Lynn *'was a habitable place, and patchily pretty, and it had hopes'* but he seemed more interested in the gangs of motor cyclists that he considered were *'as much a part of the find old market towns in provincial England as the period houses and the graceful windows'*. They were at least alive and kicking, the very antidote to conservation *'roaring down quaint cobblestone streets on their Japanese motorbikes.'*

Years before, John Betjeman had sampled the delights of branch line travel from Lynn to Hunstanton via the royal station at Wolferton in a programme for BBC television, but with its closure and the prospect of another trudge across marshy terrain, Theroux rode out of town on the No 6 bus to Wells.

Osbert Lancaster
(1908-86)

East Winch

A delightful vignette of childhood holidays at East Winch Hall a few miles from King's Lynn, is to be found in **Osbert Lancaster's** autobiography *All Done From Memory* (1953). Arriving on the Midland and Great Northern line, he described the odd sensation that lingered about the deserted platform before an aunt emerged from the waiting room to claim him:

There is no silence in the world so overwhelming as that which prevails on a small country station when a train has just left it. The fact that it is by no means complete, that the fading echoes of the engine are still clearly audible from the signal box behind which the guard's van is finally disappearing, that one now hears for the first time the cawing of rooks, a distant dog's bark, the hum of the bees in the stationmaster's garden, in no way detracts from its quality

At East Winch station, lost amidst the un-by-passed fields of my Edwardian childhood, this period of suspension was apt to be longer than elsewhere. The platform....appeared in the flat East Anglian landscape to be a raised island, isolated way above the surrounding elm-broken cornlands.

When Lancaster knew it, East Winch was little more than a few dull carrstone cottages strung out along the main road between the church at one end *'scraped and scrubbed into insignificance'* by Gilbert Scott and the Hall at the other, a plain late Georgian affair built for *'some modest nabob who had done well in the tea trade'*. Osbert's grandfather had taken it upon himself to animate the yellow brick facade with masks of Comedy and Tragedy and a huge wooden porch that strained to support the Lancaster coat of arms. Here under an edifice of dubious taste and uncertain structure, house parties would gather on long summer evenings even though the corridors never echoed to *'whispered speculations about the geography of the bedrooms'*.

Lancaster's picture of this eminently conventional upper class family is enlivened by a collection of eccentrics of which Wodehouse himself would have been proud. His grandfather's abiding passion, always more philanthropic than erotic, was to dispense charity to an odd assemblage of female relatives known as the Grateful Hearts. To qualify, dependents were required to display a mixture of poverty, piety and affliction *'bravely and brightly born'*, qualities exhibited in equal measure by two rival spinsters. One was elderly, bad tempered and *'suffered from advanced cataracts'*, the other was a *'kindly timid creature with curvature of the spine'* whose cavalry moustache was regarded as an asset on the strength that a great aunt had on several occasions been mistaken for Lord Kitchener. Mr Phipps, an elderly curate known as 'Filthy Phipps' from the colour of his hands and neck that *'invariably matched the greasy black of his clerical boater'* was in close contention for grandfather's dispensations, as was Frau Schmiegelow, the Prussian governess, whose obvious affliction was to have been born a foreigner.

The small country station that for Osbert Lancaster signalled the beginning of holidays with his grandparents at East Winch Hall.

Henry Rider Haggard
(1856-1925)

Bradenham Hall

Another plain Georgian mansion with what the architectural historian Pevsner described as '*substantial early 20th century additions*', Bradenham Hall stands on some of the highest land in Norfolk. When the young **Rider Haggard** lived here its pedimented brick facade looked out across wooded parkland that sloped away to West Bradenham church and beyond to the river Wissey. Behind the hall stood an octagonal game larder flanked by one wall of the kitchen garden with stables, a gardener's cottage, and woodland walks leading through the Long Plantation to a summer house where '*generations of the family had carved their names.*'

The estate itself, a modest 400 acres of rich agricultural land, contained a number of farmsteads including Wood Farm, a brick and thatch house which survives, much altered, to the north of Bradenham Great Wood. Returning early from a holiday abroad with the imminent arrival of another baby, William and Ella Haggard found the hall still occupied by tenants and Ella retired to the farmhouse where she gave birth to Henry Rider Haggard, her eighth child, on June 22nd 1856. While Henry's father led the life of a despotic country squire, his mother found time to write poetry, much of which was published, including tales of her life in India, and it was to her that Rider Haggard believed he owed much of his literary talent.

Haggard always looked back on his childhood at Bradenham with great affection, until at the age of thirteen he was sent firstly to an Oxford crammer followed by three years at Ipswich Grammar School before his father suddenly decided he should take entrance exams for the Foreign Office. At the age of 19 he finally left Bradenham to become Secretary to the new Governor of Natal, Sir Henry Bulwer, who was a family friend from north Norfolk. The move proved more significant than Haggard could have possibly imagined.

On the death of his father in 1892 Haggard's elder brother inherited the estate which he struggled to manage until, by the end of the First War, failing health and mounting debts forced him to sell up. Although Haggard had become attached to Ditchingham House, (see p137) his home near Bungay following his return from Africa in 1878 and his marriage two years later, it never won his heart as Bradenham had. The hall had been the family home for nearly 150 years and he dearly wished to continue the Haggard association but, together with the Ditchingham property it would have proved too great a burden and, with great reluctance, he accepted his brother's decision. Returning to Bradenham in 1918 he reflected in his diary:

It is odd at the end of life coming back to houses at which one has spent its beginnings, for then such become one vast and living memory. Every bit of furniture, every picture on the walls, every stone and tree bring forgotten scenes before the eye, or find tongues and talk.

Before he left, Haggard walked up to the Grazing Grounds in solemn mood knowing that this would be his last visit. It was May and the landscape, bathed in sunlight, looked more beautiful that he could remember. '*What*' he asked himself '*was the magic of these old pastures shadowed with their great trees?*'

But he also knew that both brother and father had paid dearly for the privilege of owning such an enchanted stretch of countryside. Haggard wondered how long the majestic oaks would remain once the estate was sold, little knowing that his worst fears would be confirmed so soon. The new owner was a speculative timber merchant for whom the great trees represented a handsome profit. Within the first few months they were all gone.

* * * * *

L P Hartley stayed at Bradenham Hall in the summer of 1909 as a guest of his schoolfriend Moxey whose parents had rented the Hall from Rider Haggard's brother, but it was over 40 years later before he used it as the setting for **The Go-Between** (1954), regarded by many as his most accomplished novel and, partly as a result of Joseph Losey's 1970 film version, his best known work. Set at the turn of the century against a background of rigid class distinction, this delicate study of a young boy's painful initiation into an adult world of deceit and destructive passion begins with Leo Colston's discovery of the diary he kept while the guest of a schoolfriend, Marcus Maudsley. As Leo reads the entries he made throughout that fateful heat wave in 1900, all the disturbing memories for so long buried in Brandham (Bradenham) come flooding back, although his recollections of the hall itself are now rather vague as he pours over the description copied from a Norfolk Directory : *'Brandham Hall, the seat of the Winlove family .... of an architectural style too bare and unadorned for present tastes, it makes an impressive if over-plain effect when seen from the SW'*

L P Hartley
(1895-1972)

The only feature Leo remembers clearly is the grand double staircase that so excited his imagination - *'a tilted horseshoe, a magnet, a cataract'* - but otherwise the hall, with its dreary family portraits and polished silverware, was where grown-ups gathered for dinner parties and the formalities of a strict social order were carefully observed. On the few occasions when the Maudsleys encountered the village at church on Sundays or at the annual cricket match they always assumed an air of well-rehearsed ritual. As Leo recalls, the derelict outbuildings were more attractive than the prospect of Brandham Hall and here, shortly after his arrival, he stumbled upon the beautiful but poisonous belladonna plant. Behind the hall, under the shade of a yew tree, stood the disused game larder that was still in existence at the time of Hartley's visit. Here Leo monitored the heat wave's relentless progress by daily readings from the thermometer that hung inside.

Transformed by the heat, young Leo crosses *'the rainbow bridge from reality to dream'* and enters the realm of the immortals. Enchanted by his friend's elder sister Marion, *'The Virgin of the Zodiac'*, he becomes her mercurial messenger, but even as he strides out through fields bathed in golden light to deliver his first letter to Ted Burgess at Black Farm, he feels caught in the sun's *'fierce embrace'*. Later, on discovering the real reason for Marion's lavish attention, Leo's spirit, that had once soared to new heights, comes crashing to earth, the spell broken. On his way to Black Farm, *'a bent figure, no bigger than a beetle, weaving to and fro,'* Leo knows he has been used, his loyalty betrayed, and as he pauses beside the sluice his shrunken spirit appears reflected in the receding water line:

Bradenham Hall, the childhood home of Sir Henry Rider Haggard and the setting for L P Hartley's novel *The Go Between.*

St Benet's Abbey gatehouse on the banks of the river Bure that gave Sylvia Townsend Warner the idea for Oby nunnery in *The Corner That Held Them.*

The dunes at Horsey Gap and *'the whistling bent-grass on the leeside'* of John Betjeman's poem
East Anglian Bathe.

Horsey Mere, renamed Hurle Mere by Wilkie Collins in **Armadale**, his 'Novel of Sensation',
where his anti-heroine Lydia Gwilt makes her first appearance.

The surface of the pool was still blue, but many more boulders than before showed ghostly, corpse-like, at the bottom. And on the other side, the shallow side, the change was greater. Before it had been untidy, now it was a scene of mad disorder: a tangled mass of water-weeds, all high and dry, and sticking out of them, mounds of yellow gravel, like bald patches on a head. The clusters of round, thin, grey-green rushes .... had fallen over, let down by their native element, back-broken, under their own weight; they lay pointing this way and that, all discipline gone. The army of spearmen had been routed.

Ted Burgess, the young tenant farmer whose athletic prowess had so impressed Leo just a few weeks earlier as he clubbed boundaries for the village team, was now too a fallen idol. Even then as he strode to the wicket, a large white cloud, the first for days, had drifted ominously towards the sun. Spectacular in its execution, Leo's dive in the outfield to dismiss his hero is re-enacted later in more traumatic circumstances when Ted and Marion are caught in the outbuildings.

When, near the end of his holiday, Leo goes to say goodbye, he sees Ted clearly for the first time, a young man defeated by the unbridgeable gulf between him and his lover now engaged to Viscount Trimingham. As he recalled: '*once he had reminded me of a cornfield ripe for reaping; now he was like corn that had been cut and left in the sun .... sweating though he was, he looked up, the husk of the man he had been.*' The only living thing that thrives in the heat is the deadly nightshade which by now is bursting out of the ruined potting shed:

The shrub had spread amazingly; it tipped the roofless walls, it pressed into their crannies, groping for an outlet, urged by a secret explosive force that I felt would have burst them. It had battened on the heat which had parched everything else ..... It invited and yet repelled inspection, as if it was harbouring some shady secret which it yet wanted you to know.

The game larder at Bradenham Hall that replaced the octagonal structure in which Leo measured the heat wave in *The Go Between*.

As he stands there, fascinated and repulsed by its spreading tentacles, Leo knows what he must do to break the spell Ted still casts over Marion. Fearful of the consequences, he returns at dusk to the kitchen garden and, forcing his way into the shed, struggles to uproot the plant and with the cry '*Dellenda est bella donna*', purges himself of the fantasy that has grown with it since his arrival at Brandham, The magic begins to work almost immediately as storm clouds gather on his 13th birthday, unleashing a tragic chain of events that culminates in Leo's breakdown and Ted's suicide. Forced by Mrs Maudsley to confess his role as go-between, he is dragged through the rain back to the outbuildings to confront the lovers and the frightening '*shadow on the wall that opened and closed like an umbrella*'.

Years later, his curiosity aroused by the diary, Leo Colston returns to Brandham to find the hall converted into a girl's school and Marion, Lady Trimingham, living in the village alone with memories of her illegitimate son, the 10th Viscount Trimingham. Killed in action in 1944, he is commemorated by a tablet in the family chapel at Brandham church. Before leaving Leo reflects once more on '*What an Eden Brandham Hall had been before* (that) *serpent entered it.*'

21

Bradenham church. Members of the Haggard family are buried in the churchyard. In **The Go Between** it is the absense of a memorial to the 5th Viscount Trimmingham that so intrigued young Leo.

Fiction imitating life plays an important part in Hartley's heavily autobiographical novels, especially in **The Go Between** where the circumstances of Leo's invitation to stay with the Maudsleys closely resemble those of the author's own childhood holiday at Bradenham Hall. On arrival Hartley was soon writing to his mother: *'On Saturday we had a ball, very grand indeed, or at least not very. We always have late dinners here. There is going to be a cricket match today, the Hall against the village. I am going to score'.* Years later his sister recalled how Hartley first got the idea for the novel and the theme of love destroyed by impossible class barriers from a diary he had discovered at Bradenham belonging to one of the young ladies.

As his biographer maintains, the novel includes material essential to our appreciation of Hartley but that *'what remains questionable is whether the central trauma of the book .... represents the truth.'* Hartley repeatedly refuted attempts to interpret events in the novel in terms of his own life, but at the Norwich premiere of Losey's film the year before his death, the mask finally slipped. At one point he broke down, admitting to the director that, although not dragged, he had been made to follow the lady of the house to the outbuildings. Exactly what he saw there and the extent to which it changed his life, we shall never know for certain. The diaries that may have contained the answers have been destroyed thereby consigning Bradenham to its enigmatic place in the literary landscape of Norfolk.

Dereham

The poet **William Cowper** had close family links with Norfolk and spent numerous childhood holidays on the Broads at Ludham Hall, home of his grandfather Roger Donne who claimed direct descent from the poet John Donne. The death of his mother when he was only six had a profound effect on

William Cowper
(1731-1800)

the young Cowper and later, on being given her portrait he wrote the poem *On Receipt of my Mother's Picture out of Norfolk*. As a result of these family connections he came to spend the last few years of his life in the small market town of East Dereham.

Before his move to Norfolk, Cowper had lived for many years in the Buckinghamshire village of Olney with his companion Mary Unwin. Here they had enjoyed a quiet routine of religious devotion and domestic harmony while she nursed Cowper through recurring bouts of depression, and it was here he wrote most of the works on which his literary reputation is based, including his finest poem 'The Task' as well as 'The Olney Hymns' (1779) in collaboration with the Rev John Newton.

Towards the end of her life Mary Unwin suffered a series of debilitating strokes that left her in need of almost constant attention. Seeing the strain that her affliction was having on Cowper and fearful it could induce another bout of melancholia, his young cousin Johnny Johnson persuaded the couple to stay with him in Dereham where he was curate. They left Buckinghamshire in 1795 staying firstly in the rectory at North Tuddenham, from where Cowper could walk the four miles to visit his cousin Anne Bodham at Mattishall. But Johnson, believing that sea air and frequent changes of scene would be good for their health, arranged moves between Mundesley on the coast (see p59) and Dunham Lodge, a small country seat between Swaffham and Dereham. Cowper, who spent most of his time reading novels, found the house too grand for his taste, referring to it as that *'rambling, dreary Lodge upon the Hill at Dunham.'* Johnson could also see his beloved friend failing rapidly and they returned to his house in Dereham overlooking the Market Place, where Mary died on December 17th 1796. Cowper was grief stricken and rarely spoke of her again.

Dunham Lodge, completed a few years before William Cowper stayed here in 1796.

The bleakness of Cowper's last years was alleviated by daily visits from his cousin who sat and read to him and from Johnson's friend Margaret Perowne who devoted herself to caring for the poet in his decline. In December 1799 they all moved to another house in the Market Place where the Cowper Congregational Church now stands. Writing to a friend, Johnson explained *'we have been fortunate to hire a house three doors down from this with a charming garden well planted with wall fruit'* It was here on April 25th 1800 that Cowper died peacefully. He lies buried near Mary Unwin in the parish church, commemorated by Flaxman's memorial which bears an inscription by the poet's friend and biographer William Hayley. The memorial window erected 100 years later in St Edmund's chapel depicts Cowper in morning cap and dressing gown near his mother's portrait and with his pet hares and a dog at his feet.

Cowper's memorial by Flaxman in St Withburga's church Dereham.

Three years after Cowper's death, Dereham's other literary figure, the novelist and adventurer **George Borrow**, was born in a farmhouse rented by his parents at Dumpling Green on the southern edge of the parish. His father had been stationed in the town as a recruiting sergeant in the West Norfolk Militia and had married Ann Perfrement in St Withburga's church in the presence of James Philo, the Parish Clerk. In his autobiographical work **Lavengro** (1851) and its sequel **Romany Rye** (1857), Borrow recalls with affection his early years in Dereham, *'a beautiful little town'*, especially the church services and the tall, dignified presence of James Philo.

The farmhouse at Dumpling Green where George Borrow was born in 1803.

Parson Woodforde
(1740-1803)

Weston Longville

The gently rolling landscape east of Dereham known as 'Woodforde Country' still retains the atmosphere of comfortable prosperity that first tempted the merchant classes out of Norwich. In search of more spacious surroundings in which to display their newly acquired wealth, the nouveaux riches chose the more elevated positions overlooking the Yare and Wensum valleys for their new Jacobean halls. By the time **James Woodforde** presented himself to the living at Weston Longville in 1776, the surrounding countryside had already become a mosaic of well-timbered estates, with each country house the centrepiece of parkland designed in the style of the Norfolk landscape gardener Humphrey Repton. Elegant brick rectories appeared in almost every parish, dispensing faith and charity, but little hope, to the small congregations of labourers and their families who trudged dutifully to church each Sunday.

Woodforde slipped easily into this orderly world, a world in which religious duties proved somewhat inconvenient to the pursuit of his preferred role, that of country squire - at a time when the '*spiritually comatose base of the Church of England* (was) *still unawakened by Wolsey.*' News of momentous events in the outside world eventually filtered through to Weston Longville, but failed to ruffle the tranquillity of life at the rectory. Once jilted by a lady in Somerset, Parson Woodforde remained unmoved by affairs of the heart, his bachelor ways attended to by Nancy, his loyal niece, and a variety of servants. Unlike his contemporary, the Rev George Crabbe, the good parson maintained a healthy indifference to the world of literature and the plight of the poor. His one abiding passion was food, consumed in large quantities, preferably in the company of that small group of fellow clergymen and local gentry who took it in turns to organise 'rotation' days when, after a heavy meal, they would retire to the backgammon board or a round of quadrille.

The orthodox view we have of rural society in late 18th century Norfolk comes largely from Woodforde's meticulous record of daily life that fills the 68 notebooks now in the Bodleian Library. He began keeping a diary in 1758 while at Oxford, a daily habit he maintained with hardly a break throughout several curacies in the West Country and his years at Weston Longville. The notebooks remained in the Woodforde family until their discovery by John Beresford who, on recognising their importance, arranged their publication in five volumes between 1924 and 1931. A fascinating source for social historians and students of 18th century cuisine, Woodforde's diaries offer little insight into the lives of his contemporaries or the moral welfare of his parishioners. Entries such as '*we breakfasted, dined, supped and slept again at home*' or '*I read Prayers and Preached this afternoon at Weston Church*' become part of a familiar sequence concluding with a list of the dishes eaten, the company kept and the bills paid.

If Woodforde's diaries sometimes appear dull, we should not expect more of the worthy parson who is, after all, a victim of historical accident. Many more revealing pictures of life in Georgian England have doubtless been lost, but Parson Woodforde, thanks to the efforts of Beresford, now stands a little reluctantly alongside Pepys, Evelyn and Boswell as one of the most celebrated

The house at South Green Mattishall where William Cowper visited his cousin Anne Bodham when staying at North Tuddenham rectory. 'Rotations' held here by the Bodhams were attended by Parson Woodforde, and recorded in his diaries.

diarists of his age. Whereas these eminent men of letters immersed themselves in the mainstream of political and social life, Woodforde's shopping trips seldom took him beyond Reepham. His quiet rural backwater beside the Wensum comes slowly to life, pieced together from a series of accidental and amusing episodes recorded during his 27 years in the parish. We know the price of his new wig and the cost of reglazing his cucumber frame; the severity of winters that troubled his gout and froze the chamber pot under his bed; the pain he suffered when the local farmer broke his jaw while drawing a tooth and the occasions when contraband liquor appeared on his doorstep.

Sometimes humourous - once his pigs became drunk on the dregs of homemade beer but recovered sufficiently the next day to enable Woodforde to declare '*my 2 piggs are tolerably sober* '- the effect seems unintentional and due to the rather stilted way in which such incidents are recounted. He was certainly no story teller but some of the more bizarre encounters such as the girl in Norwich with no arms '*and yet wonderfully clever with her feet,*' require little embellishment. On another occasion, the evening after Nancy had been busy making raspberry jam they were interrupted by:

a black with a french horn, blowing it all the way up the yard to the kitchen door, to know if we would like to see a little woman only 33 inches high .... as we did not give our Dissent, she was taken out of the cart and brought into our kitchen where we saw her and heard her sing two songs. I don't think she was any taller than represented, but rather deformed, seemed in good spirits, sang exceedingly high with very little judgement and was very talkative.

Woodforde dispensed charity to the odd collection of vagrants, beggars and old soldiers who regularly beat a path to his door. None were turned away empty-handed, one shilling being the regular sum, but they were rewarded more from a sense of Christian duty than compassion. Baptisms and weddings were often held in the comfort of the rectory, and long before he was impaired by ill health, Woodforde paid a curate to officiate at services. The burial of a five week old child in the depths of winter was recorded with the indifference of a man more concerned for his own welfare - *'I think that I never felt the cold more severe than when I buried the above infant.'*

Unlike his contemporary, Gilbert White, Woodforde's curiosity in the natural world extended only to his enjoyment of country sports; fishing and hare coursing were among his favourite pastimes. Wildlife is otherwise only ever referred to as vermin. Beset by a plague of toads in his pond, the parson spent *'most of the morning in killing them, I dare say I killed one hundred'*, and in the winter of 1784 he wrote: *'I rejoiced much this morning on shooting an old woodpecker which had teized me a long time in pulling out the Reed from my house....to Goody Doughty for 7 lemons pd.0.0.6.'*

East Tuddenham rectory where Parson Woodforde often visited his friend Mr Du Quesne.

Although Woodforde's rectory has gone along with Weston House, the home of his friend Mr Custance, the landscape around remains remarkably unchanged despite the turkey-rearing sheds at the edge of the village that would have have made the parson's mouth water. It is still possible to retrace the journeys he made on horseback to visit friends in nearby villages - the Bodhams at South Green, Mattishall; Mr Du Quesne at East Tuddenham rectory and an assortment of clergy at Great Witchingham, Honingham, Sparham and Hockering. The Mill at Lenwade and the old workhouse at Gressenhall that he knew so well have also survived. Weston Longville church, outwardly plain, solid and enduring like its famous parson buried in the chancel, contains a portrait of the diarist by his nephew Samuel Woodforde RA.

Norwich

Throughout the first weeks of May 1373 a thirty year old woman, name unknown, lay dying in a room somewhere in the city. Days later in the early hours of sunday May 8th, having received the last rites, she gazed upon the cross and God's love became known to her in a series of revelations or 'showings' as she preferred to call them. Profoundly moved by these experiences and her return to health, the woman withdrew from the world, taking refuge in an anchorite cell attached to St Julian's church and overlooking the river Wensum, where she remained in prayer and contemplation until her death in 1413. Although she wrote down the first abbreviated account of her showings at the time, many years of quiet reflection passed before she understood their meaning well enough to produce the much longer version known to the world as *The Sixteen Revelations of Divine Love*.

Because St Julian's church was controlled by the Benedictine Priory that lay just outside the city walls at Carrow, it is commonly assumed that the person referred to simply as **Julian of Norwich** received her education there, but nothing more is known about the author of the earliest surviving text by an English woman and one of the great medieval mystics. There are no relics and no tomb to enhance her reputation, the original late 14th century manuscript of her 'Revelations' has been lost - the earliest surviving copies in the British Museum are much later - but the absence of tangible evidence is somehow consistent with her wish to remain anonymous and allow readers to find Christ's love through her writing.

The solitary religious life supported by bequests and donations became popular in medieval England, but while hermits often retired to rocky outcrops on the coast, anchorites withdrew within the community where their reclusive life was a constant example to those who sought guidance on spiritual and moral issues. Norwich with its procession of pilgrims to the cathedral, was a prosperous religious centre and cells became attached to the city gates and most of the 50 or more medieval churches within the walls. Julian, like other anchorites, probably lived her life according to the 13th century Ancrene Rule which allowed for three cell windows; one into the church to receive the sacrament, one onto the churchyard to counsel those in need and a third through to the servant's quarters.

Parson Woodforde's memorial in Weston Longville church.

Julian lived through a period of unprecedented strife and to her refuge above the Wensum, pilgrims brought fragmentary news of the Hundred Years' War and, of more immediate concern, reports of the Peasants' Revolt, the latest visitation of the plague and the fate of heretics burnt in the city at Lollards' Pit. Although her book of 'Revelations' was then virtually unknown, Julian welcomed among her many visitors the young Margery Kempe from King's Lynn. This worldly figure who travelled extensively abroad in search of religious fulfilment, received wise counsel over 'many days' knowing that Dame Julian through her own inner journey had acquired a vision of God more profound that anything she had experienced, without stepping outside her cell.

Today, down an alley between the high rise flats in Rouen Road and the King Street 'red light' district, stands the Catholic church of St Julian, a faithful reconstruction of the medieval building destroyed by a German bomb in 1942. Built into the north wall is a Norman doorway rescued from the church of St Michael at Thorn in Ber Street that had suffered the same fate. It leads through into the new Julian shrine on or near the site where for over 600 years the faith inspired by her remarkable showings is still kept alive.

St Julian wrote her *Revelations of Divine Love* in an anchorite cell attached to the medieval church. Destroyed in the last war, a new shrine has been incorporated in the present building.

Sir Thomas Browne had already completed his most famous work 'Religio Medici' before moving to Norwich in 1636, even though it was not published until 1643, and he is still regarded by many as the city's most distinguished scholar and one of England's finest prose writers. He established his medical practice in a sumptuously panelled Jacobean house formerly owned by a mayor of Norwich, that stood at the junction of the Haymarket and Orford Place. Browne lived and worked here for the rest of his life surrounded by his specimens and an impressive library of over 2000 volumes that reflected a wide ranging interest in philosophy, religion, linguistics and the natural sciences. Following a visit in 1671 John Evelyn described Browne's *'whole house and garden being a paradise and cabinet of rarities, and that of the best collection, especially medals, books, plants and natural things.'*

Although, as the leading practitioner in Norfolk, he always regarded himself firstly a physician, he always found time to pursue his amateur interest in natural history. Renowned for his collection of eggs, Browne also identified several new species of wild flowers and made important contributions to the study of marine life from specimens brought to him by local fishermen. As an antiquarian he was fascinated by the Roman urns found in a field at Brampton and several years later the discovery of a Saxon burial ground at Gt. Walsingham inspired his **Urn Burial** (1658), the *'leisurely excursion of a scholarly mind into the burial customs of past nations'* that for *'richness of imagery and majestic pomp of diction can hardly be paralleled in the English language.'*

Pegram's statue of **Sir Thomas Browne** (1605-82) on Hay Hill.

Knighted by Charles 11 in St Andrews Hall, Browne died eleven years later in 1682 and was buried in his local church, St Peter Mancroft. Despite his request that *'at my death I mean to take a total adieu of the world, not caring for a monument, History or Epithaph'*, his wife arranged for a memorial tablet to be erected on the wall of the sanctuary near his vault. He lay here peacefully until the accidental disturbance of his tomb in 1840 and the removal of his skull to the museum of the Norfolk and Norwich hospital. It remained there until 1922 when it was finally returned to St Peter Mancroft. Three years after its removal Browne's house in the Haymarket was replaced by a savings bank.

It was not until 1905 that the corporation, conscious of how the memory of its most illustrious citizen had thus far been commemorated, elected to celebrate the tercentenary of his birth with a statue erected on Hay Hill. But even this display of civic pride failed to prevent another outburst of rampart idolatry when in 1961 the timber frame building known as Sir Thomas Browne's garden house was demolished to make way for Littlewoods department store. In 1972 the statue itself was relocated to make room for a fountain of dubious taste that has since been paved over, and shortly afterwards the meadow between the Cathedral and Pull's Ferry where Browne planted fruit trees and grew his herbs was turned into a car park. Today all that remains is the invaluable collection of Browne's manuscripts and letters assembled last century and Pegram's bronze statue of Browne contemplating a shard of pottery with all the bemused abstraction of a man grown used to the indifference of the world around him.

* * * * *

There is a long history of dissent in Norwich and the city is, as Malcolm Bradbury acknowledges, *'proud of its radical heritage.'* Kett's Rebellion of 1549 was probably its most graphic expression but throughout the next two centuries Norwich accepted refugees from religious persecution in Europe in a mood of tolerance that helped create the city's Non-conformist tradition in the early 19th century. Just north of the river in Colegate stand two monuments to that particular brand of religious radicalism. Tucked away down an alley is the

Old Meeting House, a sophisticated design in red brick with early sash windows and a series of Corinthian pilasters founded in 1643 by Protestant refugees from Holland. Nearby and more impressive is the Octagon built in 1755 as a Presbyterian chapel. Its theatrical interior, full of columns and panelled galleries, became the meeting place for the city's freethinking intellectuals that earned it the reputation of *'the Devil's cucumber frame.'*

The Octagon chapel in Colegate attended by Harriet Martineau, became the centre for radical dissent in Norwich during the early 19th century.

Writing from her home in King's Lynn, Fanny Burney was mindful of the Octagon group when she wrote in 1792 '*I am truly amazed and half alarmed to find this county filled with little Revolution Societies'*. Prominent among its members was the Quaker and popular novelist Amelia Opie who, like others, supported the French Revolution. Her husband was John Opie, the Royal Academician who painted Robert Southey's portrait in 1806 during the poet's return visit to the Octagon. Well pleased with his stay, Southey wrote to a friend: '*For Society, of all places I have ever seen, Norwich is the best.'* Among those he came to see was the linguist William Taylor who taught German to the young George Borrow. Taylor, another republican who attended the Octagon, lies buried in the little churchyard behind the chapel.

Gurney Court off Magdalen Street, birthplace of Elizabeth Fry and Harriet Martineau.

Harriet Martineau
(1802-76)

A short distance from here in Gurney Court is the birthplace of the city's two most notable libertarians, Elizabeth Fry (1780) the Quaker prison reformer and **Harriet Martineau** (1802). The Martineau family of Huguenot descent, moved across the road to No 24 Magdalen Street, *'a handsome, plain brick house .... prosaic to the last degree. Except the vine on its back gable there is not an element of naturalness or poetry about it.'* But there in the walled garden, Harriet's *Autobiography* recalls the imaginative world of her childhood:

our plan was to dig completely through the globe till we came out at the other side. I fully expected to do this, and had an idea of an extremely deep hole, the darkness of which at the bottom would be lighted by the passage of stars'. Thwarted by an impenetrable layer of rubble the children simply adapted their hole to the shape of a grave in which they laid, eyes shut *'having an extreme desire to know what dying was like.*

Harriet Martineau attended services at the Octagon where her eyes wandering up to the windows in the roof *'looking for angels to come to me and take me to heaven, in sight of the congregation'.* Despite being able to pray alone, she could never manage to do so in chapel, *'and the hypocricy of appearing to do so was a long and sore trouble'.* Not surprisingly in the light of these revelations, she began writing moral tales for children, but today her literary reputation rests with her essays on social reform and her work as a campaigning journalist.

* * * * *

George Borrow's early years spent moving around the country with his father's regiment, stirred in the young boy a desire to travel which lasted most of his life and provided the material for a series of autobiographical works. The recall of the West Norfolk Militia from Ireland after the Battle of Waterloo, signalled the end of his father's military career and the family settled in Norwich, leasing a house that still stands in Willow Lane, off St Giles Street. At the age of 13, he attended the King Edward VI Grammar School in the Cathedral Close for three years, but his peripatetic life and early encounters with gypsies had not prepared him for the strictures of formal education. *Lavengro* remains silent about the school years that proved an unwelcome interruption to his self-education. The only account comes from James Martineau and illustrates Borrow's rebellious nature as much as the brutal regime *'under the rod of Dr Edward Volpey'.* Having been discovered leading a group of boys on some mutinous adventure, Borrow was hoisted onto the back of a fellow pupil and flogged in front of the whole school.

George Borrow
(1803-81)

Whenever possible Borrow escaped to the fairs in Tombland where he mingled with the gypsies and tinkers whose life and language he found so fascinating. In *Lavengro* he salutes the sport of bare-knuckle fighting and recalls a gathering the country's greatest prize fighters in Chapel Fields. At a horse fair on Castle Meadow, where several gypsies were displaying their riding skills in an improvised ring, a wild-eyed man with locks of shiny black hair spotted the young boy in the crowd and Borrow became reacquainted with Jasper Petulengro, the gypsy he had met years before. Leaving the fair together they made for the gypsy encampment on Mousehold Heath.

King Edward VI Grammar School in Cathedral Close where George Borrow felt the rod of Dr Volpey.

The open heath that Borrow knew stretched for miles to the north east of the city and, intersected by drovers' tracks, looked very much as Cotman had painted it a few years earlier. The two friends '*arrived at a small valley between two hills or downs, the sides of which were covered with furze; in the midst of this valley were various carts and low tents forming a rude kind of encampment*' Here, roaming about the heath, or at one of the many fairs in the neighbourhood, Borrow soon came to admire Petulengro's tribe and through his remarkable gift for languages became so proficient in the Romany tongue, '*spoken by people who dwell among thickets and furze bushes, in tents as tawny as their faces'*, that he was given the name 'Lav-engro' which *'in the language of the gorgios meaneth Word Master'.*

On his leaving school in 1818 Borrow's parents attempted to rescue him from a life of vagrancy by securing him the position of clerk articled to Simpson and Rackham, a firm of solicitors in Tuck's Court, St Giles Street. Here he sat behind a deal desk and copied documents in *a strange old house, occupying one side of a long and narrow court, into which, however, the greater number of the windows looked not, but into an extensive garden, filled with fruit trees, in the rear of a large, handsome house'* To relieve the boredom, Borrow used every opportunity to teach himself languages and after five years he remained *'a novice in law but a perfect master in the Welsh tongue'.* On the death of his father in 1823 Borrow left for London and, failing to find work as a translator, set off on his travels before joining the Bible Society. (see p143)

Mousehold Heath c.1810 by John Sell Cotman, looks much as George Borrow would have known it when he visited the gypsy camp a few years later.

The building known as Anna Sewell House stands at the junction of Church Street and Spixworth Road in Old Catton, a modest 18th century residence named after the author of **Black Beauty** (1877) who lived there from 1866 until her death in 1878. Confined to bed for much of her adult life by a mysterious illness not unknown among educated Victorian spinsters, **Anna Sewell** wrote her only published work *'to induce kindness, sympathy and an understanding treatment of horses'* among those who worked with them. But this *'autobiography of a horse',* full of incident and simple moral values, soon became a children's classic and remains one of the best loved animal stories, although the author never lived to enjoy its success.

The house at Old Catton where Anna Sewell lived and wrote ***Black Beauty.***

Born in Yarmouth in a house that still stands overlooking Church Plain, she moved soon after to London with her parents and then to Bath where they remained for many years before returning to Norfolk. The family connection was renewed each summer when Anna and her brother travelled to stay with their grandparents at Dudwick Farm near Aylsham. The farm was part of the Dudwick estate owned by their uncle and it was here that Anna first learned to ride.

Characters in ***Black Beauty*** were drawn from members of her family and incidents of cruelty to horses were often taken directly from her own experience of city life. Sewell was quick to make the distinction, prevelant in the 19th century, between the evils of urban existence and civilised society in the country epitomized by Birtwick Park (Dudwick) where the loyal bond between servant and master, man and animal, was recognised as the highest virtue. True to her Quaker upbringing, Sewell used the book to affirm the evils of drink and work on the sabbath as well as concern for the welfare of others.

Each week her brother would ride Black Bess, the model for Black Beauty, from his home in Norwich via Old Catton and Spixworth out to his uncle's house. Today the route passes close to Redwings Horse Sanctuary, a reminder that although horses are now kept largely for pleasure, neglect and cruelty still persist over a century after the publication of Sewell's influential tale.

* * * * *

Arnold Wesker
(1932 -)

Unable to get a grant to enter RADA in 1950, **Arnold Wesker** left behind in London a failed relationship and a pile of rejection slips to stay with his sister Della and her husband in south Norfolk. Once at Wacton he applied for the post of kitchen porter in The Bell Hotel on Timber Hill where, having abandoned any hope of becoming a writer he recalls, '*I began to write behind my back*'. Although odd incidents found their way into his first play, ***The***

Kitchen was based largely on experiences that came later at Le Rallye restaurant in Paris, but descriptions in his diary of the lost souls who drifted through The Bell, grew into ***The Terrible Valley,*** his unpublished trilogy of hotel life.

These autobiographical stories with their gallery of rogues and ruffians, capture the strange underworld where workplace dramas were played out, quite literally, at the kitchen sink. There was Tom the chef, opinionated, prone to gross exaggeration and hungry for affection, who taught Wesker elementary cooking; Albert the gay washer-up who fell in love with him and the head waiter, *'the most lecherous of young men who fucked all the female staff he could pin down in passages, storerooms, on the edge of dining room tables* and who *somewhere on the East Anglian coast runs a country house of monstrous decor.'* Harry, always drunk, on the scrounge, and on the road before finding work as a porter at The Bell, became the central character in ***Hal Scratch***, the second of Wesker's stories, while Robbie the waiter *'a well-spoken, semi-cultured gambling alcoholic'* resurfaced in ***The Terrible Valley***.

Of all the lonely, damaged individuals who sought temporary refuge and a regular meal in the hotel kitchens during the fourteen months Wesker worked there, Gordon was perhaps the most vulnerable, *'very shaky some mornings over the kitchen sink peeling potatoes, often still with make-up smudged over his face.'* Gordon was gay and worked each evening as a drag artist in The Blue Room near Thorpe Station, a place of dubious reputation that catered for minority tastes. Understandably Wesker put some distance between himself and his workmates, preferring to record observations in the privacy of his attic bedroom, but through his humanity, his Jewishness and ironically, his own sense of failure as a writer, he came to identify with this sad collection of misfits. Their *'failed, impoverished lives'* began to assume a fictional reality in Wesker's trilogy, out of which emerged a new self-confidence that he could write something of lasting quality. In this extract from his recent autobiography Wesker acknowledges the importance of his time in the city in what amounts to his own writer's manifesto:

all these characters .... made an impression on me that I only now realise .... was deep and seminal. I concluded .... too many people chase second best too often: their perplexity, fear and frustration, rendered them naked, exposed: they were bereft of the wherewithal to defend themselves against grubby exploitation .... The hotel, where I came to find peace, ... drew me slowly into a vortex of lives abounding with petty intrigues, short tempers, self-righteous extremes .... But I stumbled upon some of the themes for a lifetime of writing: lives wasted accepting second best

But Wesker hadn't bargained on Dusty Bicker. This *'vivacious country girl'* from Starston had left school at fifteen to escape the privations of life in an isolated village on the Norfolk-Suffolk border and took her chance in the city where, having worked in several hotels, she arrived at The Bell amid the kind of speculation that greeted every new chambermaid. There was no escape for Wesker once she had become installed at the other end of his corridor, and despite attempts to thwart her infatuation, *'the country girl got under his skin.'*

The Bell Hotel. Wesker's attic bedroom is on the left where, from his experiences as a kitchen porter the idea for his play **Roots** began to take shape.

They made love as church bells rang out across the city announcing the death of another wasted Sunday. It was church bells that first so enraged Jimmy Porter in John Osborne's 'Look Back in Anger'; the play that established the credibility of working class theatre in which Wesker's **Roots** was soon to flourish. Out of the passion of those afternoons an image began to form in the young playwright's mind. Beatie Bryant, the central character in his first Norfolk play, was even then beginning to take on the personality of Dusty Bicker and, as Wesker acknowledges, her 'triumphant outrage' at the end of the play had its seeds in his Bell Hotel diary even though he had yet to meet Dusty's family. (see p132)

2
Shelter from the Storm
Yarmouth &
The Broads

There after supper lit by lantern light
Warm in the cabin I could lie secure
And hear against the polished sides at night
The lap lap lapping of the weedy Bure,
A whispering and watery Norfolk sound
Telling of all the moonlit reeds around.

How did the Devil come? When first attack?
The church is just the same, though now I know
Fowler of Louth restored it. Time, bring back
The rapturous ignorance of long ago,
The peace, before the dreadful daylight starts,
Of unkept promises and broken hearts.

From *Norfolk* by **John Betjeman**

Itteringham

In the late 60s, when **George Barker** spotted an advertisement for a National Trust property to rent in Norfolk, he was already a legendary figure among the Bohemian set who frequented the Colony Club and other Soho drinking haunts. In the 1930s, along with other aspiring poets, Barker drifted into David Archer's bookshop on Parton Street and from there to T S Eliot at Faber who admired his work. Barker and Dylan Thomas were among the first generation of working class poets to challenge the blue line that led straight from Oxbridge to the London publishing houses, and the appearance of 'Poems' when Barker was still only 22, represented a significant breakthrough.

Barker had 'invented himself from the least likely material', and came to Norfolk with a fearsome reputation for outrageous behaviour and passionate, witty conversation, a celebrated love affair with Elizabeth Smart (see p135), and Elspeth Langlands, the beautiful young woman he eventually married. He also brought with him an unshakeable belief in his own literary talent that earned him many admirers but very little money. Bintry House, a 17th century flint and brick farmhouse on the Blickling estate, was damp and draughty but beautifully positioned on the banks of a reluctant stream. Barker's arrival failed to ruffle the lethargic waters of the Bure but the two swans that floated *'like blobs of ice-cream on* (its) *black surface'* hissed a warning, as the countryside around prepared to pass judgement on the rapscallion tribe that

Bintry House, George Barker's home from the late 60s until his death in 1991.

was Barker's extended family and odd assortment of friends. The very place names bristled with indignation; Tuttington disapproved, Erpingham exploded and Itteringham twitted irritably.

Life at Bintry House seldom mirrored the tranquillity of Barker's ***Morning in Norfolk*** when *'The crimson / December morning brims over / Norfolk, turning / to burning Turner / this aqueous water colour / idyll that earlier gleamed / so green that it seemed / drowned.'* More often, after one of Barker's drinking evenings when 'the house smouldered angrily', the dawn was shattered by the sound of breaking glass and *'The hanging fire of the day'* became a blazing hangover. Barker's 'Icelandic' rage came from his father and grandfather, a Lincolnshire farmer who, when the drink was on him, would stagger into the yard and wrestle with the cattle. But the next day all would be forgotten: *'For then the mind / Looking backwards upon its / too sullied yesterday / that rotting sack of / resolution and refuse / reads in the rainbowed sky / a greater covenant, / the tremendous pronouncement: / the day forgives.'*

As **Raffaella Barker** is quick to point out, *'most of the time the chaos was warm and familiar and comforting'* although she often craved the orderly life of friends. In ***Come and Tell Me Some Lies*** (1994) she offers an amusing and affectionate picture of life in the Barker household where danger lurked round every corner. Children fell off motorbikes or wrote off cars and ended up in hospital; her brothers plundered the wreckage of planes that fell out of the sky and hoarded live ammunition in the barn and chickens succumbed to mysterious diseases or were slaughtered by deranged dogs. Babies were born amid the chaos to a mother who, affecting a blond wig to avoid detection when driving around the country lanes, *'looked like a mad woman'*. For Raffaella, unsure of the difference between truth and fable, her father's stories became *'fairy-tales, fantasies grown from a seed of truth into something wild and overblown'*, to re-emerge in several collections of children's verse, notably ***To Aylsham Fair***.

Barker wrote with 'a tiger in his loins' that threatened to devour those around him, but he remained dedicated to the muse, 'his only real mistress' until his death in 1991. Anthony Thwaite attributes his neglect as a poet firstly to the towering presence of Dylan Thomas, another poet of 'personal concern and extravagant gesture', and then to changes in poetic fashion that saw the emergence of anti-romantic Movement poets like Philip Larkin in the 50s and the trend towards performance poetry a decade later.

Barker's line drawing in
At Thurgarton Church.

*As I stand by the porch
I believe that no one has heard
here in Thurgarton Church
one single veritable word
save the unspoken No.*

*The godfathered negative
that responds to our mistaken
incredulous and heartbroken
desire above all to live
as though things were not so.*

*Desire above all to live
as though the soul was stone
believing we cannot give
or love since we are alone
and always will be so.*

*That heartbroken desire
to live as though no light
ever set the seas on fire
and no sun burnt at night
or Mercy walked to and fro.*

*The proud flesh howls: I am not
caught up in the great cloud
of my unknowing. But that
proud flesh has endowed
us with the cloud we know.*

*To this the unspoken No
of the dead god responds
and then the whirlwinds blow
over all things and beyond
and the dead mop and mow.*

All his life Barker was engaged in the creative process of dying. As long ago as 1939 in his essay 'Therefore All Poems Are Elegies' he asserted that the poet *'embroiled daily in his own decease, is caught in the toil of reality as profoundly and as hopelessly as the consumptive who drowns in his own saliva'*. This was Barker's central theme; he disdained the professional poet who avoids death and writes clever, technical verse because *'the best poems leave him so much more short of blood'*. He was also haunted by Catholic guilt and fear of an authoritarian father he only forgave years later in the moving and eloquent poem *At Thurgarton Church*, dedicated to his memory.

Sloley

The novelist **Sylvia Townsend Warner** and her lover Valentine Ackland made frequent visits to Norfolk after Valentine's mother had moved to Winterton (see p51). In May 1933, on Valentine's birthday, they were out touring the countryside when Sylvia navigated the car up a track in the parish of Sloley. She may simply have been intrigued by the name, but Valentine's more purposeful eye picked out Frankfurt Manor, *'a mouldering grange'* tucked away in a wooded tributary of the river Ant. Their excitement grew when they discovered it was empty and to let. The 17th century house had a Dutch gable and reed thatch, but what struck Sylvia was how beautifully it had aged:

its good looks sobered by age and usage - It gave an impression of .... being worn smooth and thin like an old spoon. The doorway was narrow and severe; the mullions and transomes of the windows remarkably delicate. Their white paint was worn to a dandelion dock silver. The house was of brick, it had been coated with a yellowish limewash, ... the colour of the brick showed dimly through, so the general tint of the house was that of a ripening pear with streaks of vague rose and pale madder flushing its sallow stain.

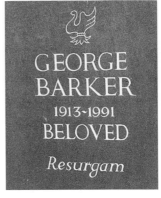

GEORGE
BARKER
1913-1991
BELOVED
Resurgam

*I hear the old bones in me cry
and the dying spirit call:
I have forfeited all
and once and for all must die
and this is all that I know.*

The faded limewash has gone but otherwise Frankfurt Manor looks much as Sylvia and Valentine knew it in 1933.

Bea Howe and Sylvia Townsend
Warner at Frankfurt Manor.

This description, written nearly thirty years later, appeared in her
Introduction to **The Cat's Cradle Book** (1960), a collection of short stories
written from a cat's-eye view of the world and based on an idea which took
shape at Frankfurt Manor where a family of 'rough' cats had taken up residence
in the outbuildings. Here for the next ten months Sylvia and Valentine were
blissfully happy gardening, writing or just pottering about. Sylvia's letters are
full of enchanting descriptions:

*The house looks out on a great rampart of trees; all day they are motionless
in the strong sun, but at dusk they seem to creep silently across the lawn, until
looking from my window I seem to see their enormous foreheads pressed to the
pane .... I have never lived with trees before. They take some mastering; but I
think I shall be on good terms with them even before I see them naked.*

In her autobiography **For Sylvia** Valentine conveys the mounting excitement
as they explored their new domain:

*At Frankfurt Manor, then, we lived in a kind of solemn, fairy story
splendour. The first spring and summer brought nothing but miraculous days.
Every day a fresh discovery; one day I found white currants .... another day we
met a hedgehog walking up the drive, another day I was picking green peas
into a colander and saw the earth near my feet heaving and a mole emerged
and I caught it instantly in the colander and carried it in to Sylvia and set it
down beside her typewriter on her table.*

The grounds included a walled kitchen garden, a nuttery, orchard and
paddock, but as the summer wore on they found it increasingly difficult to
attend properly to the garden and find time for their writing. They left the
house in November 1934 with heavy hearts both knowing '*we were never again*

so unimpededly good as we were at Frankfurt Manor.' Valentine wrote '*I shall never forget how I felt as I drove the car out of the gate for the last time. I dream of it now, too often, and when I am dead for sure my ghost will haunt there, loving and grieving.* Their only joint literary venture, a collection of poems entitled **Whether a Dove or a Seagull**, published anonymously the previous year remains a fitting memorial to the love which blossomed in this secret corner of Norfolk, 'the corner that held them'.

Oby

Prior to their stay at Frankfurt Manor, Sylvia and Valentine had taken a houseboat on the river at Thurne which with their numerous trips to Winterton and excursions in the surrounding countryside, gave Sylvia an intimate knowledge of the Broads that she used later in **The Corner That Held Them,** a chronicle of life in the 14th century nunnery of Oby:

under the enormous vault of sky, perched on the little rise of ground which gave the place its old name and half encircled by a loop of the Waxle Stream it looked like one of those maps into which the draughtsman has put every detail and coloured the whole to represent life.

Written in Dorset with numerous interruptions during the war, Sylvia began this, her favourite novel, in 1941, even though its completion and publication were to take another seven years. With no plot and no protagonist the nunnery becomes the central character where the more dramatic events; an outbreak of the plague, the collapse of the convent spire and the bishop's visitation, are interwoven with daily life during the years 1345 to 1382, and where the Waxle Stream becomes a metaphor for the pace and shape of the book:

a muddy, reluctant stream, full of loops and turnings and constantly reversing its course, for the general lie of the land imposed no restraints on its vagaries. In some places, it had hollowed for itself long pools where the current seemed to have ceased altogether, in others it skulked through acres of rushes and spongy moss.

The convent and its manor lie in the parish of Wivelham, some nine miles from the coastal town of Waxalby. Both Oby and Lintoft on the further side of Oby Fen are connected to Waxalby by '*the only indication of man's will to thwart nature*', a high earthen causeway called the Hog Trail. By her careful choice of place names with their Scandinavian endings ('by' and 'toft') and their approximation to real places (Waxham and Lowestoft), Sylvia managed to create a convincing context for the novel. Oby is itself an interesting choice for the nunnery; a place which now exists only as a name on the map beside the river Bure. A mile or so upstream stand the ruins of St Benet's abbey gatehouse, the subject of so many Norwich School watercolours, that may have given Sylvia the idea for her nunnery.

* * * * *

When **George Macbeth** moved out of London in 1979 it was part of a more general exodus by writers in search of fresh inspiration and cheap property deep in the East Anglian countryside. He arrived at Oby rectory, -'*I defer to* *country ease'*- having spent the last twenty years presenting poetry anthologies on BBC radio. These broadcasts, together with his readings in performance, had done much to popularise poetry over the last twenty years

Isolated on a low rise, the plain late Georgian house with its *'two acres of weed and woodlands'* protected by huge beech trees, looks out across large, windswept beet fields to the Bure marshes. This was the Isle of Flegg, an area of early Scandinavian settlement where Macbeth immediately felt at home: *'All arrogance is human, hot black pride of the Vikings is mine.'*

> *The long-ships drove up the Bure, and the horned men were*
> *here to rape and to burn,*
> *Seeding their names, Rollesby and Billockby, Fleggburgh,*
> *Clippesby and Thurne,*
> *Ashby and Oby. Our church roofs came from the rot of each*
> *oak-warped stern.*

George Macbeth against one of the massive beech trees in the grounds of Oby rectory.

45

Macbeth had a strong sense of being rooted to his piece of land and of feeling secure there with his young wife, the novelist Lisa St Aubin de Teran. Here he published his first children's story, ***The Rectory Mice,*** followed by a new collection of verse, ***Poems from Oby*** (1982) that he acknowledged were *'the fruit of a new understanding with the countryside'*. In **Renewal** Macbeth looks back on previous homes with former lovers before his thoughts return to new love and the desire to begin again.

> *I needed somewhere with a flirt of grace*
> *To match your fervour for long acerage.*
> *I found it, here at Oby. Naked space*

Rich in imagery from the natural world and domestic bliss, this collection reveals the diversity of Macbeth's verse from ***Thoughts on a Box of Razors***, a lengthy discussion on violence prompted by a purchase at Stalham sale, to the pleasure of breathing new life into the damp old house. Familiar themes of love and death recur but are here explored in a calmer, more consistent style that reflects Macbeth's connectedness to the place:

> *I saw the future, and our children stand*
> *Mirrored against those blackened, further trees*
> *In the cold December night: and, hand in hand,*
> *At ease with us, gather their flying dreams.*

But by then Macbeth's own dream had begun to fade with the death of Lisa's mother and the 'traumatic' birth of their son. From Oby the couple retreated to a Victorian gothic manor house on the edge of the Fens at Wiggenhall St Mary where his wife *'sank, at first imperceptibly, into the mud'* and *'felt the grey*

Oby rectory, the setting for Macbeth's children's story ***The Rectory Mice***.

mould of the Fens settle on (her) *mind*.' The marriage finally broke up in these bleak surroundings the day Lisa set off for Italy with a young painter. Macbeth left for Ireland where he later dealt with the experience in the only way he knew. *Another Love Story*, published the year before he died, is the thinly disguised and acrimonious account of their marriage.

Yarmouth

Charles Dickens
(1812 - 70)

For admirers of **Charles Dickens** the port of Yarmouth will always be associated with the opening chapters of *David Copperfield*, the author's thinly disguised autobiography. He had originally meant to set the story against the more familiar background of the Isle of Wight, and he did write some of the novel there in 1849 while staying at Bonchurch, but the trip planned earlier that year was cancelled because of bad weather. Instead Dickens travelled to Norfolk intent on visiting Stanfield Hall near Wymondham, scene of the notorious Rush murders. From there he travelled to Yarmouth, recording his impressions later through the eyes of the young Copperfield:

It looked rather spongy and soppy, I thought, as I carried my eye over the great dull waste that lay across the river; and I could not help wondering if the world was really as round as my geography book said, how any part of it came to be so flat. But I reflected that Yarmouth might be situated at one of the poles, which would account for it.

The following day Dickens ventured out from the Royal Hotel on Marine Parade to explore '*the strangest place in the world*.' The sounds and smells of this busy fishing town provided the author with just the atmosphere he wanted for the novel that was already taking shape in his mind. The story opens with the birth of David Copperfield at the Rookery in Blunderstone (Blundeston), a village south of Yarmouth through which Dickens had passed on his way to visit Sir Morton Peto at Somerleyton Hall. Overlooking the churchyard, The Rookery is almost certainly the rectory, even though the rooks had already vacated the trees at the bottom of the garden:

As the elms bent to one another, like giants who were whispering secrets, and after a few seconds of such repose, fell into violent flurry, tossing their wild arms about, as if their late confidences were really too wicked for their peace of mind, some weather-beaten old rooks' nests burdening their higher branches, swung like wrecks upon a stormy sea.

Here Davy is brought up by his mother and Peggotty his nanny, the wife of a Yarmouth fisherman who was proud to call herself a 'Yarmouth bloater'. Recalling his early childhood, Copperfield describes the house in vivid detail:

On the ground floor is Peggotty's kitchen, opening into a backyard, with a pigeon house on a pole in the centre, without any pigeons in it; a great dog kennel in a corner without any dog; and a quantity of fowls that look terribly tall to me, walking about in a menacing and ferocious manner.

Inside, the long hall from Peggotty's kitchen to the front door and the dark storeroom '*to be run past at night*' suggest the interior of Blundeston Hall which Dickens also visited. Outside where sheep grazed in the churchyard, the

47

The Saxon round tower remains unaltered, but the church at Blundeston has otherwise been heavily restored since David Copperfield's boyhood in The Rookery. Even the sundial is a brass replica of the original.

sundial over the porch is real enough, but the high backed pews from where Peggotty reassured herself that The Rookery had not been robbed or set on fire, are more like those in the church at Chatham that Dickens attended as a child.

Following the appearance of the infamous Murdstone who quickly befriends Davy's frail and impressionable mother, the young boy travels to Yarmouth on Barkis's carrier's cart to spend a holiday with Peggotty's family. Here Davy is made welcome by Ham and Little Em'ly in the upturned boat on the Denes which serves as their cramped but delightfully snug home. Dickens probably took the idea for this ingenious habitation from the Thames estuary where improvised dwellings of this sort clustered together on the edge of the marshes:

To hear the wind getting up out at sea, to know that the fog was creeping over the desolate flat outside and to look at the fire and think that there was no house near but this one, and this one a boat, was like enchantment.

On his return home Davy finds great changes have taken place at The Rookery; his mother has married Mr Murdstone who promptly installed his equally formidable sister and the empty kennel now houses a fearsome beast. The transformation signals the beginning of a miserable episode in the life of young Copperfield at the hands of the tyrannical couple. Retreating to his bedroom, Davy finds consolation in the characters that inhabit his adventure stories, including Robinson Crusoe whose shipwreck off Yarmouth presages the storm sequence near the end Dickens' novel.

Davy is then packed off to school in London where further misfortune awaits him in the shape of Creake, the sadistic headmaster. Here he meets Steerforth and together they embark on a series of adventures. Soon after Mrs Copperfield, bought low by her son's departure and Peggotty's dismissal, dies in labour and is buried alongside her husband in the churchyard. Some time later, while visiting his adoptive family, Davy makes a final pilgrimage to Blundestone. Walking in the churchyard, he reflects on the scene before him:

The ragged nests, so long deserted by the rooks were gone: and the trees were lopped and topped out of their remembered shapes. The garden had run wild, and half the windows of the houses were shut up. It was occupied only by a poor lunatic gentleman and the people who took care of him. He was always sitting at my little window looking out into the churchyard; and I wondered whether his rambling thoughts ever went upon any of the fancies that used to occupy mine, on the rosy mornings, when I peeped out of the same little window in my night clothes, and saw the sheep quietly feeding in the light of the rising sun.

Davy's decision to invite Steerforth to accompany him to Yarmouth sets in motion a train of events which lead to disaster. Ham is about to marry little Em'ly when she becomes captivated by Davy's friend and agrees to run away with him. Mr Peggotty, after travelling through many countries, eventually finds her abandoned by Steerforth and together they return to England. Towards the end of the novel Yarmouth becomes the setting for the final tragedy during a violent storm long remembered as '*the greatest ever known to blow upon that coast.*' Dickens reserves his most dramatic prose to convey the awesome power of the waves whipped up by this raging tempest:

As the high watery walls came rolling in, and, at their highest, tumbled into surf, they looked as if the least would engulf the town. As the receding wave swept back with a hoarse roar, it seemed to scoop out deep caves in the beach as if its purpose were to undermine the earth .... Undulating hills were changed to valleys, undulating valleys (with a solitary storm bird sometimes skimming through them) were lifted up to hills; masses of water shivered and shook the beach with a booming sound;.... the ideal shore on the horizon, with its towers and buildings, rose and fell; the clouds flew fast and thick; I seemed to see a rending and upheaving of all nature.

The following day a Spanish schooner runs aground within sight of the shore. Crowds gathering on the beach watch helplessly as the ship is pounded by tumultuous waves, when a lone survivor appears clinging to the broken mast, waving his red hat in a gesture familiar to Davy. At the same time Ham breaks through the crowd and, with a rope around his waist, battles through mountainous waves in a vain attempt to rescue his former rival. Ham is drowned as the ship sinks and sometime later a second body is washed ashore:

And on that part of it where she and I had looked for shells, two children - on that part of it where some lighter fragments of the old boat, blown down last night, had been scattered by the wind - among the ruins of the home he had wronged - I saw him lying with his head upon his arm, as I had often seen him lie at school.

Writing to his friend and biographer on completing **David Copperfield**, Dickens confided '*Oh, my dear Forster, if I were to say half of what Copperfield makes me feel tonight, how strangely, even to you, I should be turned inside-out! I seem to be sending some part of myself into the Shadowy World.*' It was the book he most enjoyed reading in public and in a later preface he admitted '*Of all my books, I like this the best.*'

Boats in Distress c1820 by the Yarmouth artist William Joy.

Winterton

Winterton Ness has always been a notoriously dangerous spot and the scene of countless shipwrecks. **Daniel Defoe** cites the occasion in 1692 when upward of 200 Newcastle colliers bound for London were driven aground in a storm with the loss of over 1000 lives. Travelling north from Yarmouth in 1724 he described the widespread use of wreckage:

Country people had scarce a barn, or a shed, or a stable; nay nor the pales of their yards, and gardens, not a hog stye, not a necessary-house, but what was built of old planks, beams, wales and timbers etc, the wrecks of ships and ruins of mariners and merchants' fortunes; and in some places were whole yards fill'd and piled up very high with the same stuff laid up, as I suppos'd to sell for the like building purposes, as there should be occasion.

Defoe's *Tour Through England and Wales* was in fact an amalgam of various trips made as a government official rather than the record of a single journey, and enabled him to draw directly on experiences along this stretch of coast in *Robinson Crusoe*. Having run away to sea against his father's will, Crusoe finds himself on a boat six days out from Hull and anchored in Yarmouth Roads awaiting a following wind when another storm breaks. Mountainous seas batter the ship which sinks shortly after the crew are rescued. The lifeboat labours towards shore *'till being past the lighthouse at Winterton'* it begins to pull more easily under the shelter of land. Once ashore Crusoe walks to Yarmouth where he lodges for the night. In scorning the opportunity presented by the storm to return home, Crusoe seals his fate and on arrival in London, boards a ship bound for Africa.

* * * * *

Shortly after **Sylvia Townsend Warner** and Valentine Ackland had first met at the home of the Dorset novelist T F Powys, they went to stay in Winterton, in an Edwardian villa owned by Valentine's parents. She remembered as a child sitting for hours in the branches of a tree in the garden writing poems and letters to imaginary friends. Beyond, the dunes stretched for miles along the coast in either direction, and in the summer of 1930 the *'lovers lounged in the inn and on the quay, played childish games on the beach, writing their initials in the sand'*. Years later Sylvia drew on these memories:

> *Across the dunes and brushing through the marram*
> *Grass the holiday strangers loiter*
> *Happy and idle and a little solemn*
> *Sobered by so deep a sky and so straight a horizon;*

The following year Valentine took Sylvia to meet John Craske, a retired fisherman and painter whose naive seascapes she much admired. Valentine had stumbled upon his unlikely talent when her aunt, who lived in the old lighthouse at Winterton, told her about a local man who made model boats. Arriving at his cottage workshop she discovered paintings executed on every available surface - old doors, tea chest panels and pieces of driftwood. Sylvia also was struck by the directness of Craske's work and bought a number of paintings. Years later she included *John Craske's Country* in a series of poems entitled 'Five British Watercolours'.

You cannot love here as you can love inland
Where love grows easy as a pig or a south-wall fruit
Love on this coast is something you must dispute
With a wind blowing from the North Pole and only salt
water between.

And you cannot grieve here as you can grieve inland.
Where the dead lie sweetly labelled like jams in the grocer's store
You must blink at the sea till your face is scarlet and your eyes sore
With a wind blowing from the North Pole and only salt
water between

Seascape by John Craske.

Horsey Mere

Having visited Aldeburgh in 1861 to gather material for his second novel 'No Name' (see p171), **Wilkie Collins** was already familiar with the Suffolk coast when he returned to East Anglia three years later. Staying on this occasion with friends at the Victoria Hotel in Yarmouth he combined a little sailing with research for some of the crucial scenes in his next novel *Armadale* (1866). Being a great admirer of Defoe's work, Collins decided to retrace Crusoe's journey up the coast to Winterton where, from the dunes, a short walk inland brought him to the edge of Horsey Mere.

Armadale, is regarded by many as the classic Novel of Sensation with its convoluted plot, bewildering scene changes and gallery of unsavoury characters. Having sketched out the plot while on holiday in Italy, Collins travelled to Norfolk where much of the second half of the book is set. Here, the melancholy atmosphere of the reed beds and the still, shallow water of Horsey Mere were precisely what Collins wanted for the picnic trip to Hurle Mere and the introduction of the novel's murderous anti-heroine Lydia Gwilt:

Wilkie Collins
(1824 - 89)

The reeds opened back on the right hand and the left, and the boat glided suddenly into the wide circle of a pool. Round the nearer half of the circle, the eternal reeds still fringed the margin of the water. Round the farther half the land appeared again here rolling back from the pool in desolate sandhills: there, rising above it in a sweep of grassy shore .... The sun was sinking in the cloudless western heaven. The waters of the Mere lay beneath, tinged red by the dying lights. The open country stretched away, darkening drearily already on the right hand and the left. And on the near margin of the pool, where all had been solitude before, there now stood, fronting the sunset, the figure of a woman

The novel was written in London where Collins had for several years been living with Caroline Graves, the inspiration for 'The Woman in White', but the Hurle Mere episode may have dramatised a more recent encounter with a Winterton girl called Martha Rudd. Collins, who had an eye for attractive women, found the spirited beauty and simple virtues of this young country girl irresistible, and by the time Martha moved to London in 1868, pregnant with the first of his three children, Caroline Graves was respectably married to a younger man. Martha remained with Collins until his death twenty years later.

Eccles On Sea

Today Eccles On Sea is little more than the Bush estate, a grim little exercise in property speculation begun between the wars. According to contemporary accounts the village disappeared beneath the waves during a tempest of biblical ferocity on January 4th 1604 and almost overnight Eccles Juxta Mare had become Eccles 'Sub Mare' and a mere name on the map with only the round tower of St Mary's church visible. Partly engulfed in the sand for many years it was left exposed on the foreshore by a series of storm tides in the middle of the last century, marking the site where the early Christian fathers first established a precarious foothold on this exposed stretch of coastline - the name 'Eccles' is derived from the Latin for 'Church'.

Eccles church tower in 1882.

This lonely sentinel became a familiar landmark to sailors, the object of speculation among antiquarians and the destination for siteseers until on January 25th 1895, it finally succumbed to the sea. Since then, at intervals, fragments of masonry have been left exposed by scouring tides, exciting the morbid fascination of graverobbers and attracting the attention of amateur archaeologists. In *Eccles* the poet **Anthony Thwaite** reflects on how even the name of the village, like the remains of the church and the place itself, have been cut short, silenced for ever by the sea.

Cliffs sifting down, stiff grassblades bent,
Subdued, and shouldering off thick sand,
Boulders - compacted grout and flint -
Jut from a stranded beach, a land
Adhering thickly to the sea.
Tide-drenched, withdrawn, and drowned again,
Capsized, these buttresses still strain
Towards perpendicularity

> *The place-name mimes the fallen church,*
> *Abbreviated, shrunk to this*
> *Truncated word, echo of speech,*
> *A Latin ghost's thin obsequies*
> *Carried by wind, answered by sea-*
> *Ecclesia: the syllables*
> *Curtailed, half heard, like tongueless bells*
> *From empty steeples endlessly.*

Bacton

The coastline between Cromer and Great Yarmouth provides the setting for **Devices and Desires** (1989), one of **P D James'** most enthralling detective novels. Although places peripheral to the main events are real enough - Holt is the scene of the Whistler's fourth victim at the beginning of the book, and the police incident room is set up in Hoveton - James admits that this is simply her '*cunning device to add authenticity to fictitious characters and events* ' Real and imaginary worlds are further confused by the use of local village names such as Massingham and Lessingham for some of the minor characters, but the author is quick to point out that Larksoken mill, the power station and Lydsett village, central landmarks around which the action revolves, are not to be found on any map of the locality.

P D James
(1920 -)

Using her knowledge of the area James sets about rearranging familiar elements of the Norfolk landscape to create a convincing picture of this desolate coast; its long continuous curve interrupted by a low headland fringed with pine trees. At the far end the menacing bulk of Larksoken nuclear power station governs the lives and occasionally the deaths of those on the headland. From here it presides over a landscape littered with relics from the past - the abandoned sea defences, the ruined abbey, the disused railway and the converted windmill; powerful reminders of man's arrogant attempt to impose order on the natural world:

The headland was empty and almost bare, the few straggling trees, distorted by the wind, struggling to keep their precarious hold in the uncompromising soil. And now he was passing a second and more dilapidated pillbox and it struck him that the whole headland had the desolate look of an old battlefield .... while the power station loomed over it like a grandiose modern monument to the unknown dead.

One thing that distinguishes P D James from most other crime writers is not just the brilliant dissection of a cleverly constructed plot, but the way in which the narrative is shot through with references to landmarks that exert a powerful influence over the lives of her characters. In this extract the director of the power station begins to voice doubts about its future:

For those who sought symbols in inanimate objects, its message was both simple and expedient, that man, by his own intelligence and his own efforts, could understand and master his own world .... But sometimes on the darkest nights, when the waves pounded the shingle like distant gunfire, both the science and the symbol would seem as transitory as those drowned lives and he

Stowe windmill

would find himself wondering if this great hulk would one day yield to the sea, like the wave-smashed concrete from the last war defences, and like them, become a broken symbol of man's long history on this desolate coast.

As the story unfolds the author's sleuth, Commander Adam Dalgliesh, travels up from London to spend what he imagines will be a relaxing weekend at Larksoken Mill. On arrival at his country retreat, complete with sails and an octagonal domecap remarkably like Stowe Mill near Mundesley, he climbs to the top and surveys the surrounding countryside. Lydsett with its flint and pantile cottages, its Dutch gables and round tower church looks authentic and even the name of the pub, 'The Local Hero', a colloquial reference to Nelson in the county of his birth, sounds convincing.

But the coast here is strewn with red herrings; has there been a radioactive leak at the power station or is the author simply spreading mischief among her suspects as well as covering her own tracks? From the power station the dramatic skyline of Happisburgh church tower and the lighthouse is clearly visible. The tower, rising 110 feet above the flat countryside, is a beacon of faith *'and the last sight of land for hundreds of drowning mariners'* finally laid to rest in the churchyard. They include the entire crew of HMS Invincible which broke up on March 13th 1801; over one hundred unsung local heroes on their way to join Nelson's fleet. By drawing on this macabre incident James provides an important topographical clue to the whereabouts of Larksoken. Happisburgh is only three miles south of Bacton gas terminal, but in replacing this benign source of energy with a Sizewell-type nuclear reactor, she creates a sinister focal point for a series of mysterious deaths in the wake of the Chernobyl disaster.

By contrast, the ruined Benedictine Abbey is *'the decaying symbol of a very different power.'* Perched precariously on a low cliff of crumbling sand, it sounds remarkably like the priory at Dunwich on the Suffolk coast, the scene of James' other East Anglian detective novel (see p166) but the remains of Broomholm Priory languishing in a farmyard in the nearby parish of Bacton

Happisburgh church and the lighthouse became familiar landmarks to William Cowper as well as the characters in ***Devices and Desires.***

seem a more likely reference. With a piece of the Holy Cross in its possession, Broomholm was once an important pilgrimage centre and one of the great powerhouses of monastic life in East Anglia. *'By the Holy Cross of Bromholm'* was the oath of Chaucer's Reeve. Larksoken Abbey with the nuclear reactor framed in its *'great empty arch of the east window'* holds a peculiar power for those on the headland; the scene of secret assignations and moonlight expeditions to honour the dead.

Remains of the south transept of Broomholm Priory.

The presence of the past and its ability to influence events, is a constant thread running through the novel. Martyr's Cottage is built on the site of an earlier house in which Agnes Poley lived, before burning at the stake in 1557. The plaque which commemorates the event carries the quotation from Ecclesiastes Chapter 3, verse 15: *'That which hath been is now and that which is to be hath already been, and God requireth that which is past.'* Reflecting on the novel's final conflagration and its aftermath, Meg Dennison sees *'the past and the present fused and her own life, with its trivial devices and desires, seemed only an insignificant moment in the long history of the headland.'*

Paston

The volumes of private correspondence known as the **Paston Letters** provide a unique insight into the life and aspirations of a prosperous family in the 15th century. Covering the period 1420 to 1500 they chronicle the rise of the Pastons from humble origins to become one of the wealthiest families in the region, against a background of the Wars of the Roses. The letters, above all, make clear the Pastons' chief preoccupation; the acquisition and administration of property by every means at their disposal. Pursued ruthlessly through a calculated series of marriages, alliances and the seizure of land, the family amassed huge estates in north east Norfolk with principle residences at Gresham, Oxnead and Caister Castle as well as in the village from which the family took its name.

The letters, by far the largest single collection to survive from the 15th century, present a remarkable picture of life as seen from the manor house. Essentially business correspondence written in the plain style of the day and

Oxnead Hall. The Pastons entertained Charles II here at the height of their power, but the estate was sold off in 1731 and the hall pulled down soon after.

never intended for publication, they are in no sense belles-lettres. Any literary merit they possess is, as Virginia Woolf concluded, largely accidental: *'in all this there is no writing for writing's sake, no use of the pen to convey pleasure or amusement or any of the million shades of endearment and intimacy which has filled so many English letters since.'*

The great tythe barn built for Sir William Paston in 1581.

From the letters written to her husband, many of them from Caister Castle, Margaret Paston emerges as the central character, defending the family interests with great tenacity while John Paston is in London contesting the will of Sir John Fastolf (Shakespeare's Falstaff), by which the family estates were considerably enlarged. On one occasion, the first of several violent outrages against the Pastons during her lifetime, Margaret was evicted from her manor at Gresham, and in 1469 the Duke of Norfolk laid siege to Caister Castle. Amid the turmoil Margaret never neglects her maternal duties, finding time to rail against her wayward son and to voice concern at her daughter's determination to marry beneath herself.

Today little survives of the dynasty which flourished for 300 years until, in the early 18th century, the family fortunes declined to such an extent that William Paston, Second Earl of Yarmouth, was forced to sell off the estates. Oxnead Hall, the principal family residence in the Bure valley where the Pastons entertained Charles II, was demolished shortly after. The service wing is all that remains of the magnificent Tudor mansion. Elsewhere the evidence is even more fragmentary - an overgrown mound marks the site of Gresham Castle from which Margaret was evicted and the ruins of Caister Castle are now part of a museum celebrating the achievements of the motor car.

Katherine Paston's tomb in the chancel of St Margaret's church.

For more tangible evidence the visitor must return to the village of Paston from which the family originated. Here huddled together for protection against the bitter north east winds stand the church, the tythe barn and the hall. Although the original Paston residence was replaced by the present house in about 1750, the magnificent flint and thatch tythe barn remains, empty but intact. The church contains monuments to the Pastons, notably John Paston's table tomb (1466) removed from Broomholm Priory and the ornate effigy of Katherine Paston (1628) by Nicholas Stone with an inscription by John Donne.

Ironically it was only the dispersal of the family estates that unwittingly secured the Pastons their place in English social history. William Paston's sale of the letters to a local antiquarian ensured their survival intact; John Fenn first published a selection in 1787 and in 1904 James Gairdner put together a much larger collection from various sources in the British Museum.

Mundesley

In the days when Mundesley was still a small fishing village, the poet **William Cowper** was sent here to convalesce on several occasions towards the end of his life, staying in the little double-fronted Georgian house in the High Street which bears his name. From here Cowper was encouraged to walk by the sea in the hope that the exercise would lift his spirits, but although he managed to write '*No situation, at least when the weather is clear and bright can be pleasanter*', the salt spray and cold, north easterly winds inflamed his eyelids and he was often forced to keep indoors. The letter written a few days earlier to his cousin, Lady Hesketh, reveals the true extent of his despair:

The cliff is here a height that it is terrible to look down from; and yesterday evening, by moonlight, I passed sometimes within a foot of the edge of it .... But though to have been dashed in pieces would perhaps have been best for me, I shrunk from the precipice, and am waiting to be dashed in pieces by other means. At two miles distance on the coast is a solitary pillar of rock, that the crumbling cliff has left at the high watermark. I have visited it twice, and have found it an emblem to myself. Torn from my natural connexions, I stand alone and expect the storm that shall displace me.

On another occasion Cowper's cousin, Johnny Johnson, persuaded him to walk to 'Hazeborough' to inspect the new lighthouse (built in 1791). Despite dining well at the inn near the church, the journey left him exhausted and feverish. In the year before his death, recapturing some of his old intensity, Cowper wrote his finest poem, ***The Castaway***. In it, mindful perhaps of the sailors buried in Happisburgh churchyard, he surveyed his life in terms of a sailor swept overboard, abandoned without hope in the raging sea.

No voice divine the storm allay'd
No light propitious shone;
When snatched from all effectual aid,
We perish'd, each alone:
But I beneath a rougher sea,
And whelm'd in deeper gulphs than he

Over a century later the artist **Paul Nash** recorded his own impression of the countryside around Mundesley while staying with friends in November 1912. *'We walked in a landscape entirely new to my eyes .... flat and chequered, with all the trees slanting one way, their branches welded together in tortuous form by the relentless winds.'* It would be hard to find a more apt metaphor for Cowper's afflicted soul.

3

On the Borderline
The
North Norfolk Coast

I walk on Overstrand shore
and the crab at my foot
inscribes praise in the sand.
The wave bursts with glory
because it rises up like
angels out of the sea,
and the dead starfish burns
on Overstrand promontory.

Why do I hear them cry
out from the far side of life,
those forms and impulses
unborn beyond the sky?
Why should they hope and seek
above all else to be?
Tonight on Overstrand
I know for one moment why.

From ***In Memory of David Archer*** by **George Barker**

Sheringham

Born into a comfortable middle class family, **Stephen Spender** spent much of his childhood on the north Norfolk coast following his father's decision to move out of London in 1913 and rent 'The Bluff', a large Victorian house on the edge of the cliffs at Sheringham. Here, scrambling over the rocks or playing in the woods, Stephen and his brothers and sister engaged in endless adventures like characters from an L P Hartley novel. Their father would take the boys off for long expeditions along the beach or rabbit shooting over East Runton Common, but Stephen's dearest memories were of an early fascination for wildlife and a desire to become a naturalist:

In the woods at spring there were the pale damp primroses with their scent of sublimated mould and buttery thickness which one could almost taste. Then in summer there was the heather, brittle flowers like tiny purple beads on gnarled charcoal stems, flooding over the burnt-looking soil, on which bees descended in thousands to lift away the honey. Beyond the heather, near blackberry hedges, the gorse lay like gold armour, or like fleece of fire all round me, on bushes of spiky green thorns.

At evening, floating above the flat Norfolk landscape, there appeared range upon range of mountains with gulfs and valleys between high peaks, which stayed motionless, sculptured on the sky out of clouds

Beyond the garden arable fields studied with heartsease and cornflower ran along the cliff top, broken here and there by patches of rough meadow where the young Spender would jump ditches, scale fences and wade up to his shoulders through bracken and scabious, mesmerised by the flight of delicate blue butterflies:

> *Opens now, now shuts, its wings,*
> *Opening, closing, like a hinge,*
> *Sprung at touch of sun or shadow.*
> *Open, the wings mirror*
> *All the cloudless sky.*
> *Shut, the milky underwing*
> *Cloud-mirroring, is bordered by*
> *Orange spots nailed there*
> *By a pigmy hammering.*

Spender revelled in this natural world, investing it with imaginary shapes and celestial sounds. At one time the clouds resembled a white milk jug but his sister, by association, insisted she could see a white cat. On another occasion the prevailing wind which had shaped the thorn hedges along the cliff edge was so strong the young boy felt:

I could lean against it, like an invisible door in a wall of air; it would yield slightly if I pushed it, and then spring back against me. Then I started singing into the wind. Then I stopped singing, and I heard a very pure sound of choral voices answering me out of the blowing sky. It was the angels.

For two years he attended Miss Harcourt's kindergarten in East Runton and there he loved to run to the edge of the pond, lie down and peer into the '*gelatinous stillness*' where newts, beetles and snails crawled below the surface. Here he witnessed '*naked dramas, glutinous loves, voracious murders, incredibly fertile births, taking place in the utter stillness of natural light*'.

In 1916 a family holiday in the Lake District broke the spell, the mountains here were real enough. Spender discovered Wordsworth and decided instead to become a poet. At the end of the summer the family returned to the realities of war and a monstrous armada of zeppelins gathered offshore. Stephen's father, always a remote figure, declared '*the first bomb of the war fell in a garden just behind my house*'; and busied himself organising the Norfolk Volunteers while his son lay awake upstairs listening to the troops singing in the room below. It was then he realised the significance of his mother's German connections and that the idyllic world of his childhood was at an end.

By this time Stephen's elder brother had begun to absorb the robust, manly notions of fair play and discipline encouraged by their father while his shy younger son sought refuge in his mother's company. ***My Parents*** recalls the way he was bullied by the local children who '*sprang up behind hedges*', threw mud and copied his lisp:

> *My parents kept me from children who were rough*
> *Who threw words like stones and wore torn clothes*
> *Their thighs showed through rags they ran in the street*
> *And climbed cliffs and stripped by the country streams.*

Spender's decision to follow his brother to Old School House, the prep wing of Greshams was, he felt, one of the most important of his life. Here in the shadow of Michael's academic achievements, he displayed all the symptoms of a sensitive, homesick child and retreated into the same imaginary world that had earlier shaped his response to nature. *'The one reality I could hold onto was my own inner life, my capacity to enact dramas for myself, to speak to those who would never listen to me in an impassioned language of hidden love'*. Unlike Auden who entered the main school in 1920, he was ill equipped to survive the honour system and endured years of deep personal unhappiness until his father eventually removed him to school in Worthing when the family returned to Hampstead after the war.

Greshams School. Spender and Auden were pupils here in the early 20s.

Holt

Aware that a more authoritarian public school might have made life unbearable for their sensitive and precocious child, **W H Auden**'s parents chose Greshams on the strength of its liberal reputation As they had hoped, Wystan soon made friends and under the influence of his English and Music teachers began to take an active part in the literary and artistic life of the school. He undoubtedly enjoyed his time at Greshams, although in later years when his political views had matured he saw the institution in a more critical light and claimed he had been *'A citizen of a totalitarian state'*. Referring to the honour system whereby new boys promised not to swear, smoke or be indecent and to report others who were, Auden wrote *'it meant that the whole of our moral life was based on fear, on fear of the community, not to mention the temptation it offered to the natural informer, and fear is not a healthy basis. It makes one furtive and dishonest and unadventurous'*.

Auden (left) and Spender (right) with Christopher Isherwood. The two Greshams Old Boys later became friends at Oxford.

A shared enthusiasm for poetry and an awakening of his latent homosexuality drew Auden into several influential friendships at this time. He began to read Freud and write Hardyesque verse and his contact with Michael Davidson, a sub-editor on the Eastern Daily Press, led to the publication of his first poem **Woods in Rain** in a collection entitled 'Public School Verse' (1924).

Accompanied by another schoolfriend, John Pudney, who later made his own reputation as a poet and novelist, Auden went on the sort of '*long didactic walks*' favoured by adolescent poets, and interrupted by delicious farmhouse teas. He recalled the excitement of watching a snowstorm gather over the marshes at Salthouse and walking by the mill at Hempstead in a summer's dawn, '*only two of the most vivid of a hundred such experiences*'. In his autobiography Pudney recounts the melodramatic occasion during a walk through the school grounds when Auden attempted to rid himself of poetry and turn his attentions to science:

It was a Wagnerian scene .... with East Anglian winds sounding gusty chords of doom ... As we approached the larger of the school ponds, I was commanded to stand back while the poet, tossing back his pale straight hair, drew his manuscripts from his pockets and went on alone, to commit literary suicide by casting them into the depths.

The scene turned later to farce when Wystan had a change of heart, and returned to the pond to retrieve a handful of damp verse from the stagnant water. As Auden's biographer concluded '*To suspect that they had been carefully placed earlier that day so as to facilitate their later retrieval would be unkind*' but probably true! Auden won a scholarship to Oxford in 1925 where, despite reading natural science, he emerged to become the leading poet of his generation.

Letheringsett

As part of the bright young set at Oxford between the wars **John Betjeman** was a regular guest at weekend house parties in the shire counties. The local gentry in Norfolk must have seemed dull by comparison, only interested in improvements of an agricultural kind and the ritual slaughter of pheasants. To a man in love with Victorian architecture and suburban railway stations the county held few promises but in Roy and Wilhelmine Harrod, Betjeman did at last find friendship in Norfolk.

Before her marriage to the Oxford economist Roy Harrod, Wilhelmine Cresswell had been a good friend of Penelope Betjeman, although this didn't stop John from becoming briefly engaged to 'Billa' just prior to his marriage.

John Betjeman with Wilhelmine Harrod (right) outside Blakeney church during the visit to Norfolk in 1955 that resulted in his poem **Lord Cozens Hardy.**

From that time the two families remained in close contact. Lady Harrod was preparing the Norfolk volume for the Shell County Guide series edited by Piper and Betjeman, when Betjeman went to stay in December 1955, having agreed to open an exhibition of work by his friend Osbert Lancaster at the castle museum in Norwich. Following a visit to Letheringsett Hall he wrote the poem ***Lord Cozens Hardy*** on the train back to London, inspired partly by the freezing railway carriage, and included in a short 'thank you' letter to 'darling Billa'. The poem first appeared in The Saturday Book 1956, entitled 'Lord Barton Bendish' after the west Norfolk village of that name:

> *Oh Lord Cozens Hardy*
> *Your mausoleum is cold,*
> *The dry brown grass is brittle*
> *And frozen hard the mould*
> *And where those Grecian columns rise*
> *So white among the dark*
> *Of yew trees and of hollies in*
> *That corner of the park*
> *By Norfolk oaks surrounded*
> *Whose branches seem to talk*
> *I know, Lord Cozens Hardy,*
> *I would not like to walk.*

John Piper's line drawing of the mausoleum that accompanied ***Lord Cozens Hardy*** in The Saturday Book.

Today visitors will search in vain for the mausoleum in the park because, as Lady Harrod recalls *'There never was a mausoleum! John invented it when he was staying with us at Bayfield Brecks, Letheringsett; there was a little round wood on the road there which John decided contained a mausoleum - but it didn't! The Cozens-Hardys are buried in a vault in the churchyard at Letheringsett. John Piper's drawing is also an invention. Yes, I persuaded John to substitute Barton Bendish in case of hurt feelings but it only happened once; and eventually no offence was taken and they all became friends.'*

Salthouse

Following their stay at Frankfurt Manor (see p38), it was not until 1950 before **Sylvia Townsend Warner** and Valentine Ackland came to live in Norfolk again. On one of their frequent visits to Winterton to see Valentine's ailing mother they discovered Great Eye Folly near Salthouse, built in the early 19th century by Onesiphorous Randall. This local business man lived up to his eccentric name (Onesiphorous means 'Bringing Profit') by making a fortune as a speculative builder in London. He built 'Randalls Folly' on his return to Norfolk as a place to entertain his women friends. On his death in 1873 it became a coastguard station. In a letter to Paul Nordoff, Sylvia wrote:

It is on the north coast of Norfolk, on the extremest edge of it, sea from the foreward set of windows, and marsh and saltings and the sad, stern mainland from the others. It stands on a little hummock and looks like a dear little police station.

Sylvia Townsend Warner
(1893 - 1978)

Both women were immediately taken with its eccentric appearance and exposed position. To Valentine it was *'like a hooded hawk on a clenched fist - like my family's crest indeed'*, and Sylvia recorded in her diary *'The east wind sobs and whimpers like a Bronte in the kitchen'*. They decided to take the short winter let while renting out their Dorset cottage and spent the next few months exhilarated by the wintery seas and the wildlife:

To the seaward we see gulls and sometimes seals and porpoises; to the landward, there is a heron that lives in the marsh, and a kingfisher, and three horses ... The flotsam etc is very odd, one would think that people on this north sea did nothing but eat coconuts and brush their teeth.

Letters from here are filled with excited accounts of gale force winds and high tides threatening to cut them off from the mainland. In December they were snowbound. With no electricity or drinking water they spent much of their time battling against the wind, gathering driftwood and cooking fish. During the previous year their relationship had been rocked by Valentine's affair with an American friend, and their short stay here helped heal the rift. They even talked of trying to buy the Folly but later abandoned the idea, a wise decision as it was swept away in the 1953 floods.

Back in Dorset with images of the coast still fresh in her mind and encouraged by the success of her first Norfolk-based novel 'The Corner that Held Them' (1948), Sylvia began to write **The Flint Anchor** (1954) set in the coastal town of Loseby during the early 19th century. The original fishing

Great Eye Folly at Salthouse where Sylvia Townsend Warner and Valentine Ackland spent the winter of 1950.

village with its '*narrow streets and flights of cobble steps twisting down to the harbour*' appears to be a mixture of Wells and Blakeney, onto which had been grafted the '*bracing East Coast resort of New Loseby*'. By an odd coincidence Sylvia's cousin Oliver Warner was, at the same time, working on a biography of Captain Marryat (see p.75), and an incident at the beginning of **The Flint Anchor** in which the captain of the press gang is lured to his death reads like an episode plucked straight out of 'Mr Midshipman Easy'.

The novel takes its title from Anchor House, a dignified Georgian residence near the church where an anchor of knapped flints, emblem of the Barnard family, is let into the brickwork. It traces the fortunes of its central character John Barnard, dynastic head of a successful trading company that '*imported tar and hemp and fats from the Baltic, packed and exported herrings and supplied ships' chandlery*'. A model of commercial integrity, God-fearing and faithful to his wife, Barnard devotes himself to a life of charitable works but still manages to '*spread around him a desert of mendacity and discontent*' which takes root in a doting attachment to his daughter. Following their marriage, Barnard's daughter Mary and her husband Thomas Kettle go to live in the grounds of Graveton Hall. Here Thomas finds brief happiness writing poetry and cataloguing Miss Basham's shell collection:

He was standing in the orangery, where the February sunshine fell with a watery light on swags of mussel-shell foliage and clusters of pink shell roses, when he saw a petal detach itself, and fall, and splinter on the marble floor. Enchanted by this concord of artifice and decay, he felt his whole future happiness depending on a shellwork rose.

Inspired perhaps, like Miss Basham, by a visit to the rocaille grotto of Rambouillet, Victorian aristocrats set about decorating summerhouses and private chapels with a bewildering pattern of shells collected from around the world. The suggestion that Sylvia took her idea from the Shell Museum at Glandford designed by Sir Alfred Jodrell in 1915, is strengthened by the presence of 'The North Norfolk Coast', an embroidered collage by John Craske discovered by Sylvia and Valentine in the 1930s (see p.51). In the novel Miss Basham bequeaths her entire shell collection to the County of Norfolk, a gesture reminiscent of Margaret Fountaine's decision to leave her collection of exotic butterflies to Norwich Castle Museum in 1940.

In Loseby, Thomas Kettle was popular among the fishermen who frequented the Bluefish Inn by the harbour and there, before leaving the town, Crusoe defends his love for the man: *It's the way we live, and always have been whatever it may be inland .... but in Loseby we go man with man and man with woman, and nobody think the worse'.* Although women didn't apparently go with women in 19th century Loseby, Sylvia took comfort in the knowledge that the love she shared with Valentine Ackland was safe on this stretch of coast. She was sad to return to Dorset:

I am much more a social success in East Anglia than in Wessex and I don't look forward to being just that peculiar Miss Warner again, after being loved and laurelled all the way down Holt High Street and knowing the names of everyone's cats.

The Shell Museum.at Glandford.

Wiveton

Stevie Smith
(1902 - 71)

'Born in Hull. But moved to London at the age of three and has lived in the same house ever since'. This brief statement was all the poet **Stevie Smith** could manage when asked to supply a biographical note by her publisher. Her sedentary life in the suburbs of Palmer's Green with beloved 'Aunt' became legendary, but although she remained at No.1 Avondale Road until her death in 1971, she was never a recluse. For many years Stevie enjoyed the literary life of the capital and, as her reputation grew, she became a popular figure at poetry festivals throughout the country. Her travels, usually without her aunt, may seem unadventurous today, but for someone who relied on public transport and the generosity of friends, Stevie could be surprisingly mobile. She had what Hermione Lee has called *'a passion for English places'* - the *'wild, wet Lincolnshire of the younger Tennyson'*, the subdued contours and sluggish rivers of the home counties, the sea at Swanage and parts of the Norfolk coast *'that looked like nobody has ever been there before'*.

Stevie's pleasure in the Norfolk coast grew through her friendship with Anna Browne. The two had met in London shortly after the war and Stevie soon became a regular guest at the Browne's country retreat. In 1949, having just completed her novel 'The Holiday' Stevie decided to take a holiday of her own and went to stay in Norfolk for the first time. Writing to a friend she expressed a rather childlike delight in being near the sea:

The house in Marsh Lane where Stevie Smith wrote *The Old Sweet Dove of Wiveton.*

all windmills and salt flats and - at Blakeney Point - wonderful silver sand
dunes and the most glorious bathing I think I have ever had .... The social life
was terrific, much more than in sober (sic) old London and as long as the
petrol lasted we pretty well combed up Norfolk

Wiveton was beginning to get under her skin and Stevie even felt disposed
towards the local gentry. '*We pay and receive innumerable visits and everybody*
is of the Very Nice sort, you know, almost royal, if often poor'. Several years
later while sitting in the garden, the day overcast and silent, she managed to
convey a mood of quiescent well-being in the poem **The Old Sweet Dove of**
Wiveton, admitting to Ivy Compton-Burnett '*I do adore* (this poem) *so because*
my Norfolk holidays come into it.'

> *The gray of this heavy day*
> *Makes the green of the trees' leaves and the grass brighter*
> *And the flowers of the chestnut tree whiter*
> *And whiter the flowers of the high cow-parsley.*
>
> *So still is the air*
> *So heavy the sky*
> *You can hear the splash*
> *Of the water falling from the green grass*
> *As Red and Honey push by,*
> *The old dogs,*
> *Gone away, gone hunting by the marsh bogs.*
>
> *Happy the retriever dogs in their pursuit*
> *Happy in bog-mud the busy foot.*
>
> *Now all is silent, it is silent again*
> *In the sombre day and the beginning soft rain*
> *It is a silence made more actual*
> *By the moan from the high tree that is occasional,*
>
> *Where in his nest above*
> *Still sits the old dove,*
> *Murmuring solitary*
> *Crying for pain,*
> *Crying most melancholy*
> *Again and again.*

* * * * *

Stevie Smith's holiday retreat is tucked away along a track leading to
Wiveton Hall. Protected by thick tree belts, the hall peers out across the
marshes to Cley, its flint porch and shaped gables closely resembling Meltham
House, the small Jacobean manor in **The Eagle Has Landed** (1975) that had
been requisitioned by American soldiers. Despite its network of tank traps and
land mines, this remote stretch of coast was vulnerable to invasion during the
last war. Anyone acting strangely was immediately taken in for questioning as
Henry Williamson soon discovered (see p82). It was against this background
that **Jack Higgins** chose to set his gripping wartime adventure following a
holiday at Blakeney.

In September 1943 Hitler issued the order 'Bring me Churchill out of England'. Higgins took it and transformed it into one of the most compelling adventure stories to come out of the war. Two months later Himmler received the chilling message 'The Eagle has Landed', that told him the first stage of an audacious plan to kidnap the British Prime Minister had been accomplished. A small force of crack German storm troopers had been dropped safely on the Norfolk coast in the vicinity of Studley Grange where Churchill was to spend a quiet weekend after a morale-boosting visit to King's Lynn. Higgins confirms that as least half of the tale is documented fact, but like all the best storytellers, he leaves his readers to decide which elements are '*a matter of speculation*'.

The action takes place in and around the village of Studley Constable which with its handful of cottages round the green, a water mill, the Studley Arms and a large medieval church some distance away on the hillside, contains elements of several villages in the Glaven valley. But the author covers his tracks with all the skill of an illusionist teasing the credulity of his audience:

Everything about Studley Constable was intriguing. It was one of those places that seem to turn up in North Norfolk and nowhere else. The kind of village that you find by accident one day and can never find again, so that you begin to question whether it ever existed in the first place.

The story beings years later with the author gathering material for a magazine article. His investigations take him to Studley Constable in search of the grave of a 17th century sea captain, a veiled reference to the tomb of Capt James Greeves, (1686), in Cley churchyard. The '*row of round clerestory windows*' is another feature of St Mary's Cley but the '*great Norman pillars*' in

St Mary's Cley in the Glaven valley.

the nave are a reminder that otherwise the church, like the village, is a work of fiction. Here the author stumbles almost literally, upon the terrible wartime secret that thirty years later, the village was still unwilling to discuss. Beneath the flat tombstone set in a mound of grass was another bearing the inscription '*Here lies Lt. Col. Kurt Steiner and 13 German paratroopers*'. The next words made Higgins catch his breath - '*killed in action on November 6th 1943*', but he could find no record of this extraordinary event in the burial register. Turning to leave he discovers inside the base of the tower, a line of holes filled with plaster that look suspiciously like a burst of machine gun fire. His research had suddenly found a new direction that over the next year leads him halfway round the world in search of '*the enigma that was Kurt Steiner.*'

Blakeney

Richard Mabey
(1941 -)

An invitation to spend a weekend with friends on a converted lifeboat in Blakeney harbour first brought **Richard Mabey** to the north Norfolk coast in the late 1950s when for him, East Anglia was '*an unknown country*'. Released from the tribal confines of his native Chilterns and the '*initiation grounds*' of his boyhood, Mabey's response to this strange watery landscape was immediate and lasting. Bobbing about in the swirling waters of an incoming tide after his first night aboard 'Dilemma X', he crawled to a porthole and looked out:

What I saw was an astonishing panorama - a mile of saltmarsh shimmering under a high tide. The whole landscape seemed to be on the move. Terns hovered feet above the water, and arrowed down for small fish. Spikes of cord-grass and sea-lavender bounced about in the current. Swirling geometric figures opened upon the surface of the water, stretched and then closed again. Even the mud seemed alive, and slid out of the ebbing water with the moist shine of a newborn animal ....

It was a sight that has kept me in thrall of this coast ever since, a liberating vision of being at the edge of things.

For the next 10 years 'Dilemma X' provided a refuge for Mabey and his band of fellow students who passed their time fishing, bird-watching and tinkering with boats. At first the marsh landscape was '*too huge and incoherent to be anything other than a backdrop*', but with each successive visit he grew to know its twice daily rhythms. From the harbour he would walk out along the sea wall to where the channel flowed out into The Pit, stepping out onto the saltmarshes for the first time:

It was a strange, new substance, spongy, unpredictable, full of unfamiliar plants, broken by dark pools and glistening creeks. It seemed to grow out of the bare mud and sand, the thin films of algae gluing the surface into place, the first shoots of samphire acting like a net to the tidal wash of silt. Wherever you put your feet there was a film of flotsam caught between the plants: shells, seeds, birds' wings, bladderwrack, fish-egg cases, all coated with spindrift and plankton and waiting to be .... ground down by the tides, turned back into mud.

Here, from the comparative safety of the shore, Mabey would wait entranced for signs of the turning tide:

There would be no more than a sheen at first, a satining across the surface of the flats; then fingers of water, held back by their own surface tension, would push between the shallow ripples in the sand. Suddenly the tension would break and they would turn into trickles, then thin streams, until acres of previously solid land had been turned into open water....

I sometimes wondered if the closeness of these unstable edges of the land was part of the secret of Norfolk's appeal to us, a reflection of a half-conscious desire to be as contingent as spindthrift ourselves, to stay loose, cast off, be washed up somewhere unexpected.

The thrill of being cast adrift had much to do with the adventure stories Mabey devoured as a boy. The leafy dens and tree houses in the woods around Berkhamsted had resounded to the cries of Mabey's gang rampaging through episodes from David Severn's novels, and here at Blakeney the freedom presented by this new shapeless and, at times, treacherous landscape enabled Mabey's tribe to fulfil some of their childhood fantasies. Approaching by boat or slithering through the black mud at low tide, they would often make for their own Coral Island on the remote outpost of Blakeney Point.

The dunes at Blakeney Point, a favourite haunt of Stevie Smith in the 1950s and of Richard Mabey a decade later.

an enchanted oasis of lagoons and shifting sands, fanned by the coconut and honey scents of tree lupins and sea pinks. Even when the rain hung over the mainland this three mile long peninsula often lay under its own mysterious clear strip of blue sky .... We spent whole days there, lounging amongst the dunes. We dozed by the saltwater pools (and in them sometimes), played cricket with driftwood bats, and munched crabs .... sometimes we surprised seals basking on the sands or shared a lagoon with a tern flock, raining down on the shoals of whitebait marooned there. We went gathering ourselves .... picking samphire on the mudflats or searching for cockles

Much of what Mabey learnt about gathering edible plants; mushrooms at dawn on the grazing marshes near Salthouse, fennel from roadside verges, sea spinach along the sea walls and samphire from the saltmarshes, he learnt from a local man called Crow who knew the countryside intimately. He taught Mabey what local people had been practicing for generations, the harvesting and preparation of wild foods. As Mabey admits, these forays into the marshes and their hinterland left a greater impression than he realised at the time.

During the late 60s Mabey returned to the north Norfolk coast with a friend on a bird-watching holiday, but this time he felt more connected to the place. Out of those practical experiments in self sufficiency and his own botanical knowledge he produced his first and most successful book ***Food for Free*** (1972), written appropriately in a converted slaughterhouse he was renting in Blakeney High Street. Very much of its time, this guide to the edible wild plants of Britain soon became essential reading, along with John Seymour's 'Self Sufficiency' (1973), for all those middle class professionals who had begun grappling with the harsh realities of life on remote Welsh hill farms or East Anglian smallholdings.

The lasting popularity of ***Food for Free*** lies in its ability to reawaken the hunter-gatherer instinct in us all, stirring ancient memories which linger on in the autumnal rituals of nutting and making blackberry jam. Mabey argues that using the countryside as a natural resource for fuel and shelter and as a storehouse of wild plants selected for their medicinal and culinary properties, helps us to engage more closely with nature and *'deepens our respect for the interdependence of all living things'*. Since ***Food for Free*** Mabey has developed this theme in 'The Unofficial Countryside' and 'The Common Ground', books which celebrate the diversity of familiar habitats neglected by those in search of the rare and beautiful, but which are an equally important part of our collective inheritance. Through his pioneering work the memory of Crow takes on a wider significance, assuring Mabey of a place alongside his boyhood heroes, Richard Jefferies and Gilbert White, in the literature of the English countryside.

Langham

Captain Marryat
(1792 - 1848)

On high ground above the saltmarshes stands the village of Langham, its church tower rising above a cluster of tweedy flint and pantile cottages. Here in its shadow lies **Captain Marryat,** one of Norfolk's most unusual novelists. An unadorned monument carries the inscription 'Aetat 56, Obuit August 9th 1848' but from the marble tablet in the church we discover he was a naval captain, a Fellow of the Royal Society and a member of the Legion of Honour.

Marryat spent the last few years of his life at Langham in Manor Cottage writing children's stories and enjoying the life of a country squire. He had no links with Norfolk and the circumstances surrounding his arrival on this windswept stretch of coast are typical of the man's impetuous nature. He reputedly exchanged his Hammersmith property for the Langham estate over a glass of champagne without even visiting it. His decision to forsake the fashionable literary world of London and try his hand at farming may have been prompted by Coke's agricultural experiments at Holkham and the knowledge that just along the coast at Burnham Thorpe was the birthplace of his boyhood hero, Lord Nelson. This part of Norfolk had already supplied the navy with that other notable sea dog, Sir Cloudesley Shovell as well as Sir Christopher Myngs and Sir John Narborough. Captain Marryat was more at home here than perhaps he realised.

Most of what we know about Marryat's life is contained in *Life and Letters*, those *'two little volumes with very large print and very small pages'* written by his daughter Florence some 24 years after his death. Virginia Woolf, speculating about him in her essay 'The Captain's Death Bed', concluded that *'one of the most active, odd and adventurous lives that any English novelist ever lived, is also one of the most obscure'*. For a clearer picture of his early seafaring life we must turn to the novels themselves and to the brief extracts from his private log which record a string of adventures enough to fill a whole shelf of fiction.

Marryat decided on a naval career at an early age, and after several attempts to run away to sea he finally enlisted aboard the crack frigate HMS Imperieuse at the age of 14. Although the French defeat at Trafalgar the previous year had brought an end to the war at sea, these were the days of press gangs, mutinies and smuggling on the high seas and midshipman Marryat embarked on a career packed with incidents. His captain, Lord Cochrane, was already one of the most notorious sea captains of the 19th century, at various times MP, pirate, Admiral of the Chilean navy and scourge of the British Admiralty. Not surprisingly he resurfaced as the model for several of Marryat's swash-buckling heroes. In 1806 under Cochrane, Marryat soon experienced his first skirmishes afloat harrying the French, engaging with pirates and gun-boats, blowing up signal posts and a series of other daring adventures worked into his early novels.

Marryat soon rose through the ranks to become Captain of HMS Ariadane in 1828, his only full command. At the same time he was writing his first two novels, 'The Naval Officer' (1829) and 'The King's Own' (1830). Encouraged by their success and his father's fortune, the captain resigned his command and launched his second career as a writer of popular nautical tales which included 'Peter Simple' (1834) and 'Mr Midshipman Easy' (1836). Although he acquired the Langham estate in 1830 he left its management to tenant farmers for the next 12 years while he frequented the literary circles of Europe and America.

This neglect proved costly. In 1843 he discovered that the drawing room at Manor Cottage was being rented out to vagrants and he decided to take possession. By this time the heyday of the nautical novel was over and his writing took a new direction, that of children's fiction. With 11 children of his own he was very easy in young company, never restrictive or patronising. 'Masterman Ready' one of his most popular children's stories, was published the year before his move to Norfolk, but was followed at Langham by *Settlers in Canada* (1844) and his most famous story *Children of the New Forest* (1847) set in the Civil War, which follows the fortunes of four aristocratic children forced to hide from Cromwell's troops in the depths of the forest.

Marryat's tomb at Langham.

Manor Cottage was rather a grand affair designed in the Tudor Gothic style by the architect Copeland. With tall chimneys and lattice windows under a thatch roof it resembled George IV's royal pleasance at Virginia Waters. Marryat preferred to write seated in the garden on an artificial mound when the weather permitted, surrounded by an odd collection of tame partridges, dogs, ponies and his favourite bull, Ben Brace. But as more than one literary exile in East Anglia has learnt, a love of pets and a theoretical knowledge of agriculture do not always make a successful farmer. He took the job of estate management seriously enough, building model cottages and model pig sties, draining Fox Covert and flooding Decoy Meadows, but just when the rearing of wildfowl threatened to show a profit the project was abandoned in favour of a scheme to drain Cley marshes which fortunately never got beyond the drawing board.

Marryat's restless energy was ill-suited to the seasonal routine of farming and 17 years after resigning his command he applied to re-enter the navy in 1847 but was rejected. Receiving the news in a fit of rage he burst a blood vessel and died after an illness of several months. His boudoir at Manor Cottage, painted with trellis work, adorned with roses and the ceiling with birds, was known to villagers as the 'room of a thousand pillars' because of the effect of mirrors let into the doors. Lying here on his deathbed, Captain Marryat dictated these last simple reflections:

Tis a lovely day and Augusta has just brought me three pinks and three roses, and the bouquet is charming. I have opened the windows and the air is delightful, it is now exactly nine o'clock in the morning and I am lying on a bed in a place called Langham, two miles from the sea, on the coast of Norfolk .... To use the common sense of the word I am happy .... and God is love .... It is now half past nine o'clock. World adieu.

A born story-teller, influenced by the works of Defoe, Smollett and Fielding, Marryat's great strength was in characterisation and a fast-moving plot. To Conrad, another seafaring novelist, his work was interesting as *'a completely successful expression of an unartistic nature'*. But whatever his limitations as a writer, Marryat created a lasting tradition of nautical fiction that later encompassed C S Forester's 'Hornblower' series set in the Napoleonic Wars in which Marryat had seen service. With his children's stories he again helped shape a literary genre developed by later Victorian novelists in East Anglia, notably Rider Haggard (see p137).

Stiffkey

Henry Williamson
(1895 - 1977)
by Edward Seago 1942.

Before his move to north Devon in 1921, **Henry Williamson** had already seen his first otter in East Anglia while on a cycling tour, but it was many years before he returned to the scene of this boyhood holiday. In 1936 his publisher, who had a cottage on the north Norfolk coast, invited Williamson to stay and told him of 'The Old Castle at Creek' (Stiffkey) which was for sale with a good trout stream running through the grounds. Stiffkey Old Hall, the beautiful Elizabethan manor house, proved too expensive but the following year Williamson managed to purchase Old Hall Farm with 235 acres for £2250.

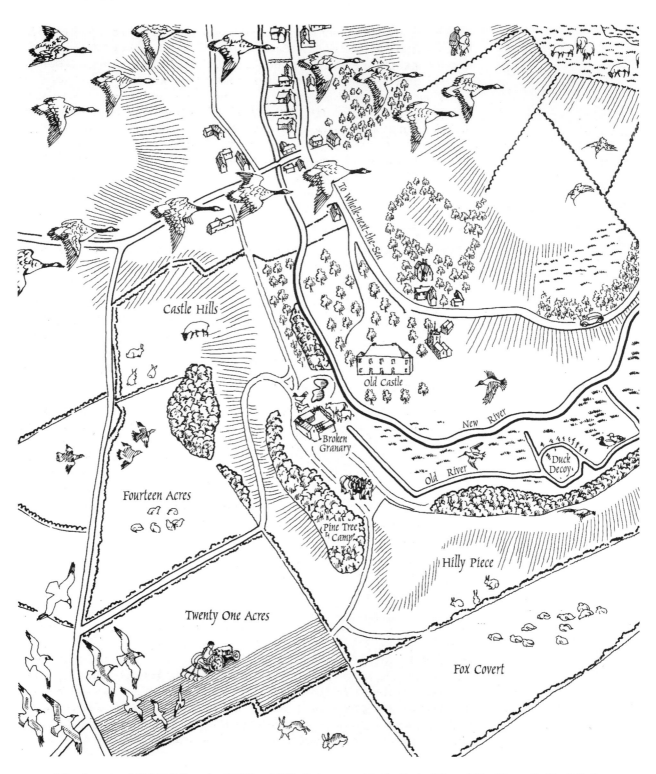

After the map of Old Hall Farm by C F Tunnicliffe that appeared in the first edition of **The Story of a Norfolk Farm.**

On Christmas Eve 1937 while his children lay asleep overhead on a heap of old sacks and rugs, Williamson climbed the hill in the frosty starlight and '*felt the earth bearing* (him) *up, the strong earth, dear earth*'. In a passage reminiscent of his mentor Richard Jefferies, he listened to the sound of wild geese flying inland:

the wild geese were the genius of the place, bringing life to it at last. Devon was alive for me because of the salmon, the mystic ocean wanderer; now life was flowing through me once more, for that the wild geese were flighting in from the sea. Beauty was come again.

Old Hall Farm by Christopher Wormwell from the illustrated edition of **The Story of a Norfolk Farm.**

Although the tales of flood and gales, of windhover and wildfowler in **The Story of a Norfolk Farm** are a reminder of Williamson's gift for describing the natural world, he was at this point in his life a farmer first and at best a journalist. In less demanding circumstances he might have written 'Guya the Goose' as his Norfolk sequel to 'Salar the Salmon'. As it was his 'Norfolk Farm in Wartime' was never published but it became incorporated in **The Phasian Bird** (1948) and was later reworked into his **Chronicle of Ancient Sunlight**.

While in Norfolk, despite his stubborn determination to become a farmer, Williamson constantly felt himself to be an outsider. His well-known Fascist sympathies and the provocative use of Mosley's lightning flash only fuelled rumour on this vulnerable stretch of coast. On one occasion he was arrested and detained overnight in cells at Wells police station on suspicion of being a German spy. Ironically, it was largely his wife's involvement in village life which helped suppress local prejudice, but the strain of living Williamson's dream finally led to the break up of their marriage. The family moved briefly to Botesdale in Suffolk but in 1945 Williamson returned alone and dejected to his beloved West Country .

Mosley's lightning strike still visible on Walnut Tree Cottage.

Wells

The north Norfolk coast with its labyrinth of marshes and mudflats contains some of the most important bird reserves in Britain, and ornithologists gather each year to witness the return of migrant waders and the great flocks of wild geese that winter on the salt marshes. Among the first was the eminent field naturalist **W H Hudson** who visited the area for the last time in the autumn of 1912 to gather material for **Adventures Among Birds** (1913). The book is concerned mainly with bird behaviour observed on country rambles and bike rides throughout southern England, but several chapters are devoted to the abundant wildlife on this stretch of the Norfolk coast: '*There are few places in England where you can get so much wildness and desolation of sea and sandhills, wood, green marsh and grey saltings as at Wells in Norfolk'*. As he travelled to the coast Hudson was struck by the number of deserted villages in north Norfolk, where even the few local inhabitants appeared to have assumed a protective camouflage:

W H Hudson
(1841 - 1922)

I caught sight of a very old man, shrunk and lean and grey, standing in a cottage garden behind its grey palings. His clothes too, like his hair and face were a dull grey, so like the hue of the old weathered lichen-stained wood of the palings as to make him almost invisible.

Men appeared in the distance like hooded crows stalking the sand at low tide in search of bait. Hudson spent his time exploring the marshes, a pair of binoculars slung round his neck, one of his favourite haunts being the belt of pine trees on the dunes at Holkham. Here in the fading light this solitary figure would wait for the grey geese to gather on the reclaimed marshes while delighting in the antics of a red squirrel or listening to indignant outbursts among '*the vast concourse*' of crows, rooks and jackdaws as they settled to roost in the trees. For Hudson was not primarily interested in those rare species blown off course which today attract their own breed of 'twitchers'. He

The pine belt at Holkham Bay.

was fascinated by the gregarious and playful nature of common birds, the erratic flight of peewits or the kestrel mobbed by starlings that formed a prelude to the main event of the evening:

United in one vast flock, numbering at least four thousand birds, the skeins extending over the sky for a length of about a third of a mile .... the heavens were without a cloud or stain and the sun still above the horizon. I could see it from the flat marsh like a great crimson globe, hanging just above the low, black roofs of Wells with the square church tower in the middle. The whole vast aerial army streamed directly over me .... then the descent began, a few at a time detaching themselves from the throng and sweeping obliquely downwards while others, singly or in small parties, with half closed wings, appeared to hurl themselves towards the earth with extraordinary violence. This marvellous wild-wing display continued for four or five minutes before the entire multitude had come to ground. Altogether it had been the most magnificent spectacle in wild-bird life I have even witnessed in England.

At the end of the book the author's pleasure is tinged with the kind of sadness associated with departure from a familiar landscape, more poignant on this occasion because Hudson realised he was unlikely to see his beloved geese again. Before boarding the train to Lynn he recalled '*I bade a simple goodbye: nevertheless my heart was heavy in me and it was perhaps a prophetic heart*'. He was then 71 and although he lived for another 10 years, failing health meant this was to be his last real adventure among birds.

Throughout his life Hudson campaigned vigorously on behalf of the RSPB, writing articles on the evils of egg collecting, wild fowling and the trade in rare species. The coast he knew so well is no longer remote, but in many ways the landscape remains unchanged. The geese return each year and the saltmarshes have since received the protection they deserve. They remain a lasting tribute to this pioneering naturalist, a man who advocated harmonious co-existence with nature long before 'conservation' and 'ecology' had become fashionable.

Wild Geese on Cley marshes.

Hunstanton

Although Hunstanton will be forever associated with L P Hartley's 'Eustace and Hilda' trilogy, the Hall made its first literary appearance some years earlier in the work of **P G Wodehouse**, thinly disguised as Woollam Chersey, the country seat of Bertie Wooster's fearsome Aunt Agatha. Between the wars, Wodehouse had been a frequent visitor to Hunstanton Hall as the guest of Charles Le Strange and during his first stay in the summer of 1926 he wrote to his old school friend Bill Townend:

The above address does not mean I have bought a country estate. It is a joint belonging to a friend of mine and I am putting in a week or two here ....

I spend most of my time on the moat, which is really a sizeable lake. I'm writing this in a punt with my typewriter on a bed-table wobbling on one of the seats. There is a duck close by which utters occasional quacks that sound like a man with an unpleasant voice saying nasty things in a undertone. Beside me is a brick wall with the date 1623 on it.

Salt marshes on the north Norfolk coast where, gathering samphire in the 1960s,
Richard Mabey began work on ***Food For Free***, the book he completed while living at Blakeney.

The west front of Hunstanton Hall, the sight that first greeted Eustace in L P Hartley's *Eustace and Hilda* trilogy.
The octagon in the park was used in *Jeeves and the Impending Doom* when P G Wodehouse stayed at the Hall in 1926.

The striped cliffs at Hunstanton where Eustace and Hilda played among the rock pools in
The Shrimp and The Anemone.

The icehouse in Quidenham Park that Virginia Woolf decided to consecrate as a Saxon burial ground while on a visit to Kenninghall from Blo' Norton Hall in 1906 where she was staying with her sister Vanessa.

Before Wodehouse took up permanent residence in America in 1951, Hunstanton Hall was one of the few country houses he knew well. The place provided a peaceful refuge and always claimed his affection, referred to as his *'beloved Hunstanton'*. Not surprisingly he used it as the setting for several country house stories including 'Money for Nothing' (1928). Although the action takes place on the Worcestershire-Gloucestershire border, Wodehouse confided to Townend that the scene was laid at Hunstanton. In **Jeeves and the Impending Doom** Bertie Wooster offers this description:

My Aunt Agatha's husband, Spenser Gregson, who is on the stock exchange, had recently cleaned up to an amazing extent in Sumatra Rubber, and Aunt Agatha, in selecting a country estate, had lashed out on an impressive scale. There were miles of what they call rolling parkland, trees in considerable profusion well provided with doves and what not cooing in no uncertain voice, gardens full of roses and also stables, outhouses and messuages, the whole forming a rather fruity tout ensemble.

Aunt Agatha's house guest is the Rt. Hon A B Filmer, Cabinet Minister and president of the Anti Tobacco League, who has caught Bertie's young cousin Thomas smoking in the shrubbery Having been severely reprimanded by Aunt Agatha, Thomas exacts his revenge. The President of the Anti Tobacco League has decided to row out to the island in the lake where he is marooned by Thomas who sets his boat adrift leaving Filmer to the mercy of an agitated swan. On approaching the island to rescue the minister, Bertie is greeted by shrieks of terror coming from somewhere above the bushes: *'In the middle of the island was a building know as the Octagon and in the middle of the Octagon, seated on the roof and spouting water like a public fountain was the Right Hon. A B Filmer'*

The octagon at Hunstanton Hall.

P G Wodehouse posing as the country squire in 1928, possibly at Hunstanton Hall.

In the park a few hundred yards south of Hunstanton Hall is an octagonal moat choked with weeds surrounding an octagonal island where, almost hidden by undergrowth stands the octagonal garden house exactly as Wodehouse described it. Built in 1655 for Sir Hamon Le Strange, probably by William Edge the stonemason engaged at nearby Raynham Hall, the design is surprisingly sophisticated '*A notable reflection of the Court Style of Inigo Jones in a remote country setting*' and an early architectural folly. Its claim to folly status lies partly in its eccentric raison d'etre. Sir Hamon's great love was the violin but his attempts to master the instrument were pursued so strenuously that his wife is said to have insisted on him building the octagon where he could practice to his heart's content. Bertie Wooster recounts this delightful story in ***Jeeves and the Impending Doom***.

Norfolk has good reason to be regarded as 'official' Wodehouse country, not only for the assorted aristocracy that frequent his books; Lord Hunstanton in 'The Small Bachelor', Jack Snettisham and Lord Brancaster in 'Very Good Jeeves', J Sheringham Adair and a host of other titled characters, but because the head of the Wodehouse family came from Kimberley Hall just outside Wymondham. Two wild men or wodewose wielding clubs appear on the family coat of arms and the village sign, and there are monuments to the Wodehouse family in the church at the entrance to the park that offer clues to the author's own pedigree and the eccentric world of Bertie Wooster, his best loved character.

* * * * *

Although **L P Hartley** never lived in Norfolk, it is no coincidence that his two best known works, the ***Eustace and Hilda*** trilogy (1944-47) and 'The Go Between' (see p16) are both set in the county during the years of his Edwardian childhood. Brought up in the Fens, it becomes clear from his accurate depiction of Hunstanton and the surrounding countryside in ***The Shrimp and the Anemone,*** the first volume of his trilogy, that Hartley knew this corner of Norfolk intimately from family holidays and his love of church architecture. This affection was confirmed by his choice of the Norfolk Regiment in which to serve as a 2nd Lieutenant during the Great War.

Hartley's life has until recently, failed to attract the serious biographical attention which his place in 20th century fiction deserves, despite the autobiographical nature of his major novels. In the first volume of his trilogy, the world is seen through the eyes of the young Eustace, a delicate self-portrait of the novelist, and traces the complex relationship with his dominant elder sister Hilda that unfolds with disastrous consequences. The destructive nature of this relationship is beautifully captured in the opening sequence when Eustace, playing in the rock pools at the foot of the cliff, tries ineffectually to save a shrimp from the devouring clutches of an anemone.

L P Hartley
(1895 - 1972)

The Cherrington family's move to Anchorstone (Hunstanton) is prompted by the boy's fragile health, like Hartley he suffers from a weak heart. His father decides that the town's elevated position, both physically and socially, is preferable to the cramped accommodation above his accountant's office in Ousemouth (King's Lynn). Eustace, who loves statistics, is comforted by the knowledge that Anchorstone has the 9th lowest death rate in England. There are clear parallels here with Hartley's own upbringing. He was born into just such an upper middle class family, his father having abandoned his solicitor's office to become director of a local brickworks. The family fortune secured Hartley a place at Harrow and a scholarship to Oxford, but in ***The Shrimp and the Anemone*** Eustace's education is paid for out of a legacy from Miss Fothergill in recognition of the boy's friendship.

The Victorian seaside resort of Hunstanton, bleak and exposed on the edge of the cliffs, peers out across the Wash to the distant outline of the Lincolnshire coast. Shortly after the Great Eastern Railway reached the town in 1862, the Le Strange family at Hunstanton Hall developed part of the estate as a health resort. Hotels sprang up around the green, then the pier, the theatre and convalescent home followed in quick succession. Streets of late Victorian villas with turrets in the French chateau style and Edwardian Tudor semis built in local brown carrstone still give the residential areas a respectable uniformity which, as Pevsner observes, are '*not a bit cheerful*'.

In Anchorstone, houses arranged in neat formation read like a roll of honour from the Boer War; Ladysmith, Omdurman, Bulawayo and Rorke's Drift. Hartley, like his great admirer John Betjeman, manages to define social distinctions in architectural terms with great subtlety. In Pretoria Street stands Mafeking Villa '*as dingy as ever, the 'Apartments' notice still askew in the window, the front garden - a circular flower-bed planted with sea shells set in a square of granite chips - discreetly depressing*'. Further along the '*beetling heights and stately pinnacles*' of the lodgings in Palmerston Parade '*always moved Eustace to awe*'. To the impressionable child they suggested the west front of Peterborough Cathedral, but above all he was struck by the magnificence of the Wolferton Hotel where, to sit among the palms in its glass wintergarden looking out to sea, seemed to Eustace '*One of the supreme rewards of human endeavour, and its noble zigzag fire-escape had kindled in his imagination conflagrations of unparalleled splendour.*'

Hartley evokes the seaside atmosphere of Edwardian Anchorstone with great charm. Eustace and Hilda play out their childhood dramas on the sands against a backdrop of the town's famous striped cliffs; a layered cake of white chalk and gingerbread carrstone filled with that thin band of red chalk peculiar to the locality. The zigzag path to the top, the 'Try your Grip' machine and the three shelters between the pier and the lighthouse mark their territory. Later Eustace gazes out over the accumulating clutter of cheap entertainment which threatens the safety of a world he is about to leave behind:

One of the Victorian shelters on the cliff top at Hunstanton.

Eustace turned round to look at the two promenades, stretching away with their burden of shops, swingboats and shabby buildings dedicated vaguely to amusement; next came the pier striding out into the sea, and beyond it the smoke-stained sky above the railway station.

Throughout the narrative is punctuated with references to the town's landmarks, those 'anchorstones' which both excite and comfort the sensitive child. As the family leaves for a trip to the downs, Eustace surveys the town from the top of the carriage, noticing with pleasure: '*Certain interesting and venerated landmarks such as the soaring water tower, a magnificent structure of redbrick which he never passed under without a thrill, thinking it might burst with the weight of the water imprisoned in it*'. Receiving the news that he

The soaring water tower, one of the town's *venerated landmarks* that impressed young Eustace.

is to leave Anchorstone for boarding school, Eustace clings to those features which, until then, have structured his world. He *'felt as if the landscape of his life was streaming by him while he, perilously balanced on a small white stone in the midst of the flux, searched in vain for some landmark which would confirm his sense of the stability in existence.'*

As a child Anchorstone Hall, enclosed in its landscaped grounds, had always seemed beyond the reach of Eustace, but returning from a picnic, the Cherringtons take a detour round the edge of the park. Eustace catches his first glimpse of the building and in that instance recognises his ambition:

Suddenly a great sheet of water opened out before them, and beyond it rose the chimneys and turrets and battlements of Anchorstone Hall. The moon made a faint pathway on the water, but the house was still gilded by the setting sun, Eustace was enchanted 'Oh isn't it lovely? If I ever made enough money to buy it, will you come and live with me there Hilda?'

Sooner than expected, Eustace finds himself briefly within the ancient walls of the Hall having been rescued in the park by Dick Staveley after he had become lost in a storm. Contact is renewed shortly afterwards when Dick is out riding on the sands. Eustace is greatly impressed by the announcement that his family are Lords of the Foreshore, a direct reference to the head of the Le Strange family who held the hereditary title, Lord High Admiral of the Wash, a position which allowed him to claim anything on the beach or in the sea as far as a man could ride a horse or shoot an arrow. In the novel this archaic rite becomes a metaphor for the way that the lives of Eustace and Hilda fall claim to the Staveleys.

In the second volume, **The Sixth Heaven**, Hartley draws heavily on his experiences as an undergraduate to recreate the dazzling social life of Oxford in the 1920s. Here Eustace finds doors open into a world of privilege to which he has always aspired. Hartley, too moved easily in some of the most glamourous literary and social circles. A frequent guest at Garsington Manor, the home of Lady Ottoline Morrell, he transposed her weekend house parties to Anchorstone Hall in his trilogy. Here Eustace is befriended by Lady Nelly Staveley, a character based partly on his life-long friend Lady Cynthia Asquith. He eventually persuades Hilda to join him, determined that she should marry Dick Staveley, heir to the family seat, thereby fulfiling his desire to enter that grand monde of elegance and tradition at the pinnacle of English society.

Later in the company of Lady Nelly he explores the grounds, taking in the architectural splendours of the hall's main front which comes as a relief from the '*self conscious Elizabethanism*' of the Victorian wing: '*The image of the house was spread out before them, the pink of the Banqueting Hall, the glinting, lively grey of the flint-flecked front; elongated and wavey, inflexions of the chimneys trembled into the rushes at their feet. The house had the mirror to itself'*. On another occasion Eustace stumbles across a ruined chapel in the grounds. Here he is disturbed by Dick who casually breaks off a fragment of carved stone from the font, handing it to Eustace as a memento, but for Eustace it comes to assume a greater significance. Later in Venice with Lady Nelly, his thoughts return to this precious spot:

of all the places in Anchorstone Hall this was his favourite, perhaps because, being a roofless ruin and belonging to the past, it did not repel his imagination with the pride of alien ownership. They had laughed at him, at home, for bringing away the carved fragment .... But Eustace had a strong feeling for relics and it should even earn its passage by acting as a paper-weight. The stability of paper-weights appealed to him. They tethered things down, they anchored the past. The Anchor Stone!

Throughout the weekend the pleasure Eustace experiences as a guest of the aristocracy is tainted by the feeling that they share a life within the carefully structured defenses of Anchorstone Hall that he can never really penetrate. After church he stops in front of the duck pond: '*So strangely did he feel his childhood pressing round him, usurping his present self, that the Tudor gateway seemed a barrier against him, the public.*'

The Jacobean archway at Hunstanton Hall gave access to a world of priviledge from which Eustace felt excluded.

Eustace only experiences a real sense of belonging at the end of the trilogy, while revisiting the scenes of his childhood for the last time. Riding out through the park which '*welcomes him into the past*' he is at last happy in the knowledge that he has Sir John's permission to go wherever he chooses. Passing the ruin which all those years ago heralded the approaching downs and their picnic: '*the roofless, gabled church which the sky poured into, made him feel as if a lid had been taken off his own mind. He passed by it slowly, his eyes dwelling with pleasure on all its broken but enduring surfaces.*'

Hartley returned to the theme of desecration when Eustace finds the *'mysterious round white summit of the lighthouse'*, Anchorstone's most potent landmark, has been decapitated. Painted a hideous maroon, it has become the Old Lighthouse Tea Rooms: *'The god has deserted his shrine and commerce has taken over'*. But before Eustace drifts into unconsciousness the reader is left with a single image of lasting beauty:

The old lighthouse.

Over the Lincolnshire coast the sun was going down in calm magnificence. A few clouds, bars of indigo, bright at the edges, rested on the lower part of the great orb; below, the sea already shimmered with the opalescence of approaching twilight. The wind had dropped but the water was still ruffled by the energy of its breath. A procession of ripples, tipped with palest gold, rolled purposefully towards Eustace

The commercial pressures, symbolised for Hartley by the tea rooms, have finally transformed Hunstanton from an attractive Edwardian town, into the kind of resort found anywhere along the coast. The railway station and the Sandringham Hotel have both gone, the pier swept away and the water tower, built with those same Fletton bricks that made the Hartley fortune, has been converted into flats. Only the striped cliffs, the rock pools and the view out to sea remain as Eustace would have remembered them. Death duties and another disastrous fire eventually forced the Le Strange family to vacate their ancestral home, but Ringstead Parva church survives, the most ancient and ruinous of the landmarks so dear to Eustace. Its *'enduring surfaces'* a little more eroded by time, it stands abandoned and unapproachable in the middle of a wheat field guarding the entrance to Ringstead Down.

The ruins of Ringstead Parva church made Eustace feel as though *a lid had been taken off his own mind.*

96

Snettisham

Renamed Frontisham by **Hartley** in *The Shrimp and the Anemone,*
Snettisham is memorable as the scene of Eustace's mystical experience. It was
often the destination for excursions by the Cherringtons in the landau, and on
arrival they would take tea in the garden of the Swan Hotel from where the
west window of the church was clearly visible. The magnificent west window
was for Hartley, a knowledgeable ecclesiologist, simply unsurpassed and by
way of confirmation he quotes from the guidebook to Frontisham church:

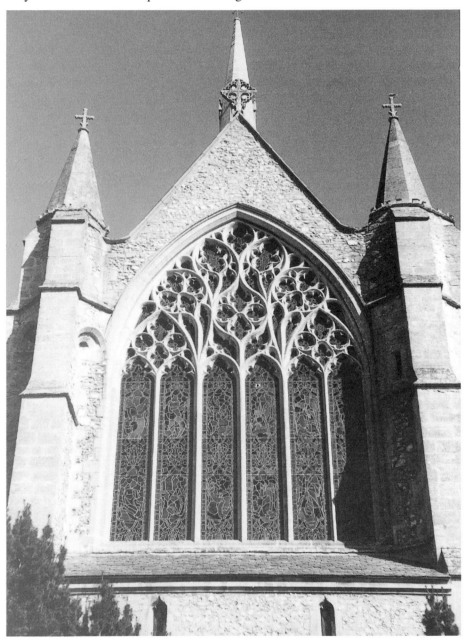

The Decorated west window of
Snettisham church.

Inferior in mere size to the west window of York Minster and to the east window of Carlisle Cathedral, the window at Frontisham easily surpasses them in beauty, vigour and originality. It is unquestionably the finest example of flamboyant tracery in the kingdom; confronted with this masterpiece, criticism is silent.

Eustace knows this passage by heart and gazing transfixed at the tracery he becomes overwhelmed in the presence of perfection; a realisation evoked as much by the language of the guidebook as by the window itself. In a descriptive passage of sustained power, Eustace's reverie intensifies into something akin to a religious experience as his tortured body is born aloft and we witness the martyrdom of the boy saint.

Disengaging himself from the tea table he floated upwards. Out shot his left arm, caught by some force and twisted this way and that; he could feel his fingers, treble-jointed and unnaturally long, scraping against the masonry of the arch as they groped for the positions that had been assigned to them .... Splayed, spread-eagled, crucified (but for fear of blasphemy he must only think the shadow of that word) into a semblance of the writhing stonework.
Meanwhile the interstices, the spaces where he was not, began to fill with stained glass. Pictures of saints and angels, red, blue and yellow, pressed against and into him, bruising him, cutting him, spilling their colours over him. The pain was exquisite, but there was rapture in it too. Another twitch, a final wriggle and Eustace felt no more; he was immobilised, turned to stone. High and lifted up, he looked down from the church wall, perfect, pre-eminent, beyond criticism .... to be admired and worshipped by hundreds of visitors .... Eustace, Eustace of Frontisham, Saint Eustace

Even the exciting ascent of Frontisham Hill on the way home fails to compensate the boy for an experience so abruptly terminated by the sound of his father's voice ordering more tea.

4
The Innocence of Youth
Breckland

This is meeting-house country, chapel country; the churches are decayed or badly restored, and the sense of the past is strong, seeping and sinister. Halls and churches have perished, fire eaten thatch, air eaten stone; buildings rejoin the landscape, their walls reduced to flint and rubble strewn across the fields ..... In this country, man's work seems ephemeral, his influence transitory.

Between settlements, there are still tracts of heather and furze, and black pine plantations: barren, monotonous, funereal, like the contents of an East European nightmare. But the bowed, arthritic pines that line the roads creep to the edges of the small towns, intruding themselves among the DIY merchants .... they gather round the new housing estates, like witches at a christening.

From *A Change of Climate* by **Hilary Mantel**

M R James
(1862 - 1936)

Great Livermere

A few miles north of Bury St Edmunds on the edge of Livermere Park stands the childhood home of two distinguished antiquaries. 'Honest' Tom Martin was brought up at the rectory and attended Thetford Grammar School before writing his 'History of Thetford' in 1779 while, from 1865 to 1909, the rectory became the home, if not always the dwelling, of **M R James** best known for his ghost stories. Although Livermere Hall was pulled down many years ago, the estate broken up and the great oak trees felled, Ampton Water still threads its way through what remains of the park and as daylight fades the place assumes that same eerie atmosphere which stirred young Monty's imagination and helped shape a fascination with the supernatural that remained throughout his life.

All through the rushes, and in the bushes,
Odd creatures slip in the dark,
And sulky owls with feathery cowls,
Go sweeping about the park.

You hear on the breeze from behind the trees,
The Ampton clock begin,
And when it is still, how thin and shrill,
The bell of the Hall chimes in.

Then the horses stir and sleepy cats purr
And something moves in the fern.
And did you not see in the hollow oak tree
Two eyes begin to burn?

You heard a foot pass, it trailed over the grass,
You shivered, it came so near.
And was it the head of a man long dead
That raised itself out of the Mere?

Great Livermere Rectory, the childhood home of M R James.

James *'apprehension of unknown forces at work behind the facade of everyday life, forces that could break through the thin fabric of what we call 'reality' at any moment'*, owed much to his childhood vision of the world. Filled with the evangelical force of his father's sermons, his dreams became troubled with religious imagery:

There was a time in my childhood when I thought that some night as I lay in bed I should be suddenly roused by a great sound of a trumpet, that I should run to the window and look out and see the whole sky split across and lit up with glaring flame: and next moment I and everybody else in the house would be caught up into the air and made to stand with countless other people before a judge seated on a throne with great books open before him.

In this remote corner of Suffolk, local people still clung to superstitious remnants of the 'old faith' referred to by the rector as *'the quasi-religious beliefs of some who have an esoteric confidence in witchcraft'*. Stories that filtered through to the young boy only heightened his sense of life as a battleground across which the forces of good and evil struggled for ascendancy. The battle raged just beyond the safe confines of the rectory grounds where his imagination conjured grotesque shapes from the eerie sounds that arose at dusk out of the reed beds by the lake to threaten the outer reality of religious instruction and devotional piety created by the Rev James.

From Livermere, James went first to Eton and then to Kings Cambridge where, *'living a life of quiet distinction'* he established a formidable reputation as a medievalist, paleographer and biblical scholar; achievements later recognised by his election as Provost and Vice-Chancellor of the University. Ironically, despite his academic reputation, James will be remembered for the ghost stories he began writing to amuse fellow undergraduates who gathered in his candlelit study on winter evenings to hear the latest gruesome tale. He is widely regarded as the finest writer of ghost stories this country has produced on the strength of the four collections published between 1904 and 1925.

The stories are notable for their authentic sense of place, historical accuracy and pervading sense of evil (see p175 & 212). Livermere was used only once, for the setting of *The Vignette* (1936), the last of James' ghost stories, but childhood memories resurface in several others, notably *Lost Hearts*, sharpened by the apprehension of dark forces gathering in the park at twilight:

The wind had fallen, and there was a still night and a full moon. At about ten o'clock Stephen was standing at the open window of his bedroom, ... Still as the night was, the mysterious population of the distant moonlit woods was not yet lulled to rest. From time to time strange cries as of lost and despairing wanderers sounded from across the mere. They might be the notes of owls or water-birds, yet they did not quite resemble either.

The Black Bourn Valley

Robert Bloomfield
(1761 -1823)

From Ixworth northward the Black Bourn stream drifts slowly through water meadows on its way to join the Little Ouse just outside Thetford. This gentle valley, its slopes dotted with the clumps and groves of Euston Park, provided the pastoral setting for the works of **Robert Bloomfield**, and in particular his remarkably successful poem *The Farmer's Boy*. Published in 1800 it drew extensively on boyhood experiences of life on his uncle's farm at Sapiston and its immediate popularity not only ensured his place in English literature but helped create the vogue for 'peasant' poetry which culminated in John Clare's 'The Shepherd's Calendar' (1827).

Bloomfield was born in 1766 in a cottage near the church in the village of Honington. Here his mother struggled to bring up six children at a time of widespread rural poverty following the death, from smallpox, of Robert's father. Hard working and resourceful, Elizabeth Bloomfield took in spinning and found time to run a local dame's school. Her precocious son received his elementary education here until, at the age of 11, he began attending school in Ixworth, walking there and back each day along the banks of the Black Bourn. He made good progress, but when his mother remarried and began a second family there was no money to continue his education and he was sent to lodge with his uncle William Austin, at The Grange in the next parish. Here he became a farmer's boy entrusted with minding the sheep, fetching cattle, scaring birds and a whole range of jobs around the farm, all the while acquiring an intimate knowledge of the countryside that he recalled later with great affection in the one poem by which he will be remembered.

Honington. Bloomfield was born in a cottage that still stands near the church.

As Bloomfield grew older, it became clear to his uncle that this short, frail youth was not built for heavy work and at the age of 15 he was packed off to London to join his two elder brothers in the shoe trade, sharing a garret in the heart of the city. Here, while serving his apprenticeship he took every opportunity to further his own education, reading newspapers and anything else he could lay his hands on, but despite the excitement of his new life, letters to his mother revealed just how homesick he was for his native Suffolk. In 1784 he returned to his uncle's farm and spent the summer revisiting familiar haunts, Fakenham Great Wood, Lanket's Grove and Euston Park in the Black Bourn valley. He fell in love for the first time with a local girl, Nancy Bantock, but more importantly the visit reawakened an ingrained love for the countryside of his youth and the idea of celebrating it in verse began to take shape.

Once back in London, Bloomfield's life changed rapidly. He married a London girl, they found new lodgings in the city and started a family while he began working for a high class ladies shoemaker. Several years later despite the noise of his workshop, the general squalor of his lodgings and those bouts of melancholia and bad health necessary to the aspiring poet, Bloomfield began work on his long pastoral poem. Some years earlier James Kay, himself something of a scholar, had introduced Bloomfield to a wide range of literature including Thompson's poem 'The Four Seasons' from which he took the idea of dividing **The Farmer's Boy** into four parts. By this time Bloomfield was already familiar with Goldsmith's 'The Deserted Village' (1770) and adopted the same metric form - rhyming couplets in iambic pentameter - for his own narrative poem. Coincidentally, Goldsmith in his later years often stayed at Livermere Hall as the guest of Sir Charles Bunbury, a gentleman of some literary taste who held Bloomfield's poem in high regard and introduced him to a wide circle of aristocratic admirers including the Duke of York.

Having completed the manuscript by 1798, Bloomfield's attempts to find a publisher met with little success until a chance meeting with Capel Lofft, another influential patron who lived at Troston Hall near Honington. Lofft, a barrister and philanthropist, was so impressed with the poem that he arranged for its publication, wrote the preface and introduced Bloomfield to the Duke of Grafton who, on seeing the Euston estate described in such affectionate terms, became equally enthusiastic:

> *Where noble Grafton spreads his rich domains,*
> *Round Euston's watered vale, and sloping plains,*
> *Where woods and groves in solemn grandeur rise,*
> *Where the kite brooding unmolested flies;*
> *The woodcock and the painted pheasant race,*
> *And skulking foxes, destined for the chase;*
> *Through every copse, and grove, and winding glade;*
> *There his first thought to Nature's charms inclined,*
> *That stamps devotion on th' enquiring mind*

Sappiston Grange where the young poet began work as a farmer's boy.

Published in 1800, the poem became an unparalleled success so that within three years it had run to seven editions and sold over 30,000 copies. Its huge popularity lay in the delightful evocation of country life as seen through the eyes of Giles, the farmer's boy. This authentic, if uncritical, rural voice celebrating the farming year in simple, unaffected language, reaffirmed the social order in a way that appealed to the landed classes. Unlike his predecessor Stephen Duck, the Wiltshire peasant poet, Bloomfield's benign view of the countryside ignored the harsh realities of poverty and injustice into which he was born, reflecting rather the happy incidents of his youth. Memorable among his descriptions of country pursuits is the joyous account of fox-hunting through the Duke of Grafton's estate. The death of Trouncer, one of the Euston pack's best-loved hounds is an incident taken from real life.

Trouncer's memorial set in a wall of the park at Euston.

The success of **The Farmer's Boy** enabled Bloomfield to move his family into more comfortable accommodation in the City Road, where he enjoyed the lifestyle of a man of letters receiving calls from members of London's social and artistic circles. Here in 1802 he brought out 'Rural Tales, Ballads and Songs' a tribute to the rich oral tradition of his Suffolk homeland including his version of the local folk tale **The Fakenham Ghost** encountered by an elderly servant in Euston Park on her way home from the hall. Bloomfield's third collection of poems 'Wild Flowers' contained **The Horkey**, his only dialect poem which recalls harvest celebrations on a Honington farm, and **Barnham Water** a record of his journey through the Black Bourn valley to Thetford.

In 1812 declining health and a desire to be in the countryside with friends, persuaded Bloomfield to move out of London not back to Suffolk but to Shefford in Bedfordshire where he remained until his death and where he lies buried. Despite an abiding love for the childhood scenes immortalised in his poetry and the generous financial help he gave to relatives, Bloomfield found the idea of close proximity to his family unattractive. There had been much wrangling over his mother's affairs and her funeral in 1805 proved to be his last visit to the Black Bourn valley. Writing shortly afterwards he said: *'Honington I have done with and it seems effectively to have done with me.'*

Euston Hall. Scenes from **The Farmer's Boy** are set on the the Duke of Grafton's estate.

Although the vogue for 'peasant' poetry was short-lived, ***The Farmer's Boy*** continued to be read long after Bloomfield's death as cheap editions found their way onto the shelves of second hand bookshops across the world. Brought up on the wild pampas of South America, W H Hudson discovered a copy on a visit to Buenos Aires half a century later. He was so moved by Bloomfield's account of farming life in the English countryside that he resolved to travel to the 'land of (his) desire'. Like Bloomfield he eventually found himself in London where he struggled to earn a living before establishing a reputation as an eminent field naturalist and writer (see p82).

Thetford

Thomas Paine
(1737 - 1809)

The most remarkable political writer and radical thinker of the late 18th century was born and brought up in Thetford, the son of a Quaker staymaker. As a result of a series of influential pamphlets and books which advocated political and social change and championed the rights of the common man, **Thomas Paine** played a prominent part in both the American War of Independence and the French Revolution. Described by Michael Foot MP as *'the greatest exile that has ever left England's shores'*, he was eventually outlawed in this country because of his views on religion and the abolition of the monarchy, and disowned by his native town for years after his death.

Following their marriage, Joseph and Frances Paine moved into a cottage at the top of what is now Whitehart Street where Tom was born on January 29th 1737. Today visitors in search of his birthplace will find the row of cottages has been replaced over the years by buildings which now form part of the Thomas Paine Hotel. The decision to baptize Tom in St Cuthbert's church was in deference to his mother's Protestant religion, but it was to the Quaker Meeting House in Cage Lane that Tom went each Sunday with his father. The Society of Friends drew its congregation from the lower middle classes, that group of tradesmen and artisans to which Joseph Paine belonged, and although it was no longer the evangelical sect founded by George Fox, the humanitarian principles of his father's faith were to have a profound effect on Tom Paine's political radicalism. His condemnation of war, his sense of justice and individual liberty were all part of his Quaker inheritance in a region well known for its dissenting politics. Even so, he never forgot the gloomy atmosphere of those early days in the Thetford Meeting House: *'if the taste of a Quaker could have been consulted at the Creation, what a silent and drab-coloured creation it would have been!'*

In the early 18th century the 'Antiq Burg' of Thetford was a classic example of a 'rotten borough', returning two MPs to Westminster despite a population of barely 2000, at a time when much larger industrial cities often had no political representation. Thetford was effectively controlled by the Dukes of Grafton from their family seat at Euston Hall. With the support of the Bidwell family, the town's most powerful industrial dynasty, the Graftons secured the support of corporation members in the selection of MPs through a system of lavish bribes. The corporation was itself *'exclusive, indolent, venal and undemocratic, its behaviour a source of scandal and notoriety, its affairs a synonym of dishonesty even in an age well accustomed to such conduct'.* Young Paine whose father had been made a freeman of the town, was left in little doubt about the level of corruption in political life. These early impressions, later confirmed by experiences elsewhere, undoubtedly influenced the direction of his political philosophy. In **The Rights of Man** Paine asserted:

> *Every chartered town is an aristocratic monopoly in itself..... (where) a man coming from another part of the country is hunted from them as if he were a foreign enemy. An Englishman is not free in his own country, every one of these places presents a barrier in his way and tells him he is not a freeman - that he has no rights.*

Joseph Paine's modest income as a staymaker enabled him to send his son to the Free School in Bridge Street but the financial strain led to his removal at the age of 13 when he became apprenticed to his father's trade. Tom appears to have enjoyed his schooling, reading the classics in translation and developing a taste for history, maths and the sciences. He later acknowledged '*My father being of the Quaker profession, it was my good fortune to have an exceedingly good moral education and a tolerable stock of learning.*'

Tom Paine's sense of history was nurtured in Thetford by the many reminders of its distinguished past. An important Saxon town, it became a major religious centre following the foundation of the Cluniac Priory in 1104 with several religious houses and no less that 22 medieval churches. Like all

Remains of the Dominican Friary and the Free School attended by Tom Paine from a contemporary engraving.

small boys Tom spent many hours clambering among the Priory ruins just yards from his home and wandering along the banks of the Ouse to the remains of St George's Nunnery. He sometimes played within the massive earthworks of Castle Hill, of which his contemporary Thomas Martin wrote, *'no one knows what race of men raised this heap of chalk'.* His own school, a seat of learning endowed by Sir Richard Fulmerstone in 1566, rose from the ruins of monastic scholarship. The remains of the Dominican Friary were still clearly visible in the grounds and it pleased Tom to know that the Rev Francis Bloomfield, author of 'A Topographical History of the County of Norfolk' (1739), was one of his school's most famous pupils.

Thetford's legacy of medieval ruins was also a graphic reminder of a prosperity which had deserted the town long ago. The new agricultural industries that were to revive its fortunes in the late 18th century were still some way off and during Tom's youth it remained stagnant and isolated in a desperately poor rural area, a mixture of cottage industries operating in run-down, antiquated buildings. As he grew older Paine began to find his home town increasingly parochial and restrictive. From an early age he had a strong desire to travel and the sight of the London stage coach pulling up at the Bell Inn reminded him of a more exciting world as he walked to school each day . His teacher the Rev Knowler, once a chaplain in the navy, fuelled his imagination with tales of voyages to distant lands and Tom's discovery of 'A Natural History of Virginia' in the library made him resolve to visit America as soon as he was able.

Although he was thirty seven before he finally set sail for the New World, Paine did eventually manage to escape Thetford at the outbreak of war with France in 1756. Armed with a letter of introduction from the American statesman Benjamin Franklin he enlisted on a privateer, 'The King of Prussia'. The break proved decisive and he returned only briefly to visit his parents and to study for a position in the Customs and Excise office. Despite his eventual success as political thinker firstly in America and then in France, Paine's last work ***The Age of Reason***, a deistic rejection of organised religion, made him so many enemies in England that he never dared return:

Nothing better illustrates the way in which Thetford remained a deeply conservative town .... than its attitude to its most famous and most illustrious son. He was vilified in his own lifetime and two centuries later attempts to commemorate his local connections met with condemnation and hostility. Even today there are many who regard his links with Thetford as a source of shame rather than pride.

Even the gilded statue by Sir Charles Wheeler erected in front of the Town Council offices in 1967 was paid for by the Thomas Paine Foundation of America, in the teeth of opposition from several members of the Tory council who attempted to have details of Paine's trial and conviction as a traitor engraved on the plinth. In 1972 as a result of London overspill, the Town Council had a Labour majority for the first time and has remained a Labour outpost ever since, ensuring that belatedly, Thomas Paine now receives the respect due to him in the town of his birth.

The statue of Thomas Paine by Sir Charles Wheeler that caused such an outcry among members of the Tory council.

Although Paine's radicalism was never likely to engage the critical attention of a writer whose outbursts against the servant classes became something of a joke in literary circles, when **Virginia Woolf** visited Thetford in 1906 she seemed genuinely unaware of his connection with the town. Paine was still very definitely 'persona non grata' and unworthy of a mention in the guide book she consulted before setting out from Blo' Norton Hall (see p120). It did refer to the steep grassy slopes of Castle Hill beyond the '*girdle of wall* (sic) *and river'* that suggested to her the outskirts of a small Italian town. Exhausted by the ride and mesmerised by the river, Virginia found herself questioning the reality of the scene that drifted before her eyes:

No one has ever been able to say exactly what does go on in these medieval towns set in the heart of England at about this hour on a summer's afternoon .... For when you come upon stalwart men leaning their elbows on a parapet and dreaming of the stream beneath .... you reconsider what you mean by life. Often in London shall I think of Thetford, and wonder if it is still alive, or whether it has really ceased, peaceably, to exist any longer. No one would notice if the whole town forgot to wake up one morning.

Castle Hill and the ramparts that greeted Virginia Woolf on her arrival in the town.

Weeting

Ghostly reminders of its turbulent history lie scattered about the large Breckland parish of Weeting. The Saxon earthworks known as the Foss Ditch that runs along its western boundary, the remains of William de Warrene's castle in Weeting Park and even the site of Weeting Hall now a bungalow estate for American airmen, all speak of more troubled times. In the same way Weeting's place in the literary landscape of Breckland is territory disputed by scholars and antiquarians

Bromehill Farm which stood just north of Brandon was reputedly the birthplace of **Thomas Shadwell** (1642-93), poet and dramatist who became Poet Laureate after Dryden and with whom he conducted a long-standing feud in print. The proximity of Shadwell just east of Thetford would appear to lend weight to Weeting's claim, but Shadwell is also a corruption of St Chad's Well. St Chad was a Northumbrian saint which may help explain why some accounts of the poet's life favour Brandon in Durham as his birthplace.

Weeting also appears in *Hereward the Wake* (1866), and was used by **Charles Kingsley** as the setting for one of his hero's most daring escapades against the Normans. In the story Hereward has chosen the Isle of Ely in which to make his last stand against the French. William the Conqueror, having failed in his attempt to take the Isle and plunder the cathedral, withdraws to Weeting Castle to consider his next move. The Isle has enough fresh food to withstand a long siege but fearing a renewed attack, Hereward disguised as a potter, leaves Ely on his horse Swallow, intent on discovering the king's plans. Before entering Weeting Castle he stays the night in a hut on the edge of Brandon Heath where he overhears two old crones foretell the time and place of William's next attack. The following day Hereward enters the king's court and becomes involved in a brawl in the kitchen. He is spared by William and escapes on Swallow before his identity can be discovered, skirting the Fens in a great arc before throwing off his pursuers and re-entering the Isle beyond Cambridge.

The remains of Weeting Castle used by Charles Kingsley in ***Hereward The Wake***.

Unlike many episodes in Kingsley's saga there is no record of the event in the medieval manuscripts he used to construct his own story of Hereward's resistance. The incident was set in Weeting purely on the basis of its ruined Norman castle, even though the archaeological evidence suggests that it was built a century later. Moated, but without a curtain wall and consisting of a hall and substantial tower, it was more like an early fortified manor house than a castle, but there on the edge of the Fens it served Kingsley's purpose.

Northwold

John Cowper Powys
(1872 - 1963)

The most famous of three literary brothers, **John Cowper Powys** was born in Derbyshire but spent his youth in Somerset before going up to Corpus Christi, Cambridge. His younger brother Littleton was his constant companion both at school and during the summer holidays when they were packed off to maternal grandparents in Northwold where Canon William Cowper Johnson was rector from 1880 to 1892. These annual trips to the rectory were eagerly awaited by the two brothers and in his extraordinary *Autobiography* (1934) written during long periods of exile in America, John recalls intensely happy memories of these boyhood adventures fishing and boating on the river Wissey. Forty years later he returned for the last time in the company of Littleton and the two men bid farewell to their youthful paradise *'exchanging wordless signals with these two little boys* who *receded from this momentary reincarnation .... till they faded into the branches of the cedar on the lawn, into the bushes by the fishpond, into the poplars along the river, into the alders of Alder Dyke.'*

A Glastonbury Romance is generally regarded as the greatest of Powys' six major novels. A work of immense range and psychic power, it is in every sense a novel on a grand scale in which the Grail legend exerts a supernatural influence on the life of the Somerset town. On its publication in 1955 J D Beresford considered it to be *'one of the greatest novels in the world to be classed with Tolstoy's War and Peace.'* Although the book is set firmly in the Somerset Levels, the exiled author reaffirms his East Anglian roots in the opening chapters as John Crowe alights from a third class carriage of the London train at Brandon station to attend the funeral of Canon William Crowe, rector of Northwold and the author's thinly disguised grandfather. With his black travelling bag and his hazel walking stick, an indispensable Powys appendage, Crowe sets out across the ancient landscape of Brandon Heath spread out against the distant prospect of Ely Cathedral, to walk the seven miles to the village:

He saw them (the cathedral towers) *against old, stunted lichen-whitened trees. He saw them against the curved up-pushing new born horns of the sap-yellow bracken .... crouching low like the heads of innumerable mottled snakes, the better to leap at the throat of life. He saw them against the reddish gnarled trunks of intermittent clumps of scots firs and against scuttling white tails of rabbits and the hovering wings of solitary kestrel-hawks.*

On his journey, John Crowe is reacquainted with cousin Mary, his childhood companion on holidays at the rectory. At this point Powys begins to draw heavily on his own boyhood memories as the two cousins revisit the pond at Harrod's Mill on the morning of the funeral. Here John Crowe falls into a reverie in which the past and present drift together like the waters of the river:

the sensation which these two returning natives got from looking into its depths was unforgettable by both of them. On its outer rim the water was a pale, neutral colour, a sort of ashen grey, but as the eye moved from circumference to centre it got darker and darker, a faint bluish tinge mingled there with the grey and there appeared a sort of mysterious luminosity as if there had been a subterranean light at the bottom of the pool.

But what a thing it was to see the great fish, one after another, rise up slowly from unseen depths .... a longing seized him that seemed to carry with it some primordial phallic tremulousness to grasp with his hands these slippery creatures, to hold them tight, to feel their fins, their scales, their sliding coolness, their electric livingness.

After the funeral relatives gather in the large drawing room of the rectory to hear the will read by Lawyer Diddlington. Looking across the lawn to the spreading cedar tree John Crowe becomes aware of a '*peculiar chilliness*' moving towards the house. Through an open window '*the presence of night flowed in, sweetscented .... and diffusing through the air a sense of something inexplicable, something beyond hope and beyond despair, full of pardon and peace.*' Once the guests leave, the peaceful atmosphere is absorbed into the silence as the empty house resumes its own life:

Childhood holidays by the Wissey were recalled many years later by John Cowper Powys in the opening chapters of *A Glastonbury Romance.*

18th century headstones in the churchyard at Northwold.

Silent and alone the broad staircase fell into that trance of romantic melancholy which was its invariable mood when the hall lamp was first lit. The oil paintings on its walls, looked out from their gilt frames with that peculiar expression of indrawn expectancy - self centred and yet patiently waiting - of which passers by catch only the psychic echo or shadow or after taste, for a single flicker of a second, as if they had caught them off guard.

The next day the two cousins pay a last visit to the river before saying goodbye and near Dyes Hole his desire for Mary becomes entangled with those same images from his past:

it was that his possession of Mary had become a calm-flowing tidal stream which released and expanded all the antennae of his nature. These responses leapt up towards the unknown, like those great slippery fish at Harrod's Mill. Tom Barter, marigold stalks, fish scales, dough-pellets - all these, and the secret that they held, depended, like the long shining river weeds upon which his eyes now rested, upon the flow of that stream of contentment which was his possession of Mary.

The Wissey flowing gently through the Fens to its appointment with the Great Ouse remains one of the purest chalk streams in Norfolk. Threading its way through cattle strewn meadows and overshadowed by aspen poplars, the Wissey still evokes a world of lost innocence and the pastoral idyll:

The river weeds below the tide that bore them on, gleamed emerald green in the warm sunshine. Across and between the weeds, darted shoals of glittering dace their swaying bodies sometimes white and sometimes slippery black as they turned and twisted, rose and sank, hovered and flashed by. Beds of golden marigolds reflected their bright cups in the swift water; and here and

there, against the brownish clumps of last years reeds, they caught passing glimpses of pale, delicate-tinged cuckoo flowers. Every now and then they would come upon a group of hornless Norfolk cattle, their brown and white backs, bent heads and noble udders giving to the whole scene an air of enchanted passivity through which the boat passed forward on its way, as if the quiet pastures and solemn cattle were the dream of some very old god into which the gleaming river and the darting fish entered by a sort of violence, as the dream of a younger and more restless immortal.

In this open landscape of large fields and ruined churches, Northwold is still recognisably the same village that John Cowper Powys knew. The large cedar in the grounds of the rectory has gone but the house itself, now The Grange, remains hidden by enormous beech and horse chestnuts. In the churchyard the beautiful collection of 18th century headstones remain a tribute to the stonemason's craft which once flourished in these Breck-Fen villages and the grave of one Robert Crow is a reminder that here in the Wissey valley lies the genesis of *A Glastonbury Romance*.

Great Hockham

Born in 1885 on the eastern edge of Breckland, the son of the village pig-killer and barber, **Michael Home** won a place at Thetford Grammar School and from there went on to King's College, London. A prolific author, he published over fifty detective novels under his real name Christopher Bush which, although popular at the time are now out of print. Today Michael Home is best remembered for his books about Breckland life at the turn of the century, based on his own boyhood memories of Hockham (Heathley) and the vast tracts of empty heath that surrounded the village:

For miles there was nothing but bracken and heather, broken here and there by clumps of pine whose trunks were gnarled and twisted and saffron red. Among the young plantations of larch or in the bracken hollows, hamlets lay hidden, and around them nestled the fields that maintained an impossible and retreating fight against bracken and cankerweeds and rabbits.

This extract is from Home's first novel *God and the Rabbit* (1934). It tells of a local boy made good, an autobiographical theme developed in several later novels, against a background of isolation and rural poverty. Home's family, like many in the village, was Methodist and Nonconformity became an important element in his fiction, epitomising the tensions in a closed rural community between the high church squire and his chapel-going labourers.

Having moved to Sussex, Home never returned to the scenes of his youth, preferring like so many writers to rework his early life in a series of reminiscences. Home's trilogy began in 1944 with *Autumn Fields* followed the year after by *Spring Sowing* and completed in 1967 by *Winter Harvest*. They present an unsentimental chronicle of life in a remote community during the early 20th century which, like the landscape itself is almost unrecognisable today. These volumes have ensured Home's place alongside Adrian Bell in the tradition of rural literature which flourished between the wars.

A part of the bracken heath that covered vast tracts of Breckland when Michael Home was a boy.

Mary Mann
(1848 - 1929)

Shropham

As a writer of romantic fiction **Mary Mann** enjoyed considerable success in her own lifetime. All her 35 novels and four volumes of short stories were published at regular intervals from 1883 until the end of the First War, but despite this prolific output and critical acclaim at the time - D H Lawrence enjoyed her work - her most accomplished novels have failed to attract the attention they deserve.

Born in Norwich, the setting for some of her earlier stories, notably ***Grandma's Jane*** (1903), Mary Mann remained in Norfolk all her life, moving first to Shropham in 1871 on her marriage to a local farmer. She remained here at the Manor House before retiring to Sheringham in 1913 following the death of her husband. It was largely through the encouragement of her nephew

Tom Ordish, a Shakespearian scholar who helped with the publication of her earlier work, that she endured the many years of isolation at Shropham and the indifference of her husband's family to her literary talent. Her numerous letters to Ordish reveal the extent of her debt to him as well as her own wide reading.

Mary Mann lies buried in the churchyard at Shropham beside her husband, surrounded by the unmarked graves of those parishioners whose lives, brutalised by grinding poverty, had been cut so tragically short. Confronted by widespread suffering, the dreadful conditions in which working people were forced to live inspired her best writing, notably the remarkable collection of short stories published in 1903 as **The Fields of Dulditch**; tales of human endurance which stand alongside those of Thomas Hardy. The sense of injustice running through the collection is voiced by the author in an unpublished Foreword to the first edition:

A depressing neighbourhood certainly. As I detail its several features, I am appalled at the bleakness, the dreariness of prospect. And it is certain that we who pass our lives here in the silence and the solitude are not always content. We know that Fate has been to us much unkind. We know that the Book of Life has been for us, practically closed, that only tantalizingly and at moments have we been permitted to turn its pages

Her years at Shropham coincided with an agricultural depression which reduced the population of the parish by a third as farm labourers drifted away to neighbouring towns in search of work. 'Dulditch' was published in the same year as Rider Haggard's 'Rural England'. His catalogue of abandoned fields, derelict cottages and widespread poverty concluded by advocating the restructuring of British farming. The plight of the countryside affected all levels of rural society, not just the half-starved labourers at the bottom but the many tenant farmers on the verge of bankruptcy and even the local squire who, at Shropham, was forced to vacate the hall for long periods and let the shooting. Fairman Mann struggled to maintain his family on 800 acres of indifferent land but like so many he was ultimately defeated by rising prices and a succession of bad harvests.

In the absence of a local squire Fairman Mann assumed responsibility for the welfare of the poor, becoming both guardian of the workhouse and school governor while Mary Mann attended the sick and the destitute. Ironically it was the need to earn money which first prompted her to write romantic novels, but with growing confidence she began to tackle more serious issues, culminating in the stark eye-witness accounts of rural poverty which grew directly out of her daily visits.

Devoid of all sentimentality, the Dulditch stories stand apart from the 'rustic charm' school of rural literature first popularised by Robert Bloomfield's poem 'The Farmer's Boy' with its idealised images of a well-stocked countryside populated by buxom dairy maids and red-faced farm lads engaged in honest toil and harvest frolics. The mud-caked labourers of Dulditch inhabit *'an insignificant landscape, bleak fen-land, gorse-choked heath, familiar ponds and pits and puddles, rank turnip fields, flat distances'* from which there is no escape. Pared down to the daily struggle for survival, these are stories of cruelty, illegitimacy, suicide and, in a world hardly touched by religion, widespread superstition. Apart from acknowledging the evils of drink they are remarkably free from the moralising tone of so much Victorian literature. As Ronald Blythe makes clear:

By enduring the misfortune of their birth, their ignorance, their incessant toil and their malnutrition, her characters receive their own special nobility, and it is this which ultimately concerns her.' Later he writes *'there was a group of human beings in her world with the dice loaded against their fulfilment and happiness. Dulditch exercises her radicalism. She sees both the admirable and the feckless brought down by circumstances that are entirely out of their control.*

In setting out to portray the harsh reality of rural life at the turn of the century, Mary Mann can claim direct descent from George Crabbe, the region's finest poet who attempted to *'paint the cot as Truth will paint it, and as bards will not.'* Her familiarity with Shropham people over many years and her accurate record of their lives and distinctive speech patterns, anticipated the oral history techniques pioneered by George Ewart Evans in the 1950s a few miles from Crabbe's Aldeburgh home.(see p190)

Larling

John Middleton Murry
(1889 - 1957)

Remembered largely as the husband of Katherine Mansfield and for his close but turbulent friendship with D H Lawrence, **John Middleton Murry** managed to establish his own rather precarious reputation as a literary critic. His outstanding achievement was probably as editor of The Adelphi, the crusading journal he founded in 1923 to *'bypass the literary intelligentsia'* and which for the next twenty five years brought current political debate to a wider reading public. His agonising search for a personal creed between the wars led him to embrace most shades of radical thought and prompted a series of philosophical tracts on the nature of Communism, Christian Socialism and the necessity of Pacificism. He eventually achieved happiness with his fourth wife in an agricultural community at Thelnetham.

Shortly after the death of his second wife, Murry embarked on what soon proved to be a disastrous marriage with his children's nurse, Betty Cockbayne. Touring East Anglia in 1931 in search of a new home away from the painful memories of his previous marriage, they discovered the Old Rectory at Larling, a late Georgian house with walled garden and wooded grounds. Once installed Murry threw his considerable energies into renovating the outbuildings, reclaiming the vegetable plot and refurbishing the library where he could resume his writing. Here, absorbed in the practical activities of daily life which he admitted years later were all that kept him sane, he slipped easily into the role of *'the complete bucolic recluse.'* Laying aside his intellectual burden, Murry began to feel at home in this isolated community.

Working at his carpentry bench, tending his beehives and teaching himself book-binding, Murry experienced a contentment that had so far escaped him, but relations with his new wife, a passionate and possessive woman, soon began to deteriorate. Even the birth of their first child could not reconcile them and the Old Rectory *'became the scene of a struggle so elemental that Lawrence alone could have depicted it.'* The atmosphere became unbearable in what Murry described as *'the hell of Larling'* but he remained devoted to his new daughter and found it impossible to make the final break. Years later his eldest son recalled the unhappiness of this period:

It was as though we were under some terrible sentence - so terrible in fact that we hardly dared to speak of it even among ourselves. Fear crept into us like a cold fog and the form it took was the belief that a 'row' was about to break. We read the message in each other's eyes, conscious that we were engaged in a never ending conspiracy whose sole aim was to preserve, by any means, the uneasy peace .... such illusions rarely survived for more than a few days. Sooner or later I would wake to hear that terrible voice screeching abuse at my father; the sound of feet running along the landing, fists pounding on a locked door, the hysterical wailing of my small step-sister and brother.

The old rectory that for Murry became *the hell of Larling.*

Inevitably Murry's work suffered and his reputation reached a low ebb. His attack on D H Lawrence in 'Son of Woman' (1931) was greeted with *'hoots of derision,'* described by Peter Quennell as knocking *'the last nail into the coffin of Murry's never very brilliant reputation.'* In the following *'period of dryness'* he eventually found salvation in a new political philosophy. Having read 'Das Kapital' he started work on 'The Necessity of Communism' in 1932. In the same year he joined the Norwich branch of the Independent Labour Party and began advocating the idea of a religious brotherhood of equals. The Adelphi became the mouthpiece for the movement and Murry quickly rose to become one of its leading figures before he advocated an ideological split with the Labour Party which brought about the demise of the ILP.

Once again Murry had managed to destroy the very organism he helped to create. But new ideas grew from the wreckage and the pattern repeated itself. His next vision was for a small socialist community '*whose force should be measured not by the number of its professional adherents, but by the intensity and spontaneity of their devotion to the work before them*.' It was known as the Adelphi Centre with headquarters at Langham in the Dedham Vale, but relied so heavily on Murry's personal involvement that his membership of the Peace Pledge Union in 1936 nearly wrecked the community. His 'Necessity of Pacifism' appeared the following year and with the outbreak of war he poured his energies into reviving Peace News and managed to double its circulation. This constant struggle which mirrored the tragedy of his personal life, tested the patience of his friends and was scorned by his critics:

From the Old Rectory, his integrity factory, Mr Murry continues like a renegade free lance vicar to preach his lugubrious apostatical sermons .... he feels compelled at rather frequent intervals to 'change his mind' and 'bare his soul' and in general to luxuriate in the role of the very ill used but at all costs really 'sincere' man, ever eager to endure fresh spasms of martyrdom.

Thelnetham

Throughout the 1930s at Larling, brief periods of reconciliation with his third wife were followed by prolonged outbreaks of hostility that left Murry exhausted until after one especially painful period of convalescence, following an operation, he made the final break. By then Murry had met Mary Gamble, a young admirer, through the Peace Pledge Union, who had moved to Dedham to be near the Adelphi Centre. Having become interested in the idea of self-supporting agricultural communities, Murry decided that what the Centre lacked was the shared experience of working the land. His response was typically forthright. He instigated the Adelphi Farm Group and when in 1942 the Air Ministry acquired adjoining land for an airfield, he set off with Mary in search of more suitable premises.

Later that year they found Lodge Farm Thelnetham a few miles south of Larling; 185 acres of rundown land, some derelict outbuildings and a farmhouse, '*a roomy old stud and plaster affair with a thatched roof*' large enough to accommodate themselves and members of the Farm Group. Over the next four years there were endless debates about the nature of collective responsibility even though Murry and Mary Gamble did not regularly participate in farm work, and by the end only one of the original group remained. As a social experiment Lodge Farm was only a qualified success, but the dilapidated barns were restored, the land cultivated and the farm unit upgraded to Class A. *Community Farm* (1952) is Murry's light-hearted account of this transformation.

By then, in need of greater privacy, Murry and Mary Gamble had moved down the lane to The Poplars, another timber frame house which they renamed Lower Lodge. Here Murry began work on 'The Free Society' in which he discarded his pacifism and advocated a free society based on the law of love. With its publication in 1948 Murry's 'thought adventure' came to an end. '*The lover had found his mistress, the cleric his church. Both the great needs inspiring his urgent, all-absorbing, seemingly interminable quest for 'truth' were met, and with that, the quest subsided.'*

Murry wrote several more books but this represented his last intellectual shift and precipitated his retirement from the political arena. Resigning from The Adelphi and the Peace Union he devoted his energies to Lodge Farm and village affairs. 'Conchie Farm' as it became known, acquired a reputation for its neighbourly transactions. The play put on in the village school by the Farm Group became an annual event and Lower Lodge opened its garden for the summer fete. Thelnetham would not have been possible without the royalties from Katherine Mansfield's work and in recognition of this, Murry edited an edition of her letters to him. At Lower Lodge, sustained by Mary's devotion, Murry found happiness at last. Love had become his religion, the Church of England his place of worship and in Thelnetham churchyard, befitting one who in his last years voted Conservative, the man and his radicalism were finally laid to rest below the inscription 'Ripeness is All'.

Blo'Norton

Some years before her marriage, **Virginia Woolf** stayed on the Norfolk-Suffolk border with her sister Vanessa in the summer of 1906. An American had taken a long lease on Blo' Norton Hall because, as Virginia wrote in her journal *'it is too remote and solitary and ancestral for anyone to wish to live here, except Americans who find all these qualities, I suppose, medicinal '.* Miss Bancroft was however happy to sublet the hall for the whole of August and there, tucked away in the upper reaches of the Little Ouse valley and approached down a long avenue of lime trees, the Stephen sisters enjoyed *'a kind of honeymoon, interrupted it is true with horrible guests'* in this moated Elizabethan manor house. On arrival along dusty lanes from Diss station, Virginia immediately felt herself soothed by a wonderful tranquillity:

Virginia Woolf
(1882 - 1941)

every mile seemed to draw a thicker curtain than the last between you and the world. So that finally, when you are set down at the Hall, no sound whatever reaches your ear; the very light seems to filter through deep layers; and the air circulates slowly, as though it had but to make the circuit of the hall, and its duties were complete.

The following day the sisters set out to explore *'a strange lonely kind of country,'* an enchanted land that at first seemed both soporific and deserted. *'The corn brims, but no one is there to cut it; the churches hold up broad grey fingers all over the landscape but no one, save perhaps the dead at their feet, attend to their command; the windmills sail round and round, but no one trims their sails.'* At the end of their second full day, a day spent stumbling through reeds, wading across ditches - *'the Little Ouse deserves its diminutive'* - and negotiating barbed wire fences, Virginia decided the countryside did have possibilities but that although *'a walk in the fens has a singular charm, it is not to be undertaken as a way of getting to places.* Later in a letter to Violet Dickinson, Virginia expressed her pleasure in the hall and *'this strange, gray green, undulating, dreaming, philosophising and remembering land',*

If only I had chosen a better time to write to you I would describe this place. Which now I shan't do. It is 300 years old, striped with oak bars inside, old staircases, ancestral vats and portraits; there is a garden and a moat. You see people of taste can get houses cheap; the station is 6 miles off and there is nothing to do. Nessa paints windmills in the afternoon, and I tramp the country for miles with a map, leap ditches, scale walls and desecrate churches making out beautiful brilliant stories every step of the way ....

Nessa and I have to go now and call on the parson and we haven't been inside the church, ... Really this is a charming country, and even beautiful, or rather quaint as we say of things that are long and attenuated and more grotesque than shapely - because their hearts are so good.

Blo' Norton Hall, the setting for Virginia Woolf's short story *The Journal of Miss Joan Martyn.*

As a way of getting to places unscathed, Virginia took to the lanes on her bicycle, an ordnance survey map tucked under her arm. Out one day in search of a Saxon burial ground at Kenninghall, she arrived in the village expecting earthworks, only to discover that *'to the shame of Kenninghall'* nobody had even heard of it. Directed instead to the Christian burial ground she fell to musing on the literary possibilities of epitaphs in St Mary's churchyard, but rather than return to Blo' Norton empty handed she *'decided to consecrate a mound in some gentleman's Park,'* unaware that the burial ground she sought lay beneath a ploughed field, just yards from where she stood at the entrance to the Quidenham estate. Closer inspection would have revealed the mound to be nothing earlier than an eighteenth century ice-house but, late in the day, it satisfied Virginia's flagging curiosity.

Struck by the mellow beauty of her surroundings and the strong sense of history conveyed by the Gaudy Brampton portraits that still grace the panelled interior of Blo' Norton Hall, Virginia managed to complete one of those *'beautiful brilliant stories'* that had begun to take shape while she roamed the country lanes. In **The Journal of Mistress Joan Martyn** a Miss Merridew calls at Martyn's Hall (the Martins had been recent tenants at Blo' Norton) in the hope of finding documents relevant to her researches into medieval land tenure. There she encounters the owner, John Martyn, surrounded by ancestral portraits and unaware that, arranged in chronological order, they trace the decline of his family from men of distinction to yeoman farmers. Turning to the ledgers and estate maps, the eyes of his guest alight on the journal of Joan Martyn for the year 1485. At this point the reader suddenly finds himself in the 15th century with all the immediacy of domestic life, against a background of internal strife that could have been taken straight from the Paston Letters. Seated by the fire on a winter's night, the young woman entertains her mother and an elderly priest with readings from the poet John Lydgate before talk turns to the dangers lurking beyond the gates:

when the time for bed comes .... we have to feel our way up the great stairs, and along the passages, where the windows shine grey, and so into our cold bed rooms. The window in my room is broken, and stuffed with straw, but gusts come in and lift the tapestry on the wall, till I think that horses and men in armour are charging down upon me. My prayer last night was, that the great gates might hold fast, and all robbers and murderers might pass us by.

The ruined church at Gasthorpe in that *strange, lonely kind of country* on the Norfolk-Suffolk border when Virginia Woolf stayed at Blo' Norton Hall in the summer of 1906.

5

Common Ground
South Norfolk
& The Waveney

O beautiful February day, a fairly roguish sun coming over the ash trees in the South, and all these portents that things are about to happen, spears, shocks, signs of movement in the squashed, sodden soil, faint but certain reds in the twigs of the berberis, golden life coming into the willow, a bud swollen unnoticed, fat, waiting on the cut-leafed elder.

From the *Journals* of **Elizabeth Smart**

Brooke

George Ewart Evans
(1909 - 88)

When his wife retired from teaching in 1968, **George Ewart Evans** bought a small thatched cottage in the centre of Brooke. The move brought to an end their twenty year sojourn in east Suffolk, a time of discovery begun in the village of Blaxhall (see p190) where Evans laid the foundations of what has become known as Oral History. His years in Norfolk until his death in 1988 were the most productive with the publication of a series of books on East Anglian folklife together with his autobiography *The Strength of the Hills* (1983), all beautifully illustrated with line drawings by David Gentleman. Building on the impressive collection of material recorded in Suffolk, these volumes extended the range of his work to include the seasonal migration of farm labourers who went to work in the maltings at Burton-on-Trent in *Where Beards Wag All* (1970); the hay trade and the Lowestoft herring industry in *The Days That We Have Seen* (1975), while in *Horse Power and Magic* (1979) he returned to his main preoccupation.

The survivors of what Evans called a 'prior culture', were those born at the end of the last century. They were often pleased to talk about their lives to someone prepared to listen because the next generation, brought up in an age of the internal combustion engine and mass communication, were seldom interested in the antiquated folklore of their parents. These old farm labourers knew their way of life was dying and this made Evans' task easier, even though members of the horseman's society were still reluctant to divulge closely guarded secrets about the control of horses. It was only after numerous visits to Arthur Chaplin that Evans finally uncovered the full story of the frog's bone ritual. (see p198) Evans' success in eliciting sensitive information lay in his ability to allow a conversation to develop naturally within the general confines of a chosen topic rather than conduct an interview with a list of prepared questions. In this way his subjects would grow more confident, sometimes letting slip some chance remark that led Evans to discover a whole new body of knowledge such as the custom of going to Burton.

By employing the field techniques of social anthropology and helped by a natural affinity with working class people acquired from his boyhood in the mining villages of South Wales, Evans won the trust of his informants, people who became his friends, by living and working in the community. He often lamented the way in which earlier anthropologists had forsaken Britain in search of more exotic material in the Amazonian rainforest or the South Seas when the rich folk culture in their own backyard was more relevant and equally at risk. Evans' inability to obtain research grants to continue his work only compounded this view and his mistrust of academic institutions was only softened latterly as a result of the efforts at Ruskin College, Oxford and Essex University to establish oral history centres.

In one sense of course, Evans **was** in a foreign country. He came to Suffolk through no choice of his own and discovered by chance an older generation who spoke a strange poetic language. Once in this flat estuarine landscape, even though years of exile failed to erase the memories of those Welsh hills that '*had always formed the clearest map in* (his) *mental topography*', this perceptive Welshman stumbled upon such a rich vein of folk culture, the 'pattern under the plough', that he abandoned his ambition to become a writer of fiction. Instead, by asking the fellows who cut the hay, he enabled the rural craftsmen of Suffolk to tell their own fascinating stories in their own rich dialect. George Ewart Evans will be remembered alongside his contemporary Seamus Delargy who set up the Irish Folklore Institute and his friend Iorwerth Peate, founder of the Welsh Folk Museum, as the greatest anthropologist to work in his adopted country.

The thatched cottage in Brooke where George Ewart Evans wrote many of his books on East Anglian folk life.

Tharston

Early in the 1970s the poet **Anthony Thwaite** was literary editor of The New Statesman and was soon to begin a twelve year term as co-editor of Encounter when he and his wife, the biographer Ann Thwaite, began looking in '*a desultory way*' for somewhere old, affordable and within easy reach of London. Their search ended when they found the Mill House at Low Tharston that has been their home ever since. As one of Philip Larkin's literary executors, much of Thwaite's time recently has been devoted to editing his 'Collected Poems' (1988) and more recently a selection of the poets voluminous correspondence. Between these two publishing landmarks and his work as reviewer and lecturer, Thwaite's own **Poems 1953-88** appeared in 1989.

Stepping down into the millhouse, the visitor is confronted by books occupying every available space that announce a literary household, but most striking is the impressive collection of 17th century Bellarmine jars and glass bottles arranged in the windows. Here they begin to shed light on Thwaite's fascination with the past and a recurring theme in his poetry. More potent than the contents of these 'greybeard' wine jars from the Rhine was their subsequent use as witch bottles. Filled with a mixture of urine, nail parings and human hair they were often buried beneath the hearth in East Anglian cottages to ward off the effects of witchcraft. Hidden away in the damp meadows of the Tas valley in a house that seems to sink a little further into the ground, these stoneware jars have to Thwaite's mind '*a heaviness, something of the earth*' and a '*granular coldness*'. With their bloated bellies and stippled markings that are '*more like a toad's metallic mottling*', they begin silently to assume the likeness of an amphibious colony.

In considering some of the contradictions that underlie Thwaite's work, critics have identified '*a modern poet with a deep and abiding sense of the past*' and an '*inveterate collector who admits to the futility of life*'. He is of course aware of the baggage he carries with him, describing himself as '*an affluent magpie in a nest that creaks/with impedimenta*' but unable to explain a habit begun in his native Yorkshire where, as a boy, he would bring home fragments of carved stone from the ruins of Bolton Abbey. Elsewhere he suggests that the random process of acquiring historical evidence helps define his own brief existence in a sequence that leads inevitably to death and decay. Thwaite's poetry is littered with remains and antiquarian references, most evident in 'The Stones of Emptiness' (1967), 'Inscriptions' (1973) and his latest volume 'The Dust of the World' (1994). Images range from the plundered tumulus that is the subject of 'The Barrow' to the casual, almost brutal way in which burial sites are desecrated by nature - the bones protruding from the cliff face in 'Dunwich' or unearthed by moles. Their significance, like the layers of faith in 'Reformation' where '*the hazed meadows of England grow over chancels*', lies only just below the surface, visible as '*faint shadows among fields*'.

For many years the Mill House has offered Thwaite a welcome respite at the end of demanding lecture tours abroad on behalf of the British Council, but surprisingly few poems have sprung directly from his experience of life in the Tas valley. In those that have, the reader discovers another paradox in the work of a man with strong domestic ties. From the security of his family home Thwaite confronts the fear of death lurking, like a pike in the depths of the mill pond where '*something hidden rises / Something secret goes*' and where '*whatever you have seen there / Goes on and out beyond / Your vision or your knowledge*'. In **The Mill House**, having shown friends round the building, he is left alone to consider his own uncertain end:

> *And so they go, and leave me here, to share*
> *Something with every date, and style, and place*
> *An ownerless owner, moving towards a date*
> *No one has told me of, or yet assigned*

Anthony Thwaite by the mill house at Tharston where *under the gate the river slams its door.*

Living so close to the Tas, this sluggish river inevitably comes seeping into Thwaite's verse. With the mill wheel now still and the river choked with weeds, there is a very real threat of flooding each winter. In *At The Flood* he asks '*will the river rising, answer for us both*', but provides no answer only the ominously inevitable '*And the rain comes down*'. Thwaite's fear resurfaces once more in *By the Sluice* as he contemplates his own mortality:

> *It pulses like a skin, at dusk*
> *Is shaken like dusty silk. The current moves*
> *But takes its impetus and gathers speed*
> *Only beyond the sluice-gate. Here, the faint*
> *Shudders, the morse of water almost trapped,*
> *Perform half mesmerized, half dying too.*
>
> *Yet are not dying: those trembling dots, those small*
> *Reverberations, rise from what is hidden*
> *Scatters of minnows, nervous hair-triggered fry*
> *Grasping at sustenance, grabbing at what is given,*
> *Submerged ferocities, brute delicacies.*
>
> *What have I hidden here, or let go, lost,*
> *With less to come than's gone, and so much gone?*
> *Under the gate the river slams its door.*

Forncett St Peter

Hidden away in the Tas valley on a slight rise above the water meadows stands the church of Forncett St Peter and the beautiful Queen Anne rectory to which the Rev William Cookson brought his new bride and young niece **Dorothy Wordsworth** in 1788. As fellow of St Johns, Cambridge he had come to take up the college living and it became their home for the next six years. The subdued agricultural landscape of south Norfolk presented a bleak contrast to Dorothy's beloved Lakeland fells but otherwise she welcomed the opportunity to escape from the household drudgery of her grandparents' home in Penrith.

Following the death of her mother, Dorothy had been brought up by relatives in Halifax and here she met Jane Pollard who was to remain a lifelong friend. It is from the few surviving letters to her old schoolfriend that we learn something of her time in Norfolk. On her arrival she was soon writing to Jane: '*We are now happily settled at Forncett .... my room is one of the pleasantest in the house, I wish you were here to share it with me, some of the views are beautiful*', and later: '*I intend to be a great gardener and promise myself much pleasure in taking care of the poultry which we are to have in great abundance.*'

By the following year, Dorothy was already involved in the life of the parish, visiting the sick and caring for her aunt's growing number of children. William Wilberforce, an old college friend of the Rev Cookson, stayed on several occasions and gave Dorothy an allowance of 10 guineas a year '*to distribute in what manner* (she) *thinks best to the poor*'. Encouraged by his example, she established a school for nine pupils at the rectory and took great interest in their welfare. Excursions were rare; to Long Stratton to visit the Rev Burroughs and his wife or to Norwich to have a tooth drawn or visit the theatre, but she found the streets in such disrepair 'a*s to almost entirely take away the pleasure of walking*' and she often '*returned quite jaded*'. Her nearest neighbour was a Miss Dix of Forncett St Mary, an eccentric old maid whose '*appearance is rather remarkable as she always wears long ruffs and a common stuff gown; she is rich but lives alone in a very plain manner .... her worst fault is censoriousness.*'

With these few social distractions and her parish duties Dorothy was perfectly content with her walks in the rectory grounds, her reading and letter writing. She received visits from each of her brothers but it was the absence of dear William that caused her the greatest sadness. He was seldom out of her thoughts and letters to Jane Pollard are full of references to him, especially his travels on the continent. At the time he was an undergraduate at Cambridge and the prospect of seeing him made Dorothy's move to East Anglia more attractive. Despite this, William came only once to Forncett, for his six weeks Christmas vacation in 1790, when Dorothy recalled:

every day as soon as we rose from dinner we used to pace the gravel walk in the garden till six o'clock when we received a summons (which was always unwelcome) to tea. Nothing but rain or snow prevented our taking this walk. Often I have gone out when the keenest north wind has been whistling among the trees over our heads. I have paced that walk in the garden which will always be dear to me from the remembrance of those long, long, conversations I have had upon it supported by my brother's arm. Ah! Jane! I never thought of the cold when he was with me.

But the young poet and reluctant scholar found little favour with his uncle. Following the discovery that while in France, he had met and fallen passionately in love with Marie Anne Vallon who bore his child, Dorothy stood loyally by her brother despite the strain it placed on the relationship with her uncle. The Rev Cookson took a less charitable view of his nephew's predicament, withdrawing his offer of a curacy and refusing any further invitations to Forncett. As a result Dorothy's relationship with her uncle deteriorated and she longed even more to see William again. In one of her last letters from Norfolk in July 1793 she described her vision of them living together in idyllic seclusion, a dream fulfiled only later in the Lake District at Dove Cottage, but one born out of her lonely days at Forncett:

*The evening is a lovely one and I have strolled into a neighbouring meadow where I am enjoying the melody of birds and the busy sounds of a fine summer's evening, while my eye is gratified by a smiling prospect of cultivated fields richly wooded, our own church, and the parsonage house. But oh how imperfect is my pleasure! I am **alone**, why are you not seated with me? And my dear William, why is he not here also? I could almost fancy that I see you both near me. I have chosen a bank where I have room to spare for a resting place for each of you. I hear **you** point out a spot where, if we could erect a little cottage and call it **our own** we should be the happiest of human beings. I* *see my brother fired with the idea of leading his sister to such a retreat as fancy ever ready at our call hastens to assist us in painting; our parlour is in a moment furnished; our garden is adorned by magic; the roses and honeysuckles spring at our command; the wood behind the house lifts at once its head and furnishes us with .... a summer's noon day shade.*

Overcome by her desire to see William again, Dorothy managed to persuade her uncle to let her travel north to Halifax, a journey which proved to be her farewell to Forncett. Here she was reunited with her dear friend Jane Pollard and shortly after with William. From there the two companions set out for the Lake District where they spent several glorious days revisiting childhood haunts. The Cooksons stayed on at Forncett until 1804 when, following the death of their young daughter Anna - there is a memorial to her in the chancel of St Peters church - they moved to Berkshire. The family connection with Norfolk was continued in the same year when Dorothy's brother Christopher became rector of Ashby near Loddon.

The meadows below the rectory at Forncett St Peter. Dorothy Wordsworth dreamed of a life together here with her brother William.

Today the church at Forncett remains very much as Dorothy and William would have known it while the rectory has, if anything, grown more graceful with age, its brickwork showing through coats of faded limewash. Ravaged by recent gales, the avenue of lime trees bordering the driveway along which they so often walked, is part of the peculiar fragile beauty that lingers about the place. Following a visit in the company of Anthony Thwaite one bright and windy day in the spring of 1982, **Philip Larkin** wrote '*I shall remember Forncett for a long time: the roaring trees, the exultant rooks, the flowering* *graveyard.*' The water meadows below the rectory grounds where Dorothy pictured her country retreat with William, are still a profusion of wild flowers in spring. Saved from destruction some years ago, they are now the only ancient meadows left in the whole of the Tas valley and a fitting memorial to Dorothy's years at the rectory.

Diss

Diss is best known for its association with two poet laureates. The first, **John Skelton**, (1460-1529) was born here and went up to Cambridge before becoming tutor to Henry VII. He returned to Diss in 1498 where he remained as rector of St Marys until his death although he was never permanently resident and spent much of his time in Norwich and London. His satirical verse included 'Colin Clout' and 'Why come ye not to Court' (1522) directed at Cardinal Wolsey.

John Betjeman paid his first visit in 1963 for a BBC series on English market towns. Before leaving London he knew little about the place other than its connection with Skelton and that it was '*near the headquarters of the British Goat Society*', but later he declared it '*the perfect small English town*'. Alighting on the windswept platform the poet disappeared down a narrow passageway to find 'The Jolly Porters' not yet open and reappeared to enquire '*Where is Diss?*'. A taxi ride along Victoria Street past the gas works and rows of Italianate villas brought him to the edge of the Mere and his first memorable view of the town centre with brick and colourwashed houses stacked up around St Mary's church and gardens sloping down to the water's edge.

John Betjeman
(1906 - 84)

From here Betjeman set out to explore the town's architectural delights; the medieval corner posts carved with archangels and scenes from the nativity, the beautiful staircase and Jacobean plasterwork of the Greyhound Inn and the colossal portico of Atkin's Greek Revival Corn Hall described in reverential tones as he paused for breath at the top of Market Hill. He was equally enthusiastic about the minor vernacular buildings; the Victorian shop fronts, the Shambles and the Non-conformist chapels tucked away down side streets, that define the spaces around the Market Place. Dramatic views through alleyways to the Mere or across pantile roofs to the church tower all celebrated the '*happy inconsequence of things*', the endless variety of a place grown organically at ease with itself. Stopping briefly to pay homage to his predecessor, Betjeman recited from Skelton's 'Ware the Hawk' set in the church, before moving out along Mount Street, '*one of the pleasantest country town streets in England*' with its elevated walkway and '*little bits of country that come right into the town.*'

Betjeman knew well enough the fragile beauty of these medieval streets and was concerned for their future. He noticed the cottages rotting in back streets and around Fair Green and worried about the threat of London overspill. But thirty years later his worst fears have not materialised. There have been changes; the fate of the Fair Green cottages became something of a 'cause celebre' in the 1970s and were eventually saved following a well-orchestrated campaign that won Betjeman's support, but the recent demolition of the

Victorian brush factory on Shelfanger Road attracted little attention. The centre is today, a mixture of building societies, charity shops and hardware stores and remains choked with cars despite the pedestrianisation of Mere Street. The Shambles is now a local museum and the King's Head, the old coaching inn where Betjeman stayed, has been converted into shops. Even the Corn Hall, resplendent after its recent face-lift, no longer resounds to the shouts of farmers haggling over the price of barley, but the town still comes alive each market day.

Diss Corn Hall on Market Hill.

Betjeman returned to Diss in 1972 in the company of Mary Wilson, wife of the Labour Prime Minister who was herself born in the town, and they both wrote poems commemorating the journey from Liverpool Street. Betjeman's *A Mind's Journey to Diss* which appeared in his last collection 'A Nip in the Air' (1974) begins *Dear Mary / Yes it will be bliss / To go with you by train to Diss.*

Redenhall

Arnold Wesker
(1932 -)

Returning from Paris in January 1957, **Arnold Wesker** went to stay with his wife's parents at Beck Farm where Dusty Bicker had been brought up and where the idea for *Roots,* the second of his autobiographical trilogy of plays, began to take shape. As Wesker readily acknowledges, the Bicker family became the background and inspiration for his play. Mrs Bryant who manages to dramatise every little incident but who can never discuss anything seriously, is the obvious incarnation of Mother Bicker while her husband, a labourer at Gawdy Hall Farm, becomes 'Poppy' Bryant, the mean spirited pigman whose reward for eighteen years service and a lifelong mistrust of the agricultural union is to be put on casual labour when the other farm hands are awarded a pay rise. Wesker's other in-laws make up the cast but it is Dusty who inspires the central character Beatie Bryant.

The family live in a tied cottage on a main road between two villages, but the play opens on the other side of Harleston at Heybird, a hybrid of Weybred, in a ramshackle cottage surrounded by gravel pits that is the home of Beatie's sister Jenny Beales. Wesker compounds the local setting with dialogue written in the Norfolk dialect that has tested many leading actors, but as he rightly insists, the speech patterns and the silences are essential to a play concerned with the power of language and the inability of its characters to communicate thoughts or feelings.

The ability of Stan Mann, a senile old horseman and lone survivor of George Ewart Evans' 'prior culture', to enjoy life, elevates him above almost every member of the Bryant family. Mrs Bryant still retains the capacity to tell stories, but in a kind of garrulous chatter without the originality or the inventive language of an oral tradition that still survived among Mann's generation. Folk songs have been replaced by dance tunes as Wesker's characters become trapped in a daily routine alleviated only by gossip and the prospect of a win on the Labour tote. Their dreams and prejudices are fed by cheap entertainment that has supplanted traditional rural culture with '*the slop singers and the pop writers and the film makers and women's magazines and the Sunday papers and the picture strip love stories*'. Beatie's lament that '*I come from a family o'farm labourers yet I ent got no roots*' might have been uttered by any one of her family but without her awareness they remain stuck in lives bereft of passion or any sense of fulfilment and, cut off from their own cultural roots, they lack the ability or the desire to change their predicament.

Beatie's response was to leave home and put down new roots in London, and the play begins with her arrival back in Norfolk glowing with enthusiasm for a new life discovered through her boyfriend Ronnie Khan (Arnold Wesker); a world of art, music and political ideas that immediately sets up tensions in the

Bryant household. Attempts to share these exciting new experiences are met with a mixture of scorn and indifference; Beatie switches the radio to a Mendleson symphony only to be told by her mother to '*Turn that squit off*' and her attempt to explain the importance of learning from others is dismissed with '*There go the half past eleven bus to Diss - blust that's early*' by a woman whose days are measured by the bus timetable and enlivened by the passing of a tradesman's van.

Uncomfortable with Beatie's passion for life beyond their own limited experience, the Bryant family soon tire of her quoting Ronnie's opinions delivered standing on a kitchen chair, but as the play develops it becomes clear that she too, in the company of Ronnie and his friends, has little to say and no ideas of her own. She quotes Ronnie without understanding him while her mother repeats mindless gossip, but the difference is that Beatie wants to learn. The play reaches its climax when Beatie is interrupted in the middle of another 'speech' by the arrival of Ronnie's letter breaking off their relationship, but instead of feeling humiliated in front of her family, something snaps during the ensuing confrontation with Mother Bryant. In what has become one of the great moments in post-war English theatre, Beatie pauses triumphant in the knowledge that for the first time she has stopped quoting Ronnie and, finding her own voice, she '*stands alone, articulate at last*' as the curtain falls.

Beck Farm at Redenhall, the setting for Wesker's play **Roots**.

In London the late 1950s became a heady mixture of new working class drama and left wing politics. It was the time of the Left Review Club, the Writers Group, Bernard Russell's Committee of 100 and the first Aldermaston march. The applause which first greeted John Osborne's 'Look Back in Anger' at the Royal Court in 1956 was still reverberating round a theatre world captivated by a whole new genre of political drama. Brendan Behan's 'The Quare Fellow' and Shelagh Delaney's 'A Taste of Honey' both emerged in 1958 through Joan Littlewood's Theatre Workshop, the year that saw the first production of John Arden's 'Live Like Pigs'. Together with Osborne and Wesker and novelists Colin Wilson, Doris Lessing and Kingsley Amis, these new playwrights became known as the 'angry young men' of literature irrespective of gender.

Wesker had first seen 'Look Back in Anger' shortly after his visit to Redenhall and still maintains *the impact cannot be understated*. Six months later he began work on 'Chicken Soup with Barley' (1958), the first play in his trilogy. Its success at the Royal Court led soon after to **Roots,** written at intervals over a three month period at Beck Farm. First performed at Coventry in May 1959 with Joan Plowright as Beatie Bryant, it transferred to the Royal Court where enthusiastic reviews from Kenneth Tynan and Bernard Levin confirmed Wesker's reputation as an exciting new dramatist. Wesker gave Mother Bicker a signed copy of the play which she left out for visitors to see but, he thinks, probably never read. Had she done so, her considered opinion, entirely appropriate to the model for Mrs Bryant, may well have been 'a load of old squit'.

Arnold Wesker (right) with Mother and 'Poppy' Bicker c1962 at Beck Farm.

Flixton

In 1937 an attractive young Canadian arrived in London convinced that only through the power of love could she realise her creative potential. **Elizabeth Smart** had already begun 'stalking her muse' when she stepped into a bookshop on the Charing Cross Road and discovered George Barker. Seduced by the imaginative intensity of his verse, Smart set out on a quest to meet this young Bohemian poet in the great tradition of romantic love. Having tracked him down to the spiritual wilderness of an academic post in Tokyo, she sprung the trap by raising enough money to pay for his flight to America. Undeterred by the presence of his wife, Barker soon found Smart irresistible and together they '*leapt bellowing with jungfreud into the arms of the infinite*', rampaging across America in a vortex of sexual and imaginative passion that gave birth to ***By Grand Central Station I Sat Down and Wept*** (1945), a confessional work of ecstatic power that remains one of the great prose poems of the 20th century.

Although they never married and rarely lived together, Smart became mother to four of Barker's children. While struggling to earn a living in London through her journalism they became familiar figures among the Bohemian set of poets and painters who inhabited Soho in the 1950s. But Smart had always yearned for a writer's retreat in the country where, through the creative process of gardening and alive to the seasonal rhythms of the countryside, she hoped to rediscover the creative drive that had deserted her writing since the publication of 'By Grand Central Station'. In the 1960s having lost her job with Harpers and Queen magazine, she spotted an advertisement for The Dell, Flixton and with her remaining savings, decided to buy it while renting a small 'copy shop' in Soho as the London base for her freelance writing. Soon after, Barker answered an advertisement in The Times for a poet with family to occupy a National Trust cottage in north Norfolk (see p35) and so began their connection with the region that was to last the rest of their separate lives.

Flixton Hall, set in acres of parkland bounded by generous tree belts, had been rebuilt on a grand scale in the mid 19th century, only to be pulled down a hundred years later when the Adair family became crippled by death duties Today all that remains is one wing reduced to a single storey and converted into a range of elegant, marble-floored cattle sheds. A short distance from here, hidden away on the edge of an overgrown gravel pit, stands the pair of estate cottages converted by Smart. Approached along dusty tracks through derelict parkland scarred by flooded gravel works that '*cratered the winter landscape so that is seemd as desolate as the moon: strings of man-made lakes crusted in ice, cranes rising from pits like strange pterodactyls. It was an eccentric, labyrinthine route*' that led to Smart's refuge from the world.

Once at The Dell she set about transforming '*an old pit shaped like Australia on the map*' into '*a personal paradise, a work of art*'. The garden became her abiding obsession for the next twenty years, absorbing much of the same passionate intensity that had once impelled her love for Barker and had, in the intervening years, been used to mother his children. The kitchen table would be strewn with bulbs, seed packets and hand tools while her journals, crammed with lists of plants and changes in the weather, were evidence enough of her voracious appetite for this new world of sensuous delights. A series of small, enclosed spaces linked by winding paths and edged with an improvised mixture of shrubs, climbers and huge umbellifers, Smart's garden became a sub-tropical profusion of aromatic smells, subtle colours and sculptural shapes providing rich material for her column in House and Garden.

The publication in 1977 of her first collection of poems, *A Bonus,* triggered a slow return to writing and with the reissue of 'By Grand Central Station' the following year, designed to help launch its sequel *The Assumption of Rogues and Rascals* (1978), Smart re-emerged briefly on the literary scene, but whereas her first work, forged in the white heat of desire over 30 years ago, had flowed effortlessly onto the page, her long-awaited sequel displayed signs of laboured reworking and received very mixed reviews. As a result, the autobiography begun some years before and referred to as her 'mother book' was never finished.

Entries in the second volume of her journals, *On The Side of The Angels* (1994), so full of enthusiastic speculation as her garden took shape, tail off towards the end of her life into short recriminatory jottings. Deserted by her muse, these painful reflections on growing old, family guilt and the despair

Elizabeth Smart in the kitchen at The Dell waiting for the muse.

brought on by her prolonged writer's block are recurrent themes in the mind of a bored and lonely woman. The death of her youngest daughter Rose in 1982, a tragedy from which she never fully recovered, only compounded Smart's isolation, leaving her with two young grandchildren to look after. Escape routes back to Soho were supplemented by frequent trips to the Homersfield Swan on her moped and bouts of inebriated weeding as Smart fell silent, a prisoner in her own wild garden.

Tucked away on the north side of the churchyard at St Cross South Elmham, Smart's slate headstone carries the prophetic line from Horace 'Non Omnis Moriar' (I shall not die altogether); her immortality assured by a single work of incomparable power and a garden of exquisite beauty. Nearby, the inscription on Rose's tombstone 'Daughter of George Barker and Elizabeth' is deliberately incomplete. A fiercely independent mother, Smart was never a feminist, but unlike Barker she put the needs of others first. This left little time for writing but among friends and family she is remembered as a generous, loving spirit and 'a glory to the world'

Ditchingham

Returning from colonial service in South Africa, **Rider Haggard** met and fell in love with Louisa Margitson, heiress to the Ditchingham estate. They were married in St Mary's church before travelling back to Haggard's ostrich farm in Natal. But with the Boer War raging in the surrounding hills, they came home in 1882 and moved into Ditchingham House, a square brick Georgian building not unlike Haggard's family home of Bradenham Hall. (see p15) It was to remain their home for the next 35 years and a base from which they travelled extensively abroad until in 1917 they moved to St Leonards in Sussex where the sea air was better for Haggard's bronchitis and where he could visit his great friend Rudyard Kipling at Burwash.

Haggard was a man of boundless energy who managed to cram several careers, those of colonial settler, agricultural reformer and public servant, into a single lifetime. But it is as the writer of adventure stories that have delighted generations of schoolboys, that he will always be remembered. Having spent some time in London reading for the bar, this youthful explorer returned to Ditchingham with his imagination fired by exploits on the South African veldt. Looking out from his study across the Waveney valley to the tower of Bungay church, Rider Haggard discovered his natural talent for storytelling and sat down to write the first of over 60 novels.

Following the success of Stevenson's 'Treasure Island', a book which Haggard never greatly admired, his brother challenged him to write something better and six weeks later *King Solomon's Mines* was finished. Eventually published by Cassells in 1885 it was an immediate and overwhelming success and has never been out of print . After three early failures, the novel launched his literary career and unleashed a sustained burst of writing over the next few years. In this time he produced his best work including a string of African adventures written at 'whiteheat' that saw the publication of *She*, *Jess* and *Alan Quartermain* in 1887.

During this time Haggard made numerous trips abroad as a member of various Royal Commissions and this enabled him to gather material for more adventure stories ranging from *Cleopatra* and *Queen Sheba's Ring* which drew on his lifelong fascination with ancient Egypt, to an Icelandic saga *Eric Brighteyes* and *Montezuma's Daughter*. This last story begins in Ditchingham from where the hero, Thomas Wingfield, sets out for Mexico following the murder of his young son. He returns to marry his childhood sweetheart and end his days at The Lodge under the Vineyard Hills. It was during his own time in Mexico that Haggard's only son Jock died at Ditchingham, a blow from which he never fully recovered.

Although Haggard wrote fiction throughout his life, public works in this country took up an increasing amount of his time. He had always been interested in farming and sat on various commissions investigating the state of agriculture and conditions in the countryside, incorporating the material in a number of well-received studies such as *A Farmer's Year* (1899), *The Poor and The Land* and *Rural England* (1902). Many of his proposals for reform were later enshrined in a Development Bill (1909) which introduced grants for

Rider Haggard in his study at Ditchingham House where most of his sixty novels were written.

Ditchingham House. Haggard's study is on the far left.

agriculture and forestry and laid the basis for a system of smallholdings. It was for this pioneer work that he was awarded a knighthood in 1912, not as was popularly believed, for his literary achievements. Haggard was also a keen gardener and wrote *A Gardener's Year* (1905) based on his experiences at Ditchingham House. Kipling wrote: '*Everything in the book delights my sympathetic soul except your orchids*', an impressive collection put together by Haggard from his travels abroad. As his daughter Lilias recalled:

The garden was his hobby. It's glory was the orchid houses, where in the warm, steamy atmosphere he could forget the gloom, damp and depression of winter, amidst those strange and lovely children of the tropics, with their odd colouring and often grotesque shapes.

In 1917 Rider Haggard presented all his manuscripts, letters and diaries to the castle museum in Norwich. Now in the Records Office where they survived the disastrous fire of 1994, they remain an invaluable collection for students of this remarkable Victorian. There is no museum devoted to his life and work, but the parish church at Ditchingham where he was church warden for many years and where he and his family lie buried in the chancel, is itself a memorial. In addition to the porch restored in 1896 with money donated by Haggard, there is the church clock given by him and his wife in memory of their son Jock and the beautiful memorial window presented by his daughter Lilias with panels depicting the pyramids, Hilldrop his farm in Natal, and his favourite view of Bungay Common from Bath Hills.

Devoted companion in Haggard's later years, his youngest daughter **Lilias Rider Haggard,** inherited something of her father's literary talent. She lived most of her life in Ditchingham taking a great interest in all aspects of country under the pseudonym 'The Country Woman'. The best of these were published in three volumes during the 1940s including ***Norfolk Life*** (1943) edited and with an introduction by Henry Williamson who, while living at Stiffkey, (see p.77) had come to appreciate her sensitive and informed response to the countryside. She will perhaps be best remembered for her skillful editing of the autobiographical notes of poacher Fred Rolfe which appeared in 1935 as ***I Walked by Night*** with illustrations by Edward Seago. Four years later she brought out ***The Rabbit Skin Cap***, tales of rural life told by George Baldry the son of a Waveney shoemaker. Her engaging biography of Rider Haggard, ***The Cloak That I Left*** (1951), remains the most informative study of the man.

After Ditchingham House had been converted into flats in 1961, Lilias moved back into Bath House at the foot of Bath Hills which she had renovated before the war. Here with the river Waveney running at the foot of her garden she could enjoy the same view across Outney Common to the tower of Bungay church which her father had found the '*most quietly and consistently beautiful*' he had ever seen:

> *For the most part of the year, the plain below is golden with gorse, but it is not on this alone that the sight depends for beauty, or on the green of the meadows and the winding river edge of lush marshes that in spring are spotted with yellow marigolds and purple myriads of cuckoo flowers. They all contribute to it, as do the grazing cattle, the gabled distant roofs and the church spires but I think the prospect owes its peculiar charm to the constant changes of light which sweep across its depths. At every season of the year, at every hour of the day, it is beautiful but always with a different beauty.*

Bath House beside the Waveney from Outney Common.

Adrian Bell
(1901 - 80)

Redisham

The demands of a young family eventually persuaded **Adrian Bell** and his wife to leave the beautiful old farmhouse in the Stour valley (see p.239) that had been their home for the last ten years and move, at the outbreak of war, to more spacious surroundings at the other end of the county where he continued to farm and write about rural life. After the bosky undulations of Dedham Vale the landscape south of Beccles was an austere reminder of the stubborn boulder clay uplands of west Suffolk where Bell had served his apprenticeship twenty years before. (see p233) They found '*a plain farm and brick house (1863) amid a flat expanse of clay*' in the parish of Redisham, the Grunsham Magna of his novels, that they bought from Miss Leaf, an eccentric old lady whose garden was a profusion of cottage plants:

We learnt that this clay, the heaviest, stickiest, most boot-clogging, encouraged an extraordinary mobility - of flowers. Snowdrops marched: they proliferated like a procession of nuns to the beech hedge, where they met a migration of aconites from the other side, and fraternised under its buff, leafy winter wall. Thence they moved onwards to a sunny bank, where primroses celebrated mixed marriages: wild ones from the paddock and the survivors of Miss Leaf's rarities from the garden. I have never witnessed such a promiscuity of pollination as went on around a certain pine tree. There were even crimson cowslips.

In this ancient, intimate landscape, barns of rough-hewn oak and straw thatch lurched along rutted tracks or reared up in muddy farmyards. From the farmhouse Bell looked out across a patchwork of small meadows to where the wooden belfry of Redisham church rose above just such a group of farmbuildings. Later that year as he walked across to look inside the church he was met by the same natural abundance that first greeted him in Miss Leaf's garden. The riotous battleground between rampant nature and clusters of neatly tended graves continued unchecked as he struggled through a churchyard full of hogweed and lichen-covered headstones to witness the ancient ritual of thanksgiving for another harvest safely gathered in. In simple, evocative prose Bell described the scene on entering the church bedecked for harvest festival:

The church had a Norman doorway, with zigzag designs framing a door with iron strappings. It stood open. The church was empty as yet of humanity, but crowded with a congregation of round heads and long heads, golden tresses. There were plumped cabbages and a choir of cornsheaves, tight-waisted. Heads of oats bowed down, and turnips were in a row like the scrubbed faces of school boys. There was a tawny mangold and a scarlet beet, marrows like green hogs. Grey veils of 'old-man's beard' draped the altar rails. A cluster of lilies were preaching from the pulpit, with wild tongues.

A man stood pulling on a bell-rope. It had a fat plush grip of twined colours that made me think of swing boats. The man's face was gentle, and reminded me of T S Eliot. .... He smiled back at me, and nodded in time with his ringing.

Shortly after his arrival Bell heard of a semi-derelict farm for sale in the next parish '*that'd break any man's heart to farm it*'. Even its name, Road

St Peter's church Redisham.

Farm, seemed appropriate in that flat landscape. Bell found the challenge too great to resist and his struggle to turn round this, his third Suffolk farm, with the help of the sitting tenant George Goforth and an odd collection of land girls, Italian POWs and a Quaker pacifist, is retold in ***Apple Acre*** (1941), his picture of an English village in wartime. The new milking parlour, the first tractor and his first crop of sugar beet were innovations far removed from Bell's early days at Stradishall but his adherence to the old order of farming and the philosophy of organic production became enshrined in the 'Kinship in Husbandry' as the nation reverted to traditional values under the threat of invasion. Leading members included Bell, Edmund Blunden, H J Massingham, the rural philosopher, and Rolf Gardiner who extolled the virtues of rural crafts, estate management and the revival of folk song and dance on his Dorset estate. By embracing organic farming and self-sufficiency, this curious mixture of reactionary ideals anticipated today's 'green' movement.

Bell's time at Redisham were among his happiest farming years, but in the 1950s he and his wife retired to Beccles where he continued to write books on rural life. He took over 'A Countryman's Notebook' in the Eastern Daily Press from Lilias Rider Haggard and continued it regularly until his death in 1980. He lies buried in Barsham churchyard.

George Borrow
(1803 - 81)

Oulton Broad

When **George Borrow** moved into a cottage on the shores of Oulton Broad in 1840 he had already packed more strange experiences into his thirty seven years than most people manage in a lifetime. A gifted linguist fluent in no less than forty languages, he had lived the life of a vagrant wandering all over England and most of Europe as far as Russia, often in the company of gypsies. For the last few years he had been working in Spain for the British and Foreign Bible Society. Travelling on foot or by mule selling copies of the bible translated into Spanish proved a dangerous assignment at a time when the country was in the grip of civil unrest and on one occasion he found himself imprisoned in Madrid for several weeks.

While in Seville he had met Mary Clarke, a widow from Oulton and they returned to England together on his recall by the Bible Society. Following their marriage in London, Borrow moved into his wife's home, Oulton Cottage, where he began work on 'Zincali, An Account of the Gypsies in Spain' (1841), Encouraged by good reviews, he followed this with *The Bible in Spain* (1843), the book that established his literary reputation, based on the extraordinary escapades described in his letters home to the Bible Society. Borrow had always been a fearless traveller and often found himself caught up in armed conflicts in remote parts of the continent. A series of encounters with brigands, thieves and bare-knuckle fighters that might have sprung from the pages of a Rider Haggard thriller, are recounted in his two autobiographical works *Lavengro* (1851) and its sequel *Romany Rye* (1857), both written in the quiet seclusion of his octagonal summer house at Oulton Cottage.

For a man who had spent most of his time on the road, married life and the peaceful atmosphere of Oulton Broad failed to calm Borrow's restless spirit entirely, although he never travelled far again. Most days would begin with some form of exercise before breakfast, a demanding row across the broad or a twenty mile gallop on his Arab stallion. Always a prodigious walker, this tall figure with flowing white hair, piercing eyes and fiery temperament could often be seen striding out along the country lanes at a furious pace. Sometimes, after a bad attack of melancholia or the 'Horrors', he was known to chase rude boys and frighten young children. He was a man of unpredictable moods and after announcing a walk his wife rarely knew when she would see him again; on one occasion he was absent for three months. He did take her and her daughter to Wales with him but left them in a hotel in Llangollen while he roamed the countryside collecting material for his last book *Wild Wales* (1862).

Borrow's irritable nature was legendary; he was rarely civil with the respectable residents of Oulton Broad and took offense at the slightest provocation, maintaining a lengthy feud with the local rector because their dogs always fought and raging against the unfortunate contractor whose job was to construct the new branch line from Reedham to Lowestoft across his land. He was only truly at ease with the gypsies. They were always welcomed when they camped on waste land near his cottage and it was here one summer that he saw Jasper Petulengro, the king of the gypsies, for the last time.

Although as literature his books are often marred by repetitious and pedantic prose, he was a gifted story-teller and any faults of style are redeemed by his voracious appetite for adventure. In later life he moved first to Yarmouth, then to London and eventually back to Oulton where he died at the age of seventy eight. His cottage was demolished long ago, swept away by development and the main road which finally destroyed the peace of Oulton Broad so that:

Only the marshlands stretching away down the Waveney Valley, soothing the eye with their wild, spacious monotony, silent but for the wail of the lapwing, still speak of that solitary man who wandered so far but sought in vain for happiness.

Oulton Cottage where George Borrow wrote *Lavengro* and *Romany Rye.*

6
Precarious Pleasures
The
Suffolk Coast

Here dull and hopeless he'd lie down and trace
How side long crabs had scrawl'd their crooked race
Or sadly listen to the tuneless cry
Of fishing gull or clanging golden-eye;
What time the sea-birds to the marsh would come,
And the loud bittern, from the bull-rush home,
Gave from the salt-ditch side the bellowing boom:
He nursed the feelings these dull scenes produce

From *Peter Grimes* by **George Crabbe**

Kessingland

Following a string of best sellers, **Rider Haggard** decided to purchase Cliff House at Kessingland in 1895 as a writer's retreat. Formerly two rows of coastguard cottages which a previous owner had linked together, this rambling house on the very edge of the cliffs also provided an ideal holiday base for his children and their young cousins who came to know '*the creak of every door, the tick of every clock and the smell of every room*'. The windswept cliffs and the deserted beach became their own enchanted playground.

Despite the demands of a growing family, Cliff Grange as it became known, was large enough to give Haggard the privacy he required. In true nautical fashion he renamed each of the seventeen bedrooms after a British admiral, selecting the Nelson room as his study. In her biography of Rider Haggard his daughter Lilias recalls the peculiar atmosphere of the house which so impressed her as a young child:

The many-windowed rooms were filled with clear shadowless light and the smell and the sound of the sea. Week in and week out the gales from the north and the east roared over its low roof, cutting every living thing to the ground with their salt-laden breath .... With all its wandering passages, queer cubby holes and unexpected rooms it was like some large stationary ship

Visitors were struck by the strange mixture of naval memorabilia, sacred pictures in the drawing room, samplers in the morning room, Landseers and old prints of English kings in the dining room. The corridors were adorned with Zulu assegais and other trophies from his days in Africa, together with framed illustrations from his novels by Greiffenhagen. One visitor who immediately

Rider Haggard at Cliff Grange.

felt at home was Haggard's life-long friend Rudyard Kipling who had also spent time in South Africa and India. They would often work in the same room reading through each other's manuscripts or planning stories together as they gazed out to sea, but their shared vision of the Empire as a civilizing force has since cast a shadow over their literary achievements.

Haggard cycled the fifteen miles from Ditchingham (see p137) in all weathers, often into the very teeth of a gale. This entry in his diary, with its amusing observations on the antics of passing clergymen, records one such hazardous journey:

Very frequently I was obliged to dismount and push behind, a duty that was not made more entertaining by the vision of a curate, cigarette in mouth, sailing passed me in the opposite direction, his feet reposing on the rests. I wonder why it is, ... that most curates and many clergymen ride bicycles so madly? Thrice have I nearly fallen a victim to their rage - the last time indeed, I just escaped being run down by a coasting covey of six of them at once.

At length I turned down the lane which leads to Cliff Grange, the very eastern most dwelling I suppose, in the whole Kingdom, and as the wind was now upon my side, got along much better, until a sudden and ferocious gust blew me and the bicycle several yards into a ploughed field. The sight from the cliff was very grand - a sullen tempest-fretted sea raging beneath a low and sullen sky.

Haggard's own restless energy seemed well tuned to the noise of wind and wave, and once installed, he set about an ambitious programme of improvements. Water was pumped up by a windmill from the newly sunk well and he laid out the grounds with a croquet lawn and a vegetable garden manured with seaweed from the foreshore which, he maintained, gave the asparagus a better flavour than inland at Ditchingham. But having witnessed the dramatic effects of coastal erosion a little further north at Pakefield, his main preoccupation was to ensure that his own house did not one day slip into the sea. He was soon experimenting with marram grass which after several years stabilized the dunes at the foot of the cliffs. During the First War the house was requisitioned and used as an army barracks, and although Haggard eventually received compensation for the ensuing damage, entries in his diary suggest he no longer had the enthusiasm to renovate the property again. Ironically Cliff Grange was eventually swept away not by the sea but by a speculator who bought the house and its ten acres after Haggard's death, and replaced it with a holiday camp.

Southwold

Approached along the causeway over Buss Creek, Southwold retains all the atmosphere of a genteel resort aloof from the 'encroaching vulgarities' that afflict most seaside towns. Bounded by the sea and the Blyth estuary, the place has had few opportunities and little inclination to spread beyond the huddle of fishermen's cottages by the lighthouse or the smart Regency villas gathered around South Green. Nothing much happens in Southwold and this fiercely conservative little town seems determined to preserve intact its greatest asset. The canons arranged on Gun Hill and the town pump in the market place with its motto 'Defend Thy Ryghts' sound a warning to anyone intent on disturbing the peace. Uncluttered by romantic ruins, Southwold has managed to avoid the attention of poets attracted by the melancholy beauty of Dunwich or the literary accretions that have grown around Crabbe's Aldeburgh. The biographer Agnes Strickland (1796-1874) lived at Reydon Hall and is buried in the churchyard, but it was years later before the young **George Orwell** arrived to ruffle the sluggish waters of Southwold society.

Orwell became known to the reading public with the appearance of ***Down and Out in Paris and London*** in 1933 but he was born Eric Arthur Blair. His education followed a familiar pattern of prep school and Eton, but he was not considered clever enough for Oxford and Blair's father decided he should study for the India Office exams. With this in mind the family moved to Southwold in December 1921 on the strength of its Anglo-Indian clique and the crammer run by a Mr P Hope MA where Eric was enrolled. Six months later, having passed the entrance exams, he boarded a boat for Burma where he was to spend the next five years in the Indian Imperial Police.

Richard and Ida Blair remained in Southwold until the death of Eric's father in 1939. In that time they lived in several houses but from 1932 they were at Montague House. Eric refused to use the name, preferring the less pretentious 36 High Street on correspondence. While he was away, the family slipped easily into the genteel social life of the town. His father played golf and joined the Blyth Club for gentlemen while Ida Blair organised bridge parties and his sister Avril opened the Copper Kettle tea rooms in the High Street. The establishment remained a popular rendezvous for elderly ladies until the outbreak of war, and Eric, who never concealed his dislike for Southwold, later subjected the place to mild ridicule in ***The Clergyman's Daughter*** (1935):

George Orwell
(1903 - 50)

Blair stayed periodically with his parents at Montague House in the 30s while writing ***Down and Out in Paris and London.***

*Not to be present at Ye Olde Tea Shoppe between ten and eleven every morning to drink your 'morning coffee' and spend your half hour or so in the agreeable twitter of upper middle class voices ('my dear he had **nine** spades to the ace queen and he went one no trump, if you please. What my dear, you don't mean to say you're paying for my coffee **again**? Oh but, my dear, it is simply too sweet of you! Now tomorrow I shall simply **insist** upon paying for yours. And just look at dear little Toto sitting up and looking such a **clever** little man with his little black nose wiggling, and he would, would he the darling duck, he would, he would, and his mother would give him a lump of sugar she would, she would. **There** Toto!') was to be definitely out of Knype Hill Society.*

Perhaps in deference to his family's feelings, his most scathing comments were reserved for a description of the building's dubious architectural merits; a mixture of mock Tudor and Pagoda that bore little resemblance to the real Copper Kettle: '*The only definitively offensive buildings were Ye Olde Tea Shoppe (plaster front with sham beams nailed onto it, bottle-glass windows and revolting curly roof like that of a Chinese joss house), and the new, Doric-pillared post office.*' With its sugar beet factory and its inland location over twenty miles from Ipswich, Orwell ensured that Knype Hill would never be found on any map of Suffolk, but even so the High Street still bore some resemblance to Southwold:

After about two hundred yards (it) forked, forming a tiny market place, adorned with a pump, now defunct, and a worm-eaten pair of stocks. On either side of the pump stood the Dog and Bottle, the principle inn of the town and the Knype Hill Conservative Club. Earlier in the novel Orwell had made it clear that not only did he find the social life of Southwold restrictive but that he cared even less for the surrounding countryside:

The town pump erected by public subscription. Unveiled by Mr Grubbe Mayor of Southwold in 1873.

St Athestan's Church stood at the highest point of Knype Hill, and if you chose to climb the tower you could see ten miles or so across the surrounding country. Not that there was anything worth looking at, only the low, barely undulating East Anglian landscape, intolerably dull in Summer, but redeemed in winter by the recurring pattern of elms, naked and fan shaped against leaden skies.

The Town Hall in Southwold Market Place. The town becomes Knype Hill in Orwell's ***The Clergyman's Daughter.***

Blair returned from Burma in 1927 intent on becoming a writer, although 'Burmese Days' did not appear until 1934. Immediately, in what was to become characteristic fashion, he set about collecting material for a book on 'down and outs', living rough in doss houses or 'spikes' in both London and Paris and taking temporary work where he could. The next few years proved most difficult while he struggled to establish himself as a writer, returning to his parents home at intervals to write up his experiences. During this time he had little to show for his efforts apart from rejection slips and some articles for The Adelphi, a leading literary journal.

Blair must have been acutely aware of the social paradox implicit in drafting **Down and Out in Paris and London** from a comfortable bedroom in Southwold and his parents, if not openly hostile, found his presence embarrassing. Their tall, awkward-looking son gave rise to the usual comments about scruffiness as he strode around the town; comments which found their way back to his mother via the bridge parties and the tea shop. They were certainly relieved to find his books published under a pseudonym.

He did however manage to earn a little money from some tutoring posts arranged through family contacts; firstly a backward child in Walberswick and then the sons of C R Peters during vacations in 1930 and 1931. Based on practical fieldwork Blair's unconventional teaching methods drew on his striking observations of the countryside and his ability to enter unobtrusively into the boys' world. Together they fished in the mill pond, dug prehistoric tumuli in the hope of making some great archaeological discovery, searched for birds' nests, fought battles in the sand dunes and made bombs which were exploded in the garden of the boys' home, much to Mrs Peters' consternation.

Despite his understandable dislike of the snobbery and prejudice in Southwold society, he did enjoy exploring the beach and roaming the immediate countryside, often walking over to the partly ruined church at Walberswick where he would read in a sheltered corner of the churchyard. It was here one summer's day that he saw the figure of a man dressed in brown walk silently through the ruins, only to vanish as suddenly as he had appeared. Blair was convinced he had seen a ghost.

There were few opportunities for a person of Blair's intellect to meet like-minded people in Southwold, but he did manage to make a few friends. As gym mistress at St Felix school, Brenda Salkeld must have seemed an unlikely candidate, but she was well liked by Eric's parents. Together they would walk or ride on the heaths around the town, but their greatest pleasure was to meet, often at the Harbour Inn where they would have a room to themselves, and discuss the books they were reading. They became very close and Eric proposed marriage but Brenda refused, maintaining she was never in love with him. They remained good friends and his letters to her from the 1930s reveal much about his literary preferences and opinions.

Soon after, he turned his attentions to Eleanor Jacques. She was already involved with his friend Dennis Collings who was away much of the time in Cambridge. During the summer of 1932 they spent many hours together and

Walberswick church. Orwell would often sit and read here on summer evenings. On one occasion he saw the ghostly figure of a monk disappear among the ruins.

'*I cannot remember when I have ever enjoyed any expeditions so much as I did those with you. Especially that day in the wood, where the deep beds of moss were. I shall always remember that, and your nice white body in the dark green moss*', and in another letter: '*I hope you will let me make love to you again sometime, but if you don't it doesn't matter, I shall always be grateful to you for your kindness to me.*'

These are hardly the most passionate of love letters; the tone is rather that of the polite 'thank you' note. He may simply have felt uncomfortable expressing his true feelings because subsequent letters to her were full of proposed assignations clearly aimed at repeating the experience away from Southwold. Meetings proved difficult to arrange, Eleanor became less enthusiastic and the following year she married Dennis Collings.

Another Southwold friend was to prove a more valuable contact. Eric enjoyed painting and was often to be seen on the beach with his watercolours when he met Mabel Fierz and her husband in 1930. She was a well read Hampstead socialist and before long he was spending time at their home in Golders Green. Mabel Fierz soon realised that as an aspiring writer, Blair would gain little by remaining in Southwold and urged him to move to London. There she introduced him to Max Plowman and other Adelphi writers, but more importantly she put him in touch with Leonard Moore who was to become his literary agent. The question of an appropriate pseudonym arose while discussing the exact title for 'Down and Out' with his publisher, and it was ironic that, considering his lack of enthusiasm for East Anglia, he eventually chose the name of a Suffolk estuary because it sounded strong and distinctive.

Although he still spent time in Southwold where he roughed out ideas for 'Keep the Aspidistra Flying', the publication of ***Down and Out in Paris and London*** launched his literary career. The move to Hampstead and a flat over the bookshop where he worked, signalled the end of his association with the town. His last recorded visit was in June 1939 to attend his father's funeral, but already the town was beginning to relax in the knowledge that its most famous literary son had finally left, the disapproving clatter of tea cups still ringing in his ears.

* * * * *

The Hardborough of **Penelope Fitzgerald**'s second novel bears little outward resemblance to Southwold despite its position somewhere between Lowestoft and Aldeburgh, but in ***The Bookshop*** (1978) she explores the nature of betrayal and revenge at work in a small coastal town that Orwell would have recognised. The decision of her self-effacing heroine to open Hardborough's first bookshop in a damp old building on the foreshore is motivated by a desire to confirm her own separate existence but, out on the marshes as she watches a heron struggling to swallow an eel, Florence Green questions the wisdom of her venture.

Catering for the rather predictable tastes of Hardborough's reading public; the memoirs of ex SAS officers, sailing manuals and accounts of the royal family, the bookshop begins to prosper, but the problem lies more in Mrs Green's choice of property. Each summer with the onset of the Aldeburgh festival, the town's most formidable patron would revive her idea to transform the building into a rival arts centre. With the opportunity now gone, Violet Gamart initiates a discreet but savagely orchestrated campaign, assembling a daunting array of influential friends and local dignitaries to dispossess her adversary. What for Florence Green had begun as a modest exercise in self-assertion becomes a struggle for self-preservation, but she is finally driven from the town by an overwhelming alliance of forces that her kind heart and quiet determination are ill-equipped to withstand.

* * * * *

Southwold may seem an unlikely place to find the country's leading crime writer, but a quick glance at the figureheads in the Sailors' Reading Room or the brightly coloured heads that adorn St Edmund's Terrace, and you begin to realise why the novels of **P D James** are littered with dismembered corpses.

Figurehead in the Sailors' Reading Room.

The rectory at Forncett St Peter where Dorothy Wordsworth lived with her uncle. Letters from here are filled with excited accounts of William's visit in 1805 and her vision of a country retreat where they could be together.

St Mary's Diss from the Mere, the view that greeted John Betjeman on a visit to the town in 1963.
The church is also the setting for John Skelton's poem *Ware The Hawk* written while he was rector here from 1498 to 1529.

Southwold with its motto *Defend Thy Ryghts* became Knype Hill in George Orwell's novel
The Clergyman's Daughter and the Hardborough of Penelope Fitzgerald's novel **The Bookshop.**

On the western outskirts of Dunwich, the *immense cincture* of Greyfriars Priory is all that remains of the medieval town. Refered to by Henry James as *the visibility of mutilation* , the ruins are now very close to the receding cliff line.

Brought up in Cambridge, the high point of holidays on the coast near Lowestoft was a trip to Southwold, and James has been a regular visitor ever since she moved into her father's retirement cottage. Although she doesn't regard Suffolk as an inherently sinister place, the emptiness and sense of history continue to inspire her best work including 'Devices and Desires' (see p54) and 'Unnatural Causes' (see p166). Both are set on the East Anglian coast and one horrific episode from her futuristic novel ***Children of Men*** (1992) takes place in a deserted Southwold where one of the few survivors, an elderly landlady, could easily be mistaken for the author.

Blythburgh

Unless you take the ferry across to Walberswick, the nine mile detour round the Blyth estuary is rewarding for the stunningly beautiful view across mudflats to Blythburgh church. One of the great Perpendicular buildings in a county renowned for the splendour of its church architecture, the sight of Holy Trinity, '*like an anchored ship surrounded by the retreating tide*,' or '*an old couchant animal watching over the deserted marshes'*, has been celebrated by generations of travel writers and landscape painters. Its spacious, limewashed interior bathed in a silvery light that comes streaming in through the clerestory windows, appeals more to the poetic imagination. Here among the '*Anglican odour of wax polish, flowers and damp old hymn books,*' **P D James** introduces her detective in ***Unnatural Causes***. Dalgliesh, with two volumes of poetry to his name, stops at the church before visiting his aunt at Monksmere.

The angel roof in Blythburgh church that became the subject of a poem by Peter Porter.

Visitors often feel uplifted by the quality of light that sharpens every angle and illuminates every carved surface as though it were possible to float quite effortlessly among the angelic host arranged along the length of the nave roof. Here, with delicate wings outstretched, they have hovered over congregations for 500 years like great marsh harriers gliding over the reed beds in the fading light. Written in the mid 70s after a visit in the company of Anthony Thwaite when the effigies were being restored, the Australian poet **Peter Porter** acknowledged their presence on the ground as a symbol of mortality in a poem made more poignant by the recent death of his wife for whom there is no restoration, no resurrection.

An Angel in Blythburgh Church

Shot down from its enskied formation,
This stern-faced plummet rests against the wall;
Cromwell's soldiers peppered it and now the death-
watch beetle has it in thrall.

If you make fortunes from wool, along
The weeping winter foreshores of the tide,
You build big churches with clerestories
And place angels high inside.

Their painted faces guard and guide. Now or
Tomorrow or whenever is the promise -
The resurrection comes: Fix your eyes halfway
Between Heaven and Diss.

The face is crudely carved, simplified by wind;
It looks straight at God and waits for orders,
Buffeted by the organ militant, and blasted
By choristers and recorders.

Faith would have our eyes as wooden and as certain.
It might be worth it, to start the New Year's hymn
Allowing for death as a mere calculation,
A depreciation, entered in.

Or so I fancy looking at the roof beams
Where the dangerous beetle sails. What is it
Turns an atheist's mind to prayer in almost
Any church on a country visit?

Greed for love or certainty or forgiveness?
High security rising with the sea birds?
A theology of self looking for precedents?
A chance to speak old words?

Rather, I think of a woman lying on her bed
Staring for hours up to the ceiling where
Nothing is projected - death the only angel
To shield her from despair.

Walberswick

Always more happy in the depths of the countryside, **Virginia Woolf**'s impressions of the Suffolk coast are at best terse and occasionally scathing. In June 1912 she and Leonard Woolf had stayed at The Bell during their engagement. A short letter to Lady Robert Cecil had the following P.S. *'I'm writing in an Inn, rain outside, three old spinsters discussing the beauties of river scenery'.* Years later, writing to thank Margaret Llwellyn Davies for some gift of embroidery she enquired: *'How did it come to Walberswick. Don't tell me that it is the produce of one of those little artistic cottages which used to annoy us so - I don't want to credit the artists of Walberswick with any decent feelings.'*

Following the success of Wilson Steer's dazzling series of Impressionist beach scenes completed in the 1880s, this small fishing village had become something of an artists' colony and holiday retreat for the middle classes; a transformation which, ironically was also reshaping St Ives in Cornwall where Virginia had spent her own childhood holidays. At Walberswick the architectural shapes of the harbour which so delighted Rennie Mackintosh failed to catch her writer's eye. Her irritation with the self-consciously picturesque village and the amateur attempts to commit it to canvas was shared by **Edward Thomas** who walked over from Dunwich in 1908 when staying at one of the coastguard cottages (see p164).

I was at Walberswick today,' he wrote to George Bottomley *'pestered by inane pretty houses, paintable bits and an elderly aesthetic lady with youthful ankles and neat old cottage furniture. But the dreary intersected marshes and invisible sounding sea in twilight mists repaid me a little - with a hump of woods just visible as culmination of the mist.*

It was perhaps inevitable that in a place despised by such distinguished writers, one of the few novels set in Walberswick should take as its starting point a painting by its most celebrated artist. The acclaimed first novel by Orford-born writer **Maggie Hemmingway** is based on a picture by Wilson Steer in which a man and a woman converse on a bridge at sunset against a background of the Blyth estuary. In real life the painter's output faded into conventional landscapes after his early brilliance, but in Hemmingway's novel ***The Bridge*** (1986) his work is inspired by a brief affair with a married woman.

Dunwich

Greyfriars, built on the western outskirts of medieval Dunwich, is now perilously close to the cliff, but even the guardianship of English Heritage cannot prolong the day when, like All Saints church, it topples over the edge. What survives of the Franciscan Priory and the redbrick cottages that huddle below, are all that now stand between Dunwich and final destruction. The town has been celebrated in verse since the late 12th century when the monk Jordan Fantosme described the siege of Dunwich in his long narrative poem, but the real battle has always been with the sea that until the 14th century had enabled the town to become one of the most prosperous sea ports on the whole east coast.

On the night of January 19th 1328 most of the town and three of its 18 churches were swept away in a terrible storm, and since then the rest of Dunwich has gradually sunk beneath the waves. By the 19th century, stirred by the sight of the last abandoned church disappearing over the cliff face - by what Henry James called *'the visibility of mutilation'* - the demise of this great city had become the subject of romantic ballads by a succession of aspiring poets, but it was left to **Swinburne** to elevate Dunwich to the status of literary shrine. As Edward Thomas concluded: *'He adds Dunwich to the poet's country. By observation, not naturalistic but spiritual, and by the emphasis of reverie and meditation, simple and conventional, but rapturous, he made that coast Swinburne's country par excellence.'*

Swinburne spent much of his childhood on the Isle of Wight in a house overlooking the sea. From an early age his explorations of the cliffs and foreshore earned him the nickname 'Seamew' or seagull, and it was always the sea that Swinburne regarded as his natural mother. This fascination lasted a lifetime. The idealised images of his earlier verse became replaced by more precise coastal scenes, especially the crumbling cliffs and reed beds of the Suffolk coast that he often visited in the company of his friend Watts-Dutton. One of their favourite destinations was the stretch between Dunwich and Covehithe they explored from a cottage at Wangford in 1875 returning again two years later. Swinburne celebrated the occasion in a number of poems notably *Evening by the Sea* which Geoffrey Grigson believed to be descriptive of Eaton Wood and Eaton Broad, and *By the North Sea* in which details of the local topography assume the significance of universal truths:

Algernon Swinburne
(1837 - 1909)

All Saints church 1783 from a
contemporary engraving.

All Saints in 1919. For many writers and poets, the ruined tower came to symbolise the destruction of Dunwich.

Tall the plumage of the rush-flower tosses,
Sharp and soft in many a curve and line
Gleam and glow the sea-coloured marsh-mosses
Salt and splendid from the circling brine.
Streak on streak of glimmering seashine crosses
All the land sea-saturate as with wine.

Swinburne's visit to Dunwich prompted **Where Dunwich Used To Be**, a meditation on the town's destruction by the restless advance of an ever hungry sea where once:

Church and hospice wrought in faultless fashion,
Hall and chancel bounteous and sublime,
Wide and sweet and glorious as compassion,
Filled and thrilled with force of choral chime,
Filled with spirit of prayer and thrilled with passion,
Hailed a God more merciful than Time

The poem gathers its strength from a pervading sense of desolation made visible by the ruins of All Saints church - *'Where is man? the cloister murmurs wailing / Back the mute shrine thunders - Where is God?'*

Here is all the end of all his glory -
Dust and grass, and barren silent stones.
Dead, like him, one hollow tower and hoary
Naked in the sea-wind stands and moans,
Filled and thrilled with its perpetual story:
Here, where earth is dense with dead men's bones.

From the scenes of desecration anguished cries rise above the waves from those souls cast out so rudely from their final resting place.

> *Tombs, with bare white piteous bones protruded,*
> *Shroudless, down the loose collapsing banks,*
> *Crumble, from their constant place detruded,*
> *That the sea devours and gives not thanks.*
> *Graves where hope and prayer and sorrow brooded*
> *Gape and slide and perish, ranks on ranks.*
>
> *Rows on rows and line by line they crumble,*
> *They that thought for all time through to be*
> *Scarce a stone whereon a child might stumble*
> *Breaks the grim field paced alone of me.*
> *Earth, and man, and all their gods wax humble*
> *Here, where Time brings pasture to the sea.*

* * * * *

During the summer of 1897 **Henry James** left the capital to celebrate Queen Victoria's diamond jubilee while he relaxed in Bournemouth putting the finishing touches to 'What Maisie Knew'. Having completed the book, he decided to stay with American cousins in Suffolk. The letter of invitation, postmarked Saxmundham, arrived only the day after he had been intrigued by the name of this Suffolk market town while reading the letters of Edward Fitzgerald. Later that same day, walking on the beach at Bournemouth, he met a boatman from Saxmundham whose brother had been Fitzgerald's boatman. This series of coincidences continued when James arrived in Dunwich to discover his cousins had booked rooms for him and his typist in the very cottage where **Edward Fitzgerald** had lodged almost every summer throughout the 1870s.

People in Dunwich had gone in fear of this strange, abstracted figure who took to walking along the shore at midnight wrapped in his Inverness cape and muttering to himself. Mrs Scarlett, Fitzgerald's landlady at Albert Cottage, would fetch him home for lunch from the ruins of All Saints church where, propped against a buttress, he would spend each morning deep in thought or writing letters. She recalled how he would return, sweeping into her shop to dispatch the village gossips with a wave of his stovepipe hat. These stories were told to **Jerome K Jerome** by Mrs Scarlett when he leased her cottage after the First War, and even today an elderly neighbour can remember how, long after his death in 1927, Jerome's ashes were kept in a casket on the mantlepiece by his widow.

From this same cottage Henry James spent August 1897 exploring the countryside on foot and by bicycle, gathering material for an article entitled 'Old Suffolk'. First published in Harper's Weekly that same year it appeared later in **English Hours** (1905) a collection of travel sketches. He enjoyed the project in the knowledge that the Suffolk coast had been the home of David Copperfield and was haunted by the ghosts of Crabbe and Fitzgerald. As a writer his response to the melancholy mood of Dunwich was both immediate and perfectly attuned:

Henry James
(1843 - 1916)

I defy anyone at desolate, exquisite Dunwich, to be disappointed in anything. The minor key is struck here with a felicity that leaves no sigh to be breathed, no loss to be suffered .... Dunwich is not even the ghost of its dead self; almost all you can say of it is that it consists of the mere letters of its old name .... few things are so melancholy .... and so redeemed from mere ugliness by sadness - as this long artificial straightness' (the coast), which gave it *'a sort of mystery, that more than makes up for what it may have surrendered.*

The empty eyehole of a skull washed clean at low tide, the ruined church perched on the edge of the cliff and *'the crumbled, ivied wall of the immense cincture of the Priory'* created a powerful atmosphere. As James imagined it, the mystery of Dunwich *'sounds forever in the hard straight tide and hangs through the long, still summer days, and over the low dyked fields in the soft, thick light'*. The following year saw the publication of James' celebrated ghost story 'The Turn of the Screw' with the ghostly bells of Dunwich still reverberating in his head.

A succession of writers including Edward Fitzgerald and Henry James lodged at Albert Cottage with Mrs Scarlett.

Remains of Greyfriars western gateway. The *crumbled ivied wall of the immense cincture of the priory* became, for Henry James, powerfully associated with the melancholy atmosphere that hung over Dunwich.

Above all James most admired the fishermen whose livelihood depended on the changing mood of the sea and he '*often dreamed that the ideal refuge for a man of letters was a cottage so placed on the coast as to be circled as it were, by the protecting arm of the Admiralty*'. His dream was realised soon after by the poet **Edward Thomas** who stayed for two months in the coastguard cottage on Dunwich Heath while recovering from one of his bouts of ill health brought on by overwork. The sea air and a chance meeting with a young girl revived him enough to complete the first draft of his book on Richard Jefferies, the Wiltshire writer and naturalist.

Information about his holiday is contained in three letters to his friend, the poet and dramatist George Bottomley. In them Thomas talks about the Jefferies project, reviews of his books and Edward Garnett's abridgement of 'Arabia Deserta', written just a few miles away at Theberton by C M Doughty.

Oh Dunwich is beautiful. I am on a heaving moor of heather and close gorse up and down and ending in a sandy cliff about 80 feet perpendicular and the black, peat strewn fine sand below. On the edge of this one and a half miles away is the ruined church that has half fallen over already. Four arches and a broken tower, pale and airy. Just beyond that the higher moor dips to quite flat marsh with gentlest rises inland with masses of trees compact and dark and a perfect huge curve of foamy coast up to the red light at Southwold northwards. In the other direction, just behind us, the moor dips to more marshes with black cattle dim and far off under white sun, and three faint windmills that work a sluice and then trees - inland more gentle rises with pines. No hills (unless you lie down in a dip of the moor and fancy the moorland as part of a Welsh 'black mountain').

When not absorbed in his work, Thomas spent many hours on the beach gathering driftwood for his fire and a bizarre collection of flotsam including *'champagne corks, sailors hats, Antwerp beer bottles, fish boxes' etc*; returning with pockets filled with beautifully patterned pebbles.

During these forays he fell in love with Hope, a young local girl with long brown plaits and *'the richest grey eyes, very wild and shy'*. They would often walk together and talk of poetry but before accepting a collection of his essays, the girl wrote to Helen Thomas seeking reassurance. His wife quickly realised that the young girl was susceptible to her husband's charms and warned him against encouraging the affair. Shortly after she went away to school where Thomas wrote to her only to receive a sound rebuttle from her father. This *'beautiful creature, more a dryad or sea-nymph than a human girl'* may have inspired those visions of youthful female perfection that recur in his poetry. Thomas was certainly very affected by the girl and regretted the abrupt end to their brief relationship:

Edward Thomas
(1878 - 1917)
from a lino cut by
Robin Guthrie.

The coastguard cottages on Dunwich Heath where Thomas worked at his biography of Richard Jefferies.

I liked her for her perfect wild youthfulness and remoteness from myself and now I think of her every day in vain acquiescent dissatisfaction and shall perhaps never see her again and shall be sad to hear she ever likes anyone else even though she will never like me.

One of Thomas's last works of literary criticism, published in the year of his death, was *A Literary Pilgrimage in England*, written to order like so much of his writing and a book about which he was decidedly unenthusiastic. Although his only recorded stay in East Anglia was that one brief holiday at Minsmere, Thomas knew his regional writers and included short chapters on Crabbe, Cowper, Fitzgerald, Swinburne and Borrow; a task made easier by drawing on his earlier biography of Swinburne (1903) and the study of Borrow into which he plunged soon after completing the book on Jefferies.

* * * * *

Dunwich remains a dangerous place as anyone walking the cliff-top path will know and it is this sense of impending disaster which lurks at the heart of *Unnatural Causes* (1967), an early crime novel by **P D James** set in Monksmere. At one point in the book Adam Dalgliesh, the author's detective, is returning along this same path when, in the moonlight he stumbles upon the recently disturbed grave of Will Scrivener shot by smugglers in 1786. A little earlier he had paused to reflect on the power of local legends, lodged deep in the memory, to resurface on nights light that; the muffled sound of church bells rising from the waves or the hooves of smugglers' horses returning from Sizewell Gap. His thoughts then turn to more recent events; a naked woman wading to her death and the handless corpse drifting ashore at the bottom of a sailing dinghy. These discoveries were no more bizarre that the human bones which for centuries have been washed out of abandoned graveyards at the foot of the cliffs and would with time become part of that same macabre tradition.

P D James
(1920 -)

Nothing tangible survives for long at Dunwich, only the memories and the legends persist; fertile ground for the writer of murder mysteries in which historical fact and contemporary fiction are precariously balanced. Drawing on the fascination Dunwich still holds for writers and poets, James creates a writers' colony on Monksmere Head (Dunwich Heath) rife with literary ambition and professional jealousy. The floating corpse is that of thriller writer Maurice Seaton whose only play was killed off by Oliver Latham's savage review some years ago, and Celia Calthorpe, doyenne of the local literary festival, has never quite forgiven reclusive novelist R D Sinclair for refusing to accept the dedication of her latest romantic novel.

The main suspects are carefully positioned around the headland like unexploded bombs, seldom out of each other's sight and never far from the clifftop; the terrain criss-crossed by a network of false trails. Dalgliesh, who is himself the author of two slim volumes of verse, arrives for what he hopes will be a quiet holiday with his aunt at Pentlands Cottage which hovers on the edge of Minsmere bird reserve. As in all her novels, James creates a strong topographical reality within which the story unfolds with all the assurance of a writer familiar with her material, but often her landscapes convey a sense of growing unease:

The cliffs at Dunwich.

John Brinkley Easy
One of the last graves in All Saints churchyard. *'Uneasy on the brink '* it toppled over the edge a few years ago.

It was a lonely shore, empty and desolate, like the last fringes of the world. It evoked no memories, cosily nostalgic, of the enchantments of childhood holidays by the sea .... Here was nothing but sea, sky and marshland, an empty beach with little to mark the miles of outspate shingle but the occasional tangle of tar splotched drift wood and the rusting spikes of old fortifications. Dalgliesh loved this emptiness, this fusion of sea and sky. But today the place held no peace for him. He saw it suddenly with new eyes, a shore alien, eerie, utterly desolate.

Shortly after, a little further along the shore, Dalgliesh discovers a second body in one of the bird hides on the edge of the reserve, and as the drama builds to its horrific climax, a storm gathers force on the headland before exacting its revenge:

The wind was alternately howling and moaning across the headland and a fast running tide was thundering up the beach driving the shingle in ridges before it. Even from the sitting room at Pentlands he could hear its long withdrawing sigh. From time to time a fitful moon cast its dead light over Monksmere so that the storm became visible and he could see from the cottage windows, the stunted trees writhing and struggling as if in agony and the whole wilderness of sea lying white and turbulent under the sky.

Aldeburgh

In the summer of 1982, having just read the M R James ghost story set in the town, **Paul Theroux** decided that '*some fictional landscapes were still worth visiting*' on his journey round the British coast. But on arrival he resorted to quoting a letter from the Palace pinned up outside the moot hall thanking the town for its good wishes on the birth of a son. Local people in Aldeburgh are not always so easily impressed by royalty. On one occasion during a visit the Queen asked Benjamin Britten's friend, the fisherman Billy Burrell, where he caught his fish. 'Over there ma'am' he replied pointing to the sea. Each year during the festival the town comes to resemble a set designed for one of Britten's comic operas. Walking down the High Street you half expect to hear the price of new potatoes delivered in the sonorous voice of an Albert Herring or the booming tones of Lady Billow as she marshals her volunteers at another RNLI bazaar.

For many people Aldeburgh **is** the festival. They return each year to cherished holiday flats or the spartan comforts of Slaughden's martello tower. In the fish and chip shop a poster invites orders for smoked salmon and in the Porche outside, a sticker announces that 'Lacrosse players give it some stick'. This is Aldeburgh's saucy postcard, its end-of-the-pier joke, but there never was a pier, not even a band stand and they don't play bingo in the cinema. Walk along Crag Path and you find Edward Clodd's house, but who was he? Evidently a man of some distinction, a famous lifeboat coxswain perhaps. The elegantly lettered tablet to his memory gazes down on a ceramic plaque to the children's author, Margery Sharp. Confronted by monuments to two of the town's more esoteric celebrities, visitors might be forgiven for wondering why the place has attracted so much attention when the reviews have not always been so complimentary.

Aldeburgh is '*a bleak little place: not beautiful. It huddles round a flint-towered church and sprawls down to the North Sea - and what a wallop the sea makes as it pounds on the shingle*.' This at least was the opinion of **E M Forster** during the war. **Norman Scarfe** writing in the Shell Guide to Suffolk (1960) got it about right when he called the place '*an ugly, delightful seaside resort*', his pleasure due more to the presence of Aldeburgh's renowned music festival than to any real sense of place. It has little of Southwold's spacious elegance or the intimacy of Orford's market square, and there is no obvious focal point, just the High Street, uncomfortably wide and windswept with few buildings of note and some narrow back streets, all presided over by the church, aloof and apart on top of the old cliff. Read any guidebook and you will soon realise why the Tudor moot hall, over-restored and over-exposed, looks faintly ridiculous on the sea front. It had once occupied the centre of Aldeburgh market place, but since the middle ages half the town has been destroyed by the sea:

The beast which has eaten up so much of Aldeburgh is not wolfish, tearing out large mouthfuls at a time; rather it seems like an incalculable ancient and primitive monster, a colossal amoeba, which eats its prey by flowing round and engulfing it.

Crabbe's birthplace from an early 18th century engraving.

In **Crabbe**'s day Aldeburgh was a dying town, reduced to a huddle of fishermen's cottages in the remaining streets while along the shore *'a few scattered tenements appeared erect among the desolation'*. A century before the trade had been good and the shipbuilding flourished, but now they were gone and people turned to smuggling to augment a meagre livelihood. The land around was no better. The marshes were undrained, *'the soil poor and sandy, the herbage bare and rushy, the trees withered and stunted'*. No wonder Crabbe considered himself *'cast by Fortune on a frowning coast'*. The harsh terrain compounded the melancholy atmosphere that hung about the town and inevitably helped shape the young poet's imagination:

> *Lo! where the heath, with withering brake grown o'er,*
> *Lends the light turf that warms the neighbouring poor;*
> *From thence a length of burning sand appears,*
> *Where the thin harvest waves its wither'd ears;*
> *Rank weeds, that every art and care defy,*
> *Reign o'er the land, and rob the blighted rye;*
> *There thistles spread their prickly arms afar,*
> *And to the ragged infants threaten war;*
> *There poppies nodding, mock the hope of toil;*
> *There the blue blugloss paints the sterile soil;*
> *Hardy and high, above the slender sheaf,*
> *The slimy mallow waves her silky leaf;*
> *O'er the young shoot the charlock throws a shade;*
> *And clasping tares cling round the sickly blade;*

George Crabbe
(1755 - 1832)

The son of a collector of salt taxes, Crabbe was put to work at an early age rolling barrels in his father's warehouse on Slaughden quay. In his spare time he roamed the sheepwalks near the coast where he was free to indulge his passion for botany and dream of a life beyond the confines of his native town:

Aldeburgh Church. Crabbe was curate here in 1781 as was the father of M R James a century later.

I loved to walk where none had walk'd before,
About the rocks that ran along the shore;
Or far beyond the sight of men to stray,
And take my pleasure when I lost my way:
For then 'twas mine to trace the hilly heath,
And all the mossy moor that lies beneath.
Here had I favourite stations, where I stood
And heard the murmers of the ocean-flood,
With not a sound beside, except when flew
Aloft the lapwing, or the grey curlew . . .

He did eventually escape the wretched little fishing town, travelling first to London and then, following his ordination, to Belvoir Castle where he became chaplain to the Duke of Rutland. Drawing on his early memories of life in Suffolk, Crabbe wrote some of his most accomplished verse during his time in Leicestershire. ***The Village*** (1783) is a realistic account of deprivation among the people he knew in Aldeburgh and years later he returned to the same theme in ***The Borough*** (1810) because as E M Forster acknowledged:

he never escaped from Aldeburgh in the spirit; and it was the making of him as a poet. Even when he was writing other things, there steals again and again into his verse the sea, the estuary, the flat Suffolk coast and the local meannesses, and an odour of brine and dirt - tempered occasionally with the scent of flowers.

While living in the Alde valley (see p186) Crabbe often visited his family on the coast, but apart from one brief spell as curate in Aldeburgh, he had no desire to return. He had clearly outgrown the town and felt unwelcome among the people he once described as:

> *a wild, amphibious race,*
> *With sullen woe display'd in every face;*
> *Who far from civil arts and social fly,*
> *And scowl at strangers with suspicious eye*

* * * * *

The very same monster that had, by the 18th century, consumed much of Crabbe's Borough, proved to be its salvation when Regency society discovered the restorative qualities of a dip in the German Ocean. Aldeburgh's transformation into fashionable resort owed much to the Garrett dynasty grown wealthy from its engineering works at Leiston, who took up residence near the church in 1840. By then brightly coloured houses, balconied and bay windowed, had begun to spring up along Crag Path where it was 'de rigueur' to be seen mingling with the rich and famous. Among the most distinguished visitors was the tall figure of **Edward Fitzgerald** who liked to escape the gossip of Woodbridge society (see p206) for '*a Toss on the Sea and a Smoke with the Sailors*'. In 1855 he drove over in the gig with **Thomas Carlyle** who recommended the place to his wife as '*a beautiful little sea town*'.

* * * * *

Wilkie Collins
(1824 - 89)

Wilkie Collins arrived five years later on the newly opened railway in search of background material for his novel *No Name* (1862). Following the success of 'The Woman in White' which established the Novel of Sensation as a literary genre, Wilkie Collins was already aware of the locational possibilities offered by the East Anglian coast. 'David Copperfield' (1850) had been published the year before he first met Dickens in London and from this developed a long friendship in which the famous author became something of a mentor to Collins, offering advice on his early novels. Divided into a series of scenes each with a different setting, *No Name* contains a lengthy middle section in Aldeburgh. His description of '*this curious little seaside snuggery*' which introduces the Fourth Scene, is taken largely from 'A Guide to Aldeburgh and Adjacent Places' published anonymously the same year.

The novel as its title suggests, tackles the moral and social implications of illegitimacy through a complicated narrative in which the main characters plot each other's downfall. Magdalen Vanstone, the strong-willed heroine, refuses to accept the stigma of her birth and seeks revenge on a society which is both patriarchal and harshly judgmental. Intent on ensnaring her obnoxious cousin in marriage and thereby retrieving her inheritance, Miss Vanstone arrives in Aldeburgh and takes up residence for the season. Here with the help of the scheming confidence trickster Captain Wragge she sets about her task with an air of resignation. Together they walk along the front towards the decayed port of Slaughden where a century earlier George Crabbe had worked in his father's warehouse. Face down on the grassy bank below the martello tower, Magdalen voices her despair: *'It doesn't cast me off Mother Earth! The only mother I have left'*. Collins was a great admirer of Crabbe and his evocation of the desolate scene before them, a scene which mirrors the loneliness of his heroine, is deliberately modelled on Crabbe's verse:

It was a dull, airless evening. Eastward was the grey majesty of the sea, hushed in breathless calm; the horizon line invisibly melting into the monotonous misty sky; .... Southward, the high ridge of the sea dyke and the grim massive circle of a martello tower reared high on its mound of grass, closed the view darkly on all that lay beyond. Westward a lurid streak of sunset glowed red in the dreary heaven-blackened the fringing trees on the far borders of the great inland marsh - and turned its little gleaming water-pools to pools of blood. Nearer to the eye, the sullen flow of the tidal river Alde, ebbed noiselessly from the muddy banks; and nearer still, lonely and unprosperous by the bleak waterside lay the lost little port of Slaughden; with its forlorn wharfs and warehouses of decaying wood, and its few scattered coasting vessels deserted on the oozy river-shore.

* * * * *

Largely through its association with Crabbe, the literary world continued to be fascinated by Aldeburgh but once its novelty as a Victorian resort had begun to wear off, writers became less complimentary. At the beginning of the century while staying at Dunwich, **Henry James** rode over to *'this small break in the wide, low, heathery bareness that brings the sweet Suffolk commons - rare purple and gold when I arrived - nearly to the edge of the sea. We don't, none the less, always gather the particular impression we bravely go forth to seek.'* Disappointed to find this *'fourth-rate watering place that had elbowed away, evidently in recent years, the old handful of characters'* from Crabbe's fishing town, James conjured away *'the little modern vulgar accumulation'* that was the resort:

What is left is just the stormy beach and the big gales and the cluster of fishermens' huts and the small, wide, short streets of decent, homely, shoppy houses. These are the private emotions of the historical sense .... what a mere pinch of manners and customs in the midst of winds and waves!

Writing to Violet Dickinson the following year, **Virginia Woolf** voiced her displeasure: *'Why do you stay at Aldeburgh; there are East winds there, both of God and man'*, and later referred to it disparagingly as *'that miserable, dull, sea village'*.

In this *curious little seaside snuggery* Magdalen Vanstone plots to regain her inheritance in Wilkie Collins' novel *No Name*.

Thomas Hardy had very little to say about the place, nothing that has survived, but then he was very careful to keep secret his visits to Edward Clodd, the rationalist and agnostic who lived at Strafford House. The two men had first met in London where Hardy became a founder member of the Omar Khayyam Club established by Clodd in 1892 to celebrate the life and work of Edward Fitzgerald. Clodd lived part of the year at Aldeburgh where he regularly entertained more illustrious members of the club at his house on the seafront. In addition to Hardy, J M Barrie, Holman Hunt, George Gissing, George Meredith and H G Wells were all tempted by the prospect of stimulating company, Aldeburgh's bracing sea air and a trip in Clodd's boat. On one occasion Hardy and others sailed up the Deben to Woodbridge, followed by a brisk walk to Fitzgerald's grave in Boulge churchyard (see p193)

The presence of Clodd at Aldeburgh provided another attraction for Hardy, namely an excuse to make several visits between 1909 and 1912 in the company of his new secretary Florence Dugdale. The two had first met in 1907 and Hardy was immediately intrigued by this much younger woman with her similar social background, her self-education and literary aspirations. Unlike the rapidly declining health of his wife Emma, Hardy appeared genuinely concerned about Florence's delicate state. Clodd was the first to be told about Florence and soon became implicated in their clandestine visits where Hardy enjoyed '*the sensation of having nothing but sea between you and the north pole*' and where he considered the sea air would be good for Florence.

Strafford House on Crag Path where Thomas Hardy stayed on several occasions between 1909 and 1912 with Edward Clodd.

During this time Hardy also introduced her to Florence Henniker with whom he had once been in love and who had remained a close friend. The two women soon developed a friendship of their own and in 1912 Florence went to stay at Mrs Henniker's summer residence in Southwold while Hardy went off to see Clodd at Aldeburgh. These trips to the Suffolk coast provided a welcome relief from the gloomy atmosphere of Hardy's Dorchester home, presided over by his ailing and eccentric wife and from the local gossip which surrounded the Max Gate menage.

Hardy was so concerned that these visits should remain secret that his autobiography makes little or no reference to them. When in 1916, two years after his marriage to Florence, they learnt of Clodd's decision to publish his own autobiography, Florence, fearing the worst, immediately wrote to Clodd threatening that Hardy would expose him in the press. This extraodinary outburst proved quite unjustified when Clodd's rather restrained memoirs were published but it seriously damaged one of Hardy's longest and most valuable friendships. There were no more visits to Aldeburgh and Clodd later wrote that although Hardy 'was a great author; he was not a great man; there was no largeness of soul'.

Thomas Hardy and Florence Dugdale on one of their clandestine visits to Aldeburgh.

M R James, Cambridge scholar and celebrated writer of ghost stories, was a regular visitor to the town throughout his life. The family connection began when his grandparents moved to Wyndham House below the parish church where his father later became curate. Monty's own association started with boyhood visits to his elderly grandmother whose charitable works are commemorated by what he later described as 'the worst painted window (perhaps) in the country'.

James remained a familiar figure in Aldeburgh after the sale of Wyndham House in 1920, although increasing infirmity restricted him to short walks along Crag Path. An unassuming man, he liked to recall the occasion when, inside a paper shop, the proprietor removed a book from the shelf and enquired whether he was familiar with the work, to which the author replied with evident satisfaction 'Yes, I wrote it'. The volume in question was almost certainly James' last collection of ghost stories *A Warning to the Curious* published in 1925 and written while he was Provost of Eton.

Set in the coastal town of Seaburgh, the title story becomes an antiquarian investigation into the local legend concerning three crowns buried during the Saxon occupation of Suffolk as a protection against invasion. In an obvious reference to Dunwich, one has already been lost to the sea and a second melted down following its discovery at Rendlesham near Woodbridge, the preferred location for the Wulfinga dynasty's royal palace. An inscription in an 18th century prayer book discovered in one of the town's curio shops leads to a burial mound at the end of a low ridge overlooking the surrounding countryside and the site of the last remaining crown. Here the amateur archaeologists begin their gruesome task in an atmosphere of impending disaster:

M R James
(1862 - 1936)

Wyndham House Aldeburgh, the family home of M R James.

Pine trees on the outskirts of the town were used by James as the grim setting for the barrow digging episode in *A Warning to the Curious*.

a line of dark firs behind us made one skyline, more trees and the church tower half a mile off on the right, cottages and a windmill on the horizon on the left, calm sea dead in front, faint barking of a dog at a cottage on a gleaming dyke between us and it, the full moon making that path we know across the sea, the eternal whisper of the scotch firs just above us, and of the sea in front. Yet in all this quiet, an acute, an acrid consciousness of a restrained hostility very near us, like a dog on a leash that might be let go any minute.

The following day Paxton, who unearthed the crown, is last seen alive pursued along the shore into a swirling sea mist. His mutilated body is later discovered near the martello tower.

* * * * *

Recalling the occasion when, as a boy, he was first ducked in the waves, Edward Fitzgerald declared, '*There is no sea like the Aldeburgh Sea - it talks to me*'; a sentiment expressed by **Benjamin Britten** a century later. Born at Lowestoft within earshot of the sea, he continued listening to the voice of the waves all his life. Mingled with the cry of marsh birds, the sounds of his native coastline become a haunting refrain throughout his music; in 'Albert Herring' where the references are to Iken and Snape, in 'Curlew River' first performed in Orford church, evoking the spirit of childhood holidays at Butley Creek and most memorably in *Peter Grimes*, the opera that established Britten's reputation as a major new composer.

The exact circumstances of Britten's introduction to Crabbe's poetry and the birth of the Aldeburgh Festival have entered the folklore of post-war English music. At the outbreak of hostilities while on an American tour with Peter Pears, he discovered an article by **E M Forster** in The Listener that changed his life. Entitled **George Crabbe, The Poet and the Man**, the opening sentence struck Britten forcibly - '*To talk about Crabbe is to talk about England. He never left our shores*' Forster's advice was '*remember Aldeburgh when you read this rather odd poet, for he belongs to the grim little place and through it to England'*. He illustrated the working of Crabbe's 'inscape' by reference to **Peter Grimes** in which the sadistic fisherman is forced to live alone in a landscape that reflects exactly the oppressive mood of the poet's anti-hero.

> *Thus by himself compell'd to live each day,*
> *To wait for certain hours the tide's delay;*
> *At the same times the same dull views to see,*
> *The bounding marsh-bank and the blighted tree;*
> *The water only, when the tides were high,*
> *When low, the mud half-cover'd and half-dry;*
> *The sun-burnt tar that blisters on the planks,*
> *And bank-side stakes in their uneven ranks;*
> *Heaps of entangled weeds that slowly float,*
> *As the tide rolls by the impeded boat.*
>
> *There anchoring, Peter chose from man to hide,*
> *There hang his head, and view the lazy tide*
> *In its hot slimy channel slowly glide;*

E M Forster, Benjamin Britten and Eric Crosier working on the libretto for **Billy Budd** at Crag House in 1949.

The Listener article was in fact the transcript of a talk by Forster broadcast on the BBC Overseas Service that must have sounded like a rallying cry to every Englishman abroad. It certainly had an immediate effect on Britten who became overwhelmed by a *'feeling of nostalgia for Suffolk'*. Having bought a copy of Crabbe's verse he sailed for England determined to write an opera. As Forster reminded his audience in a lecture given at the first Aldeburgh Festival, the *'obscure and unattractive citizen'* who had been the model for Crabbe's murderous outcast was *'the first step in a series of creative events which has produced your festival'*. Forster had attended the first performance of **Peter Grimes** at Sadlers Wells in 1945 and much as he enjoyed the music he felt he could have made a better job of the libretto. As a result Britten invited him to Crag House to work with Eric Crozier on the libretto for 'Billy Budd'.

* * * * *

True to the spirit of Crabbe, poetry and literature have always been an integral part of the festival since its inception in 1948. Most of the country's literary figures have given readings at one time or another and some, like the novelist **Susan Hill**, have been drawn back to Aldeburgh by Britten's music. Brought up on the Suffolk coast, it was only on hearing his 'Sea Interludes' that she realised how much she missed the place. It proved a turning point, the beginning of an obsession with the composer that has lasted a lifetime. Renting a cottage on the seafront each winter during the 1970s Aldeburgh became for her a place of pilgrimage in which *'the beach, the marshes and the names of all the places around and about, and in, and between, was like a country invented by his genius'*. As Hill admits, without Britten's music her imaginative life would have been greatly impoverished.

Several stories sprang directly from his inspiration, notably **The Albatross**, a tale set in the small fishing town of Heype (Aldeburgh) with characters straight from the cast of a Britten opera. Duncan Pike is a misfit but unlike Peter Grimes he is one of 'God's fools', a feeble man intimidated by the sea and a possessive mother:

he knew that once they had pushed the boat out, then there would be no escape for him, and he would be alone with Ted Flint, towering above him, in the middle of the endless sky and heaving sea, and he was seized with choking panic, he turned and began to run, pounding off down the beach to get away from the menace of the waves and wind, and the chugging of the boat, out of reach of Ted Flint, he would have done anything rather than go on that sea.

Hill's essay **Aldeburgh : The Vision and the Reality** offers a moving insight into the creative process of a writer alone with her thoughts. In it she compares the real place with its shops and streets, its golf course and yacht club, with the Aldeburgh of her imagination where she *'experienced deep joy and fulfilment'*. The clear, cold air seemed charged with an intensity then, the most prolific time of her life as a novelist, and on these *'beautiful, vibrant days'* in winter she recalls:

I walked inland for miles and saw no one, I made up page after page in my head, absorbed, concentrated, taut, yet seeing things too, waders in the mud, a heron, still as a tree stump, the individual blades of grass.

Precarious Pleasures

One day all that changed as she struggled with the shock of sudden, personal tragedy. Since then, although she has rarely been back, Hill retains a vivid sense of the Aldeburgh of her emotions *'set as in the amber you may find on the beach there, it is a landscape of the spirit'*. As local fishermen will tell you, amber is hard to find on this stony shore, but Hill knew where to look.

* * * * *

More recently, in **Pat Barker**'s award-winning ***Regeneration*** (1992), Aldeburgh assumes the grim reality of a coastal town in wartime when the army psychologist W H R Rivers takes a short break from his rehabilitation unit to visit a young officer recovering from the traumas of trench warfare. There is no mention of the war as the two men walk inland up the Alde estuary, but on the seafront the sandbags piled against doorways, the dull thud of waves pounding the shore like heavy mortars and the beach strewn with bloodied fish heads recall the nightmare world that Burns is struggling to forget.

As the storm breaks, Rivers is awakened by a series of explosions that signal the launching of the lifeboat. In a scene reminiscent of 'A Warning To The Curious', he heads south with urgent steps towards the martello tower which earlier that day had felt to Burns *'like a place where people* (had) *died .... violent deaths'*. Here in the moonlight he discovers Burns staring up at the tower gleaming white *'like the bones of a skull'* as though he had seen a ghost. The ordeal enables Burns to take the first step towards recovery and he begins to talk about the horrific experience on the Somme that so nearly destroyed his life, but as Barker concludes *'he had missed the chance of being ordinary'*.

The martello tower has become Aldeburgh's most enduring literary monument.

7

Patterns Under The Plough

Suffolk River Valleys

Living at the conjunction of the Suffolk light and heavy lands gives everything an extra edge. To the north-west stretches 'the old clay' itself, life-providing and death-reminding. To the south-east lie the sandlings and the sea. The soils do not mix .... but remain sharply defined. It is one land or the other. You know where you are .... everything ecological changes, oak to pine, hawthorn to broom, arable to marsh, hills to flats. The sandlings are a subtle shading-off of all that is emphatic in landscape, a series of earth and water abstractions .... The old clay on the other hand never ceases to shout its hard-line reality .... Suffolk: the Plain Facts and Suffolk: the Transcendental.

***From the Headlands* by Ronald Blythe**

Wissett

Faced with the prospect of military service at the outbreak of the First War, several members of the Bloomsbury Group became conscientious objectors and looked for agricultural work. At the time, Virginia Woolf's sister Vanessa Bell was living with the painter Duncan Grant who with the novelist and critic David Garnett, had gone to stay at Wissett Lodge near Halesworth made vacant by the death of Grant's aunt. Here they hoped to gain exemption from military service on the strength of re-establishing the fruit garden and the orchard. Writing to Katherine Cox in March 1916 **Virginia Woolf** relayed the news:

You have heard how Duncan has become a fruit farmer in Suffolk with Bunny Garnett? He came up after a week of it and says he finds it very soothing and all his faculties sink to sleep. He is out picking Big Bud off the currant bushes for 8 hours a day; sleeps all night, paints on Sundays .... Nessa is going to keep house for him perhaps all Summer. So you see Bloomsbury is vanished like the morning mist.

Lytton Strachey had already been declared medically unfit for active service when he arrived in Suffolk. Once at Wissett he quickly became enveloped in the same atmosphere of creative well-being that helped speed Virginia's recovery a few weeks later:

Everything and everybody seems to be more or less overgrown with vegetation .... thistles four feet high fill the flower garden, Duncan is covered

Lytton Strachey
(1880 - 1932)

with Virginia (or should it be Vanessa?) creeper, and Norton and I go about pulling up the weeds and peeping under the foliage. Norton is in very good spirits having evolved a new theory of cubic roots.

Before leaving for Garsington Strachey decided to try and *'realise the events of a single and not extraordinary day'* in the form of an essay. Entitled **Monday June 26th 1916**, it captures perfectly the way his thoughts drifted through the lives of friends, literary preoccupations and a series of amorous speculations provoked by the photograph of a boxer in the morning paper. Strachey's plan to pursue the handsome young farm lad was soon thwarted in the yard by Bunny Garnett feeding animals and a discussion of the latest Dostoievsky. Undeterred he wandered off into a field and fell into a kind of reverie:

to one side of me the country dipped down at a little distance, rising again in a lovely landscape .... And the field I was in was full of splendid grasses, and there were wild flowers scattered all about, and wild roses in the hedge on my left hand. I walked entranced; that feeling of a .... sudden easy mysterious explanation of all the long difficult mysterious embroilments of the world .... I thought of my friends and my extraodinary happiness. I thought of Death, of Keats and the Ode to the Nightingale .... All the time the sun warmed me deliciously and the landscape beamed in front of me, and visions of Jimmy Hinde (the boxer), half naked, with bruised ears, floated in my imagination .... The dazzling happiness, coming, in flood after flood, over my soul, was so intense that it was like a religious conversion. And through it all there was an odd waft of melancholy - a kind of vibration of regret. A strange importance seemed to invest and involve into a unity the scene, the moment, and my state of feeling. But at last I knew it was time to go back to the house. As I walked back, I felt as if I had made an advance - as if I had got somewhere new

After lunch, having failed to ensnare the farmer's boy, Strachey returned to the scheme he had been hatching since the morning mail, namely how to meet the young postman *'with the fair hair and lovely country complexion.'* He decided to effect an assignation at the pillar box along the lane where, cutting across the fields, he would appear in time for the afternoon collection. As the time drew near Strachey began to fret over the exact circumstances of their meeting - how would he contrive to stop the youth if he approached from the **opposite** direction and swept passed him **downhill** on his bicycle? But his carefully laid plans did not allow for the postman *'with black hair, and a red presbyterian face and a most unattractive briskness'* who pulled up beside him. The following day Strachey told David Garnett that he was *'more than a little in love with* (Dora) *Carrington'.* As Garnett recalled, Strachey was *'more ready to confide a hetero-sexual attachment to me than a daydream about the postman which would have strained my powers of sympathy!'*

In July the Woolfs went to stay at Wissett . Writing at the end of the month to Strachey, Virginia declared: *'Wissett seems to lull asleep all ambition - don't you think they have discovered the secret of life? I thought it wonderfully harmonious'* and to Vanessa: *'I've seldom enjoyed myself more than I did with you, and I can't make out exactly how you manage. One seems to get into such a contented state of mind'.* She confided *'I am very much interested in your life, which I think of writing another novel about. Its fatal staying with you - you start so many new ideas'.* This was Virginia's very first reference to her idea for **Night and Day** in which Katherine Hilbery, daughter of a famous literary family, is modelled on Vanessa.

Duncan Grant and David Garnett eventually appeared before the local Blything tribunal hearing in Halesworth. Part of Garnett's case rested on the fact that his mother, who was responsible for introducing many of the great Russian classics to English readers, had also been a pacifist and had visited Tolstoy in Russia. Garnett claimed that this disclosure backfired when the chairman of the tribunal rejected their claim for exemption thinking that Tolstoy was a Russian town. A more sympathetic hearing from an appeal tribunal in Ipswich persuaded Grant and Garnett to leave for Charleston in Sussex where, by finding employment on a local farm, they deprived Wissett of a more prominent place in the history of the Bloomsbury Group.

Bloomsbury came to Wissett Lodge in 1916.

Bruisyard

On the slopes of the Alde valley in the parish of Bruisyard stands Oakenhill Hall, chosen by **H W Freeman** as the setting for his story of Crakenhill Hall between the wars and one family's struggle to make the farm prosper:

H W Freeman
(1899 - 1994)

a curious crow-stepped gable of dark-coloured stone .... was the most striking feature about the gaunt old house, and in the evening light when it stood out strongly against the darkening sky, added a touch of the grotesque to it. It was the sort of gable that, catching the eye of some seeker after the picturesque with romantic tendencies, might have inspired him with the fancy to stay and settle there; but seekers after the picturesque are rare in this part of East Suffolk

Oakenhill Hall became the setting for *Joseph and his Bretheren.*

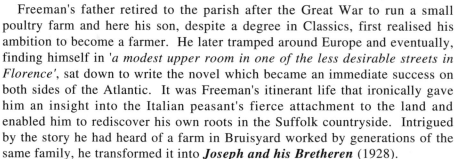

Freeman's father retired to the parish after the Great War to run a small poultry farm and here his son, despite a degree in Classics, first realised his ambition to become a farmer. He later tramped around Europe and eventually, finding himself in *'a modest upper room in one of the less desirable streets in Florence'*, sat down to write the novel which became an immediate success on both sides of the Atlantic. It was Freeman's itinerant life that ironically gave him an insight into the Italian peasant's fierce attachment to the land and enabled him to rediscover his own roots in the Suffolk countryside. Intrigued by the story he had heard of a farm in Bruisyard worked by generations of the same family, he transformed it into *Joseph and his Bretheren* (1928).

Unlike the works of his contemporary Adrian Bell who farmed in Suffolk all his life, Freeman's novel is really about the land itself and the allegiance of one family to a single farmstead. Despite the hours of unremitting toil, the work fails to brutalise his characters. The difference between them and Mary Mann's farm labourers (see p115) who are brought low by poverty and fear of the workhouse, is one of land ownership. Benjamin Geaiter began life as a labourer but through his own tenacity managed to save enough to buy a smallholding before acquiring Crakenhill Farm and one hundred acres of derelict land. Set on a steep hillside it had driven previous tenants into bankruptcy and the people of Bruisyard speculated on how long it would be before Geaiter suffered the same fate. He was under no illusion about the task ahead:

This piece of land had caused him serious misgivings although it was dirt cheap, for besides the copses and rabbits it was infested with twitch - a net of sinister, snakey white roots that choked the coulter of the plough, and the tine of the harrow till they were forced to stop.

With the help of his wife and six sons, '*the great broad-chested, lumbering man with his bushy black beard and sluggish eyes*' soon earned the respect of his neighbours. Working late into the evening this solitary muscular figure came to epitomise the dignity of hand labour celebrated by Harry Becker in his contemporary line drawings of Suffolk farm workers: '*The sight of his great bent back and long flat arms, knotted and rugged like elm branches, and the steady, measured swish of his scythe were things not easy to forget*'. But the twitch-infested clay is to exact its own heavy price. Geaiter decides that the only way to rid the field is to weed it by hand and he summons his wife and sons to begin the slow, laborious task. In a scene reminiscent of the swede-hacking episode at Flintcomb Ash in Thomas Hardy's 'Tess of the D'Urbervilles':

Emily Geaiter paused for a moment to straighten her back and knock the caked earth from her fingers, to let the breeze play in her wispy grizzled hair and cool her cheeks. Her breath came rather short nowadays and she was panting a little: it had been a hard day and she was feeling it, although she could hardly remember a day in her life which had not been hard ....

She stretched her shoulders for the last time and bending to her task once more, picked up a clod. It was riddled with sinuous, flapping strands of the evil weed, almost human in the thoroughness with which they clutched and enveloped the soil in their grip .... Suddenly her wrists went weak and the clod dropped from her hands, a feeling of sickness came over her and clouded her brain.

Minutes later Emily Geaiter pitched forward, her face buried in the broken clods. She had 'wore up' and died from years of overwork. The sons all attempt to leave but are forced back into service by their tyrannical father whose youngest son Joseph is born to Nancy Hembling, the new housekeeper. The novel traces Geaiter's declining years; the brothers drift away to work on neighbouring farms but, reunited by a common bond, they eventually buy back the farm that killed their mother.

The Alde Valley

George Crabbe
(1755 - 1832)

While exploring the heaths and marshes around his native Aldeburgh (see p169), the young **George Crabbe** became passionately interested in botany and while apprenticed to an apothecary in Woodbridge his acute observations of wild plants and their medicinal properties proved invaluable. On a visit to her uncle at Ducking Hall in the parish of Parham, the Beccles girl who was to become his wife first met the young poet, and there in the woods and meadows of the upper Alde valley Sarah Elmey came to admire his knowledge of the countryside and his emerging literary talent. As their love grew, she became his muse and the 'Mira' of his early verse. With her death years later Crabbe's pleasure in the natural world began to fade and shortly after he spent a day revisiting the scenes of their courtship:

Yes , I behold again the place,
The seat of joy, the source of pain;
It brings in view the form and face
That I must never see again.

The night-bird's song that sweetly floats
On this soft gloom - this balmy air,
Brings to the mind her sweeter notes
That I again must never hear.

Crabbe made slow progress in his chosen profession, his early verse attracted little attention and in desperation he decided to try his luck in London. The move proved decisive. With Edmund Burke's encouragement he was ordained and following the success of 'The Village' (1783), his survey of life on the Suffolk coast, he married Sarah. On the death of her uncle in 1792 the couple moved into Ducking Hall, but with the death of two young sons and continued hostility from Sarah's relatives, they moved again four years later when Crabbe accepted the curacy of Sweffling and Great Glemham. The move was made possible by the generosity of Dudley North who offered them the use of Great Glemham Hall. As Crabbe's son recalled in his affectionate biography of the poet, the family found consolation and then happiness in their new surroundings, away from the memories of Parham:

The whole parish and neighbourhood resemble a combination of groves, interspersed with fields cultivated like gardens, and intersected with those green dry lanes which tempt the walker .... in the evenings, when .... every few yards, a glowworm, and the nightingales are pouring forth their melody

But Crabbe knew well enough the harsh realities of rural poverty as he visited the sick and comforted the dying in their overcrowded hovels. Drawing on his years in the Alde valley he presented a picture of village life in ***The Parish Register*** (1807) that swept aside the pastoral tradition of the previous century with all its moralising about happy, industrious peasants. Crabbe acknowledges the law-abiding labourers who tend their cottage gardens and go to church each Sunday, but he is concerned for the plight of those brought low by grinding poverty living in *'the infected row we call our street'*.

Between the road-way and the walls, offense
Invades all eyes and strikes on every sense:
There lie, obscene, at every open door
Heaps from the hearth, and sweepings from the floor,
And day by day the mingled masses grow,
As sinks are disembrogued and kennels flow
Their hungry dogs from hungry children steal,
There pigs and chickens quarrel for a meal;
There dropsied infants wail without redress,
And all is want and wo and wretchedness.

Crabbe moved to Rendham Grove from Gt Glemham in 1801. He remained here another five years before resuming his curacy in Leicestershire. The house is the poet's only surviving residence.

187

Sweffling

T F Powys
(1875 - 1953)

Unlike his brothers John Cowper and Llewelwyn,**T F Powys** was sent from the family home in Somerset to school in Aldeburgh because the headmaster of Eaton House, the Rev W C Wilkinson, was a friend of Mrs Powys. It was through their mother's Norfolk family of Johnson that the brothers were able to trace their literary connection with the poets William Cowper and John Donne. Although the West Country exerted a profound influence on the writings of all three brothers, it was Theodore's early farming experiences in East Anglia that provided fertile material for his later fiction.

Attempts to persuade Theodore to follow his father into the Church came to nothing and he eventually chose farming as a career despite his decidedly bookish inclination. On leaving school he was allowed to stay in Suffolk, apprenticed to a farmer at Rendham in the Alde Valley, but at the age of 19 he moved, on his mother's initiative to Church Farm Warham on the north Norfolk coast where the Rev Digby, another family friend, could keep an eye on the boy's moral welfare.

A year later Powys found himself back in the Alde valley as a tenant farmer in the adjoining parish of Sweffling, where his father had acquired the lease on White House Farm. Despite his relative inexperience and small profit margin, Theodore was persuaded to take on a second smaller farm two years later.

John Cowper Powys composed *Sonnet Written in Sweffling Churchyard* while staying with his younger brother at White House Farm.

Successive droughts, the heavy boulder clay and a foreman who abused his trust all contributed to the failure of his agricultural experiment While in Suffolk he read an essay by William Hazlitt, 'On living to Oneself' which advocated a conscious retreat into a *'world of contemplation and not of action'*. It had a great effect on Theodore, providing the authority he sought to leave farming and follow his inclination to become a writer. It remained his manifesto inspiring a series of meditations in 'Soliloquies of a Hermit' (1916).

Despite this setback, his time in Suffolk proved valuable not just for the direct experience of working the land but also for certain literary influences he acquired through his continuing programme of self-education. It was perhaps inevitable that he should be drawn to the work of George Crabbe who nearly a hundred years earlier had been rector of Sweffling, *'a writer who shared not only something of his melancholy disposition but who had walked the self same country paths'*. Powys later acknowledged the importance of Crabbe's poetry on his writing with its recurring themes of rural deprivation and social injustice. While in Sweffling Theodore did manage a few early pieces, but **Sonnet Written in Sweffling Churchyard** by his prolific elder brother John Cowper is the only surviving work from this period, composed while on a visit to White House Farm.

> *There is a spirit in these ancient stones,*
> *These grassy mounds and immemorial trees*
> *That scarce seem conscious of the passing breeze*
> *So deep they brood above the sleeping bones*
> *Of happy mortals eased of toilsome breath,*
> *A power not alien to this gentle vale,*
> *Not alien to this quiet folk that fail*
> *In no observance due to life or death*
> *The spirit and the power of lives that pass*
> *Their labours ended, and their laughter fled,*
> *To mingle with the dust their hands have tilled,*
> *To take their rest beneath the silent grass*
> *Their fathers planted, and their sons shall tread,*
> *The measure of man's destiny fulfiled.*

Certain incidents were later incorporated in a number of short stories and his fellow parish councillor John Row reappeared as John Roe the persecuted ploughman in the novel 'Mark Only'. From Theodore's hermetic life, his reading of the James I bible and his admiration for 'Pilgrims Progress' were born his peculiar literary preoccupations with good and evil, love and death, rendered in a simple allegorical style that has ensured T F Powys a unique place in English literature. Farming and the cycle of the seasons provide a constant backdrop against which most of his rural dramas are played out using a large cast of familiar protagonists and a range of images of farm and field, of earth and clay which recur throughout his work, many of them inspired directly by the Suffolk countryside. Reviewing his qualification for writing 'Mr Tasker's Gods' Theodore said *'I knew the ways of the land, village customs and the right time to plant and sow, and I knew my bible.'*

Blaxhall

George Ewart Evans
(1909 - 88)

Just after the war **George Ewart Evans** arrived in Blaxhall quite unaware that his friendship with elderly neighbours in this remote Suffolk hamlet would change the whole direction of his writing and lay the foundations of what has become known as 'Oral History'. Over the next few years Evans came to realise that those residents born in the late 19th century were the last remnants of an ancient agricultural tradition - what he later referred to as a Prior Culture - that was being destroyed by the mechanisation of farm labour. The gradual replacement of horse power by the tractor was the main agent of change and for him ' *the true end of the Middle Ages is not the accession of the Tudors but the introduction of the internal combustion engine*'.

With the aid of a tape recorder he embarked on a remarkable salvage operation to chronicle this traditional rural culture across East Anglia before it disappeared, a daunting mission that preoccupied him for the rest of his life. His great achievements were to establish the value of personal recollection as a valid historical record and give the agricultural labourer a permanent voice in a series of books on East Anglian life spanning thirty years. The first of these, ***Ask The Fellows Who Cut The Hay***, published shortly after he left the village in 1956, remains a celebrated tribute to the people of Blaxhall and a way of life that had survived intact until the outbreak of the Great War.

Unlike his contemporaries Adrian Bell and Henry Williamson who were determined to carry through their own practical experiments in farming and write about their experiences, Evans came to the region by chance and with no agenda for life in the countryside. Encouraged by the publication of his first short stories before the war, he had already decided to become a writer when his wife spotted an advertisement for the post of head teacher at a village school in East Suffolk and her successful application presented a solution to their current problems: '*Looking back on our last-ditch escape to Blaxhall, we saw it as a watershed in our lives*' Evans concluded.

Blaxhall primary school before its conversion to a Youth Hostel

The sandstone boulder at Stone Farm that 'whoolly grew'.

The village remained rather cut off from the outside world and must have presented a bleak picture to this exile from the Welsh valleys. It was three miles to the nearest railway station at Campsey Ash, there was just one bus each week to Ipswich and most people relied on bicycles to get about. Conditions were still quite primitive with no mains drainage, water from a well in the playground and light from oil lamps; but the promise of a school house which went with the job decided the outcome. Evans would look after the two younger children during the day and fit in his writing when he could. He adjusted well to his new role but growing deafness compounded his sense of isolation and he seldom saw anyone but the tradesmen for weeks at a time.

Out of Evans' predicament grew a friendship with neighbours that proved crucial. His children loved to watch Robert Savage, a retired shepherd, feeding his pigs or collecting ducks eggs in his yard opposite the school house, and as Evans spent more time listening to his stories, he began to discover evidence of a rich folk culture still alive in the village. Priscilla and Robert Savage spoke a pure Suffolk dialect enriched with archaic words and phrases that, from his reading of Chaucer and Shakespeare, Evans recognised to be centuries old. Savage referred to his time as a 'page' or apprentice to a shepherd, he used the word 'tempest' to describe a thunderstorm, 'abroad' for outdoors and a whole range of technical terms associated with agriculture which the Suffolk farmer Thomas Tusser had recorded in his 'Hundreth Good Points of Husbandrie' in 1557. Evans continued to visit Robert Savage until his death and was quick to acknowledge the enormous debt he owed the old man who had become his mentor: '*He it was who gave me entry to what was a foreign country.*'

As Evans became more involved in the life of Blaxhall, partly through his active role on the Parish Council, he acknowledged the differences between the loose knit pastoral communities he had known as a boy in South Wales and the more rigidly structured and deferential nature of society in the arable villages of Suffolk. But it was ironically the aquisition of two technical advances in communication which transformed his life and work. A hearing aid ended years of personal isolation and the loan of a new portable tape recorder enabled him to make a permanent record of his early conversations with Blaxhall residents. His one regret was that Robert Savage died before he was able to record '*the rhythm and colour of his speech"* that he so admired but Priscilla Savage's memories of the domestic economy which make such an important contribution to 'Ask The Fellows', were saved.

From this tentative beginning, Evans began to construct a picture of traditional life in Blaxhall. George Messenger who worked on the barges at Snape maltings proved to be another rich source of material, describing how he cut wheat on his allotment using a serrated sickle, threshing it with a flail. Abraham Ling's father had been a member of the Blaxhall company of shearers who travelled from farm to farm clipping sheep with handshears. In both cases hand tools were being used that had survived unaltered since biblical times. Traditional dances and folk songs were still performed at the Ship Inn and Evans uncovered vestiges of ancient beliefs adhered to by the older generation that hardly seemed credible in the middle of the twentieth century, notably the origins of the Blaxhall Stone recounted by Lewis Poacher. This large sandstone boulder at Stone Farm had been transported from Lincolnshire during the last Ice Age, but to Blaxhall people who knew nothing of glaciation, the only logical explanation was that the stone 'whoolly grew'. Of this they were certain and could remember quite clearly the time when it was much smaller. Moving to Needham Market in 1956 Evans reflected:

I left the village (Blaxhall) *with mixed feelings, because I sensed it was here I had found my life's work, although I did not fully realise this at the time. It was only some years after I left that I identified the village as my second academy* (the first had been South Wales) *when I began to learn the technique of what became later known as oral history .... it was here at this time, and with the dressing and elaborating on it later, that I transposed the Blaxhall community in my own mind into its true place in an ancient historical sequence.... that had lasted well over two thousand years.*

By the time the second edition of 'Ask The Fellows' appeared in 1961 the break with the old tradition was almost complete. It seemed difficult to believe that within the space of a generation or two the old handskills had been discarded, the beliefs forgotten and the dialect impoverished. The young tractor driver listening to the Light Programme in the comfort of his new council house knew little of his father's skill with heavy horses and cared even less. But Evans understood the advantages of mechanisation and personal mobility well enough to be unsentimental about the passing of the old ways. Isolated rural communities often bred the worst kind of parochialism and he acknowledged the inevitable drift to the towns for work and entertainment.

Blaxhall cottages where Evans first discovered the survivors of a 'prior culture' and laid the foundations of Oral History.

The withdrawal of public transport, the closure of rural post offices, and the demise of the primary school have turned places like Blaxhall into retreats for Londoners drawn to the peculiar beauty of the Suffolk coast and the concerts at Snape maltings. 'Tele' cottage industries and craft workshops now flourish in those once damp, poorly lit dwellings where, nearly 50 years ago, Evans made his first recordings of Suffolk farm labourers.

Boulge

In 1835 **Edward Fitzgerald** left Wherstead Lodge and the social life of Ipswich when his parents eventually took possession of Boulge Hall, the family home just north of Woodbridge and a mile from his birthplace at Bredfield. Once there he took an immediate dislike to the spacious Queen Anne building, and despite its well-wooded park, he was equally scathing about the surrounding countryside: *'One of the ugliest places in England - one of the dullest - it has not the merit of being bleak on a grand scale- pollard trees over a flat clay, with regular hedges'* he wrote in 1844, and later that year:

Edward Fitzgerald
(1809 - 93)

I have always said that being near the sea, and being able to catch a glimpse of it from the tops of hills and of houses, redeemed Suffolk from dullness, and at all events that our turnip fields, dull in themselves, were at least set all around with an undeniably poetic element.

Life at the hall proved so distractive that soon after he removed himself to the thatched cottage by the park gates that remained his home for the next sixteen years. Here surrounded by his books, his paintings and a bust of Shakespeare he lived with his pets in chaotic seclusion, indifferent to physical discomforts and disturbed only by occasional visits from friends whom he often welcomed in dressing gown and slippers:

I live in a hut with walls as thin as a sixpence: windows that don't shut; a clay soil beneath my feet, a thatch perforated by lascivious sparrows over my head. Here I sit, read, smoke and become very wise, and am already quite beyond earthly things.

The cottage at the entrance to Boulge Park where Edward Fitzgerald lived for many years.

Fitzgerald's reputation as an eccentric recluse was not at that time entirely accurate, for he spent long periods away from Boulge visiting old Cambridge friends. W B Donne had returned to the family home at Mattishall in Norfolk where Fitzgerald and he indulged the '"vita comtemplativa'. Wanderings in East Anglia were interspersed with trips to London and here he revived friendships with Thackeray and Tennyson, offering encouragement and financial support at a time when both men were struggling to establish literary reputations. Fitzgerald was a man with no literary ambitions of his own, and although he enjoyed their company enormously, he came to feel increasingly overshadowed by their formidable success and was often glad to return to the familiar surroundings of his Boulge cottage.

As the attraction of London's literary scene began to wane, Fitzgerald cultivated new friendships nearer home, often walking across the fields to call on the Rev George Crabbe, son of the poet, at Bredfield rectory. Thomas Churchyard, a Woodbridge solicitor and water colourist in the Norwich School tradition, together with Bernard Barton the Quaker poet, completed the circle that became known as the 'Woodbridge Wits' who held regular 'symposiums' in each other's houses. Modest about his own literary gifts, Fitzgerald felt most at ease in their company playing the dilettante patron of the arts.

Fitzgerald was, by his own admission, '*a very lazy person - who do nothing*', preferring a life of wayward scholarship free from the strictures of earning a living. This financial independence, secured by a generous allowance from his mother, helps explain the undisciplined nature of his writing as well as his meagre output. He wrote occasional verse and edited, or rather rewrote Barton's poetry, displaying an early talent for free translation that flourished under Edward Cowell's guidance. But his time at Boulge is commemorated in the witty, intelligent correspondence with friends and writers of the day that confirms his reputation as one of the great Victorian men of letters.

Despite Fitzgerald's aversion to Boulge his body was brought back to the church where years earlier he recalled: '*I always put on my thickest coat .... as fungi grow in great numbers about the Communion table*'. He was buried not in the gloomy Fitzgerald mausoleum but in a solitary grave nearby covered by a granite slab which bears the inscription 'It is he that hath made us and not we ourselves'. As in life, so in death, Fitzgerald managed to avoid his family. Edward Cowell was among the few mourners, the friend who first introduced Fitzgerald to the beauty of Omar Khayyam's verse. Ten years later a small group of friends and admirers gathered at the graveside to plant a cutting taken from the pink rose on Omar Khayyam's grave at Nishapur. Today, approached through arable fields in the park where the hall once stood, old Fitz's grave is still covered in blossom each spring in this most remote Suffolk churchyard.

Edward Fitzgerald's grave in Boulge churchyard.

Charsfield

Ronald Blythe

Born into a farming family in the village of Acton near Sudbury, **Ronald Blythe** has lived in Suffolk much of his life. In the late 1950s he moved to a draughty timber frame house on the edge of Debach's old airfield, and found himself in touch with the tensions of modern village life, an experience which began his '*quest for the voice of Akenfield, Suffolk, as it sounded during the summer and autumn of 1967.*' With an influx of newcomers villages were changing faster than ever, the old ways and organisations were under renewed threat and people were becoming increasingly concerned for the welfare of England's most cherished institution.

In a sense *Akenfield* was waiting to be written. Blythe likened it to '*making a strange journey in a familiar land*', but even he was unprepared for the book's success which propelled him into the literary limelight. Almost overnight it achieved the kind of international recognition usually reserved for high profile novelists and rapidly became a best seller on both sides of the Atlantic. Blythe ascribes its popularity in the States to the fact that many Americans are descended from village people, including those East Anglians who emigrated to New England. The book grew originally out of '*a sort of compassion for farming people*' deeply rooted in the tenacious boulder clay fields where successive agricultural depressions had left the population poverty-stricken and brutalised. As Blythe explained:

I walked round the village boundaries, which are ancient ditches: very steep, dug in the clay and full of torrential winter water. And the idea came to me of the fundamental anonymity of most labourers' lives. Labourers had worked these fields for perhaps 1000 years. They seem to slip back into the earth - not quite as depressing as mud - that they had scratched for years, leaving nothing behind.

Akenfield may have begun as a homage to the agricultural labourer, but it evolved into a study of a complex rural community which carefully avoided those seductive images of the countryside perpetuated by the media and the welter of 'heritage' literature. The myth of the organic community pursued by middle class villagers in their search for identity and involvement, is still deeply rooted in the English psyche, but Blythe was more concerned to examine the conflicts that arise when these same people move into a traditional farming community. The old formalised divisions between church and chapel, farmer and labourer, become overlain by new tensions between those who work on the land and those articulate newcomers enraged by the destruction of the countryside and the ploughing up of footpaths who earn their living elsewhere. As Blythe observed: '*two contrasting concepts of* (village) *happiness - the new the literate and informed - and the old - the mysterious and intuitive - are now existing side by side in Akenfield, and with scarcely any awareness of each other*'.

Motivated by a desire to protect the real identity of its inhabitants, Blythe created a village that won't be found on any map of the area. The name 'Akenfield', chosen to suggest 'acrefield', is also a pseudonym for Charsfield where most of his country people lived, the farm labourers and fruit pickers, the commuters and the retired, the shopkeepers and school teachers who appear in his book. In one way *Akenfield* is real enough, but as a *'portrait of an English village'*, Blythe's claim is a little ambitious. It is in fact a composite picture and by attempting to make his village in some way representative, the book occasionally comes close to the kind of rural cliche Blythe was otherwise careful to avoid. In the late 1960s it would have been difficult to find a village of 300 people where the range of traditional crafts assembled in *Akenfield*, thatcher, blacksmith, wheelwright and saddler, were still practiced. The forge of blacksmith Hector Moore (Gregory Gladwell) was actually three miles from Charsfield in Brandeston and wheelwright Clifford Arbon (Judal Merton) worked in Monewden, the next parish.

The other main criticism levelled at Blythe's book was the way in which conversations with Suffolk people, particularly his 'Survivors', were rendered in dialogue from which all traces of dialect had been erased. George Ewart Evans whose 'Ask The Fellows Who Cut The Hay' relied heavily on the unedited transcripts of interviews with older Blaxhall residents and who at the time was making his own recordings of farm labourers from nearby Helmingham, was especially fierce in his reaction: *'It is like giving us cellophane-covered pap as a substitute for good coarse wholemeal bread.'* Linked together by Blythe's own narrative, some fifty cameos present a sophisticated picture of village life that lies somewhere between sociological reality and rural fiction in which *'Blythe's villagers speak with a lucidity and literary skill within an orderly framework of discourse rarely, if ever, found in the English countryside, but the content is clearly founded upon reality. At times it is the author rather than his subject who speaks, elsewhere it is impossible to discover whose voice it is.'*

Charsfield; commuter village, agricultural community and the nucleus of Blythe's *Akenfield*.

The success of **Akenfield** and Peter Hall's eloquent film have ensured that Charsfield will never be quite the same again, but with its straggle of council houses and bungalows along the main street it was never in danger of being preserved. The village has been there since the first Saxons made their way up the Deben river and, like most other villages, has survived because of its ability to absorb change. Surrounded by orchards, pig farms and broiler houses on Debach airfield where Blythe first found the voice of 'Akenfield', its real counterpart remains aloof from the traffic speeding along the nearby Roman road. A few visitors still turn off towards the church in search of the real 'Akenfield' and Peggy Cole's immaculate council house garden still draws crowds during the summer months, but otherwise twenty five years later, the people of Charsfield seem curiously indifferent to the book which remains a classic examination of village life in the late twentieth century.

Needham Market

From his conversations with elderly Blaxhall residents **George Ewart Evans** became aware that the most deep-rooted beliefs, indeed the very texture of dialect, sprang from basic working practices. East Anglia had for centuries been a region of arable farming and in **The Horse in the Furrow** (1960), Evans explored the activities and customs associated with horsepower. Completed at Needham Market with illustrations by the wildlife artist C F Tunnicliffe, it is dedicated to the old horsemen, especially those in and around the Gipping valley whose personal recollections were interwoven with contemporary farm records in this celebration of the heavy horse.

Of all Evans' many informants, Sam Friend from Framsden spoke the purest, most poetic Suffolk dialect.

The most intriguing revelations are reserved for the last section which examines the wealth of folklore surrounding the horse. Evans discovered that some old horsemen were renowned for their skill in controlling horses. Furthermore, oral evidence from the Stowmarket area identified the existence of a secret society of horsemen, an elite and powerful group with ancient origins, rather like the Freemasons, that kept alive the old beliefs and passed on the knowledge through esoteric rituals. Initiation ceremonies involved the use of a frog's bone selected by floating it upstream at midnight at the full moon. Evidence came to light for the existence of similar sects in other parts of Britain, especially in north east Scotland. Using the horse's highly developed sense of smell, members of the Society would smear a gate post or harness with an obnoxious mixture including the powdered frog's bone that would 'jade' the animal, stopping it in its tracks. Other mixtures of herbs and spices had the opposite effect, giving the horseman the power to 'draw' or call the horse at will.

Helmingham

Having endured the noise of heavy traffic through Needham Market for the last six years, Evans and his wife moved to the peace of Helmingham in 1962 when Florence found a new teaching post in the village school. Helmingham Hall had for centuries been the ancestral home of the Tollemache family and here in the mid nineteenth century John Tollemache laid out his model village complete with school, smithy and picturesque double dwellers all in the style of 'Tollemache Tudor' and each with its own neatly tended allotment garden. Within this 'closed' village estate workers enjoyed a security of tenure and a standard of living unfamiliar to those in 'open' villages beyond the Tollemache domain. But inevitably the price for improved conditions was some loss of personal freedom. Tenants were obliged by the terms of their agreement to attend church on Sunday, to dress according to their station and acknowledge the presence of Lord Tollemache and Her Ladyship. Despite his ambivalence towards the aristocracy, Evans soon felt at home in this manicured landscape and he consoled himself that at least the school house was rented to the education authority.

Helmingham estate cottages in 'Tollemache Tudor'.

In his finest book ***The Pattern under the Plough*** (1966) written at Helmingham with drawings by David Gentleman, Evans explored the pagan origins of horse cults together with the widespread survival in East Anglia of those folklore elements he discovered in Blaxhall. He succeeded in gathering together the many scattered fragments of pre-Christian beliefs associated with the home and farm; beliefs that by the late twentieth century had degenerated into superstitions but were still expounded by the older survivors of Evans' 'prior' culture. From his reading of the 'The Golden Bough' and 'The White Goddess', Evans was able to set the folklore of East Anglia within the wider context of customs and beliefs once prevalent throughout Western Europe. Impressed by its scope, Robert Graves declared that '*a single page of "The Pattern under the Plough" is worth a wilderness of folk-motifs*'.

David Gentleman's line drawing for the dust jacket of *The Pattern Under The Plough.*

The first part of the book examines the range of sympathetic magic used to protect the home against evil spirits and Evans returns to the same theme when considering the power of the 'hagstone', to ward off the 'nightmare' or 'hag' that would otherwise ride a horse leaving it 'hagridden' and in a lather the following day. Hung over the stable door, this flint with a hole through it was equivalent to the All-Seeing Eye and gave the stone its power as an amulet. Prior to its domestication the horse had been a sacred totemic animal in Britain, especially among the Celts, and the distaste of horseflesh persists to this day even though its slaughter is no longer taboo. Many folk customs that survived well into the twentieth century were descended from ancient horse cults including the Mari Lwyd, a wassailing tradition still alive in Glamorganshire when Evans was a boy. It was part of his cultural inheritance and helps explain the author's recurring fascination with the subject, a fascination at the heart of his work in East Anglia and one to which he returned in *Horse Power and Magic* (1979).

Westerfield

Westerfield Hall, a beautiful red brick house built in 1683, stands just north of Ipswich and it was here that **Matilda Betham Edwards**, author of a series of novels about Suffolk rural life, was born in 1836. The daughter of a wealthy farmer, she inherited an artistic temperament from her mother who was related to the writer and miniature painter Mary Betham. Matilda attended day school in Ipswich before travelling abroad but she was largely self-taught and by the age of twelve had read through most of the volumes in '*the small, but priceless library*' at the Hall. Her first novel 'The White House by the Sea' published in

Matilda Betham Edwards
(1836 - 1919)

200

1857, received polite attention and three years later Dickens included her narrative poem 'The Golden Bee' in Household Words. In 1864 she returned briefly to Westerfield to manage the estate on the death of her father but left soon after for Algiers in the company of Mme Eugene Bodichon, a renowned Victorian feminist. In all nearly 50 of her works were published ranging from novels to children's stories and travel guides.

Her travelling days over, Betham Edwards retired to Hastings, returning only once to Suffolk in 1892 to find how little the scenes of her childhood had changed apart from the arrival of the railway at Westerfield. The visit resulted in ***Lord of the Harvest*** (1899), the first and most notable of her Suffolk novels. Set in the early 19th century, the story begins with the choice of Elisha Sage to lead the reapers at harvest time and follows the relationship between the farmer Edward Flindell and Aimee Rougemont, the French governess at the rectory. Like her 'Mock Beggars' Hall' named after the beautiful Jacobean mansion at Claydon, in which Betham Edwards asks *'What is life but a Mock Beggar's Hall, each of us getting a snub in turn?'*, the novel is suffused with delightful character portraits. Memorable scenes of gleaning, nutting and sheep shearing are interwoven with descriptions of Ipswich on market day, but with little suggestion of the agricultural dissent that was soon to disrupt life in the region.

Westerfield Hall near Ipswich, home of the Victorian novelist Matilda Betham Edwards.

Written inevitably from the point of view of the farmer's wife, Betham Edwards was more concerned with the position of farm labourers in society than with their poverty or fear of the workhouse. But her anti-clerical views shaped in France and shared by many in East Anglia are clearly evident in her sympathy for Aimee and her struggle with the patronising Rev Pascoe. Henry James who used to visit her in Hastings, wished the novel had 'more of a tangle' while admiring it as an idyllic picture of life in a Suffolk community, and for this reason it sits firmly in the tradition of Victorian rural fiction.

Bramford

When he met Edward Cowell in 1845 the prospect of a relationship with a man of precocious intellect almost half his age excited **Edward Fitzgerald**'s curiosity. Cowell came to exert such a profound influence on Fitzgerald's emerging talent as a translator that years later he wrote: '*I have met and known many learned and clever men but Edward Cowell is the greatest scholar*'.

A brilliant linguist with a prodigious appetite for learning, Cowell had already taught himself Persian by the age of fourteen and was learning Sanskrit by the time he left Ipswich Grammar School two years later. The two scholars were first introduced at the Bramford home of Fitzgerald's friend the Rev Charlesworth, and soon fell to discussing at length their favourite Greek and Latin texts. Even Cowell's marriage shortly after to the rector's daughter with whom Fitzgerald had once briefly imagined himself in love, failed to undermine a growing intimacy based on their shared love of literature, and Fitzgerald soon became a regular visitor at the young couple's Bramford cottage.

During one of these visits Cowell showed Fitzgerald his translation of a play by Calderon, the seventeenth century Spanish dramatist. Fitzgerald's enthusiastic response to the complicated plot and 'lavish yet beautiful' poetic passages initiated a period of intense study which saw the publication of his own translation of six Calderon plays in 1853. To Fitzgerald's dismay Cowell decided to accept a place at Oxford in 1851 after determined pressure from his wife. Not only would their comfortable life at Bramford come to and end but Fitzgerald feared Cowell would have to give up his Oriental studies. But shortly after Cowell was encouraging him to study Persian.

Fitzgerald was a willing pupil and began experimenting with the kind of free translation from original texts that was to distinguish his most famous work, the ***Rubaiyat of Omar Khayyam***. His first translation was 'Salaman and Absal' an allegorical poem by Jami, one of the great Sufi poets almost unknown in the west. Published in 1856 as 'a little monument' to his 'Master of Persian', a collaboration that had given Fitzgerald such pleasure, the work was dedicated to Cowell on learning that his mentor had been offered the post of Professor of English History at Calcutta University. Written in the spirit of the poem, Fitzgerald's moving preface eulogises the many happy hours spent together in the Gipping valley, but the memories remained so poignant that years later when travelling to Cambridge on that same *'iron railway'*, Fitzgerald was forced to avert his eyes from the spire of Bramford church.

When shall we three meet again -when dip in that unreturning Tide of Time and circumstance! - In these Meadows far from the world, it seemed, as Salaman's island - before an Iron Railway broke the Heart of that Happy valley whose gossip was the Millwheel and visitors the Summer Airs that momentarily ruffled the sleepy stream that turned it as they chased one another to lose themselves in Whispers in the Copse beyond .... at such an hour drawing home together for a fireside night of it with Aeschylus or Calderon in the cottage

The view of Bramford church that in later life Fitzgerald found so distressing.

Having introduced him to the joys of Persian literature, Cowell first showed Fitzgerald his own transcript of a manuscript discovered in the Ouseley collection at the Bodleian library just prior to leaving for India in 1856. The 158 quatrains were by Omar Khayyam a little known astronomer-poet from 11th century Persia. But it was not until he received a much fuller version unearthed by Cowell in the Calcutta library that Fitzgerald began his masterful interpretation of the **Rubaiyat**, the single poem that secured his reputation.

Ipswich

In Chapter 22 of **Pickwick Papers** (1836-7) Mr Pickwick and Sam Weller board the Ipswich coach in Whitechapel to '*expose the treachery and falsehood they had suffered in Bury St Edmunds at the hands of those two deceitful rogues, Mr Jingle and Job Trotter*' (see p246), only to find themselves embroiled in one of the most hilarious adventures in the whole **Dickens** canon. On the coach they make the acquaintance of Peter Magnus, bound for the same destination in amorous pursuit of a woman of a certain age at The Great White Horse. The author's unflattering remarks about the town's principal coaching inn were based on his own visit while reporting local elections in 1835:

Charles Dickens
(1812 - 70)

The Great White Horse, rendered the more conspicuous by a stone statue of some rampacious animal with flowing mane and tail, distantly resembling an insane cart-horse, which is elevated above the principal door. The Great White Horse is famous in the neighbourhood in the same degree as a prize ox or county paper-chronicled turnip, or unwieldy pig for its enormous size. Never were such labyrinths of uncarpeted passages, such clusters of mouldy, ill-lighted rooms, such huge numbers of small dens for eating or sleeping in, beneath any one roof

The service clearly fell short of the standards Dickens had come to expect, mindful perhaps of the comfortable accommodation he had enjoyed earlier at The Angel in Bury. Having unpacked, Pickwick dines with Magnus '*in a large, badly furnished apartment with a dirty grate, in which a small fire was making a wretched attempt to be cheerful but was sinking beneath the dispiriting influence of the place*'. After dinner, while trying to revive their spirits with '*the worst possible port wine at the highest possible price*', Magnus confides the real purpose of his visit; to propose to Miss Withersfield.

Later that evening, having retrieved his pocket watch from the dining room table, Mr Pickwick becomes lost in the maze of corridors. Returning to what looks like his bedroom after disturbing most of the other residents, he discovers to his dismay the presence of '*a middle aged woman in yellow curl papers*'. Amid the embarrassing confusion, a profusely apologetic Mr Pickwick is bundled into the passage in his night cap by the outraged lady. Having recovered his composure at breakfast the following day, he is ready to advise Magnus on how to woo Miss Withersfield: '*I should commence, Sir, with a tribute to the lady's beauty and excellent qualities, from them, Sir, I should diverge to my own unworthiness*'. But on being introduced by Magnus to his betrothed, Mr Pickwick comes face to face with the real Miss Withersfield. Unable to extract a satisfactory explanation from the two dumbstruck adversaries, Magnus's mood becomes increasingly threatening and Miss Withersfield, fearing the worst, rushes off to the principal magistrate to report an impending duel.

From this point the story moves swiftly from bedroom farce to Ealing comedy when the magistrate invokes the full force of the law, and dispatches Grummer, Dubbley and six specials to apprehend Mr Pickwick at the hotel. Protesting his innocence an indignant Mr Pickwick is carried off in a Sedan chair followed by the 'unsoaped' mob. Scuffles break out as Sam Weller attempts to intervene, Grummer is knocked to the ground and the assembled company eventually arrive in a highly agitated state where the magistrate Mr Nupkins, proceeds to the swearing in of officials and the reading out of charges with all the ponderous ceremony conveyed by his position. Unable to remain silent any longer, Pickwick reveals that Nupkins too has been duped by Mr Jingle, alias Captain Fitz-Marshall and a frequent visitor to the magistrate's house. Charges are quickly dropped, honour satisfied, Jingle is unmasked and Mr Pickwick returns to London a free man.

Just before Dickens' stay the old timberframe building had been remodelled with a new grey brick and stucco facade. The landlord was so incensed by the author's remarks that he threatened legal action only to find, with the success of **Pickwick Papers**, that publicity of any kind brings its own reward. Dickens was welcomed back in 1859 and 1861 when he read extracts from the novel in the old Corn Hall. The 'insane cart-horse' still presides over the hotel entrance but plate glass windows have recently disfigured the town's most famous historic building. Today the shop units remain empty; The Great White Horse becomes The Great White Elephant.

The *insane carthorse* above the entrance to The Great White Horse as Dickens described it in **Pickwick Papers**.

Woodbridge

Preferring the company of his Woodbridge Wits, **Edward Fitzgerald** made no secret of his dislike for *'the faded tapestry of country town life'* and the gossip of local society: *'London jokes worn thread bare; scandal removed from Dukes and Duchesses to the Parson, the Banker, the Commissioner of Excise and the Attorney'*. But finding the proximity of his brother at Boulge Hall equally uncomfortable he decided in 1853 to move from the cottage that had been his home for the last 16 years to the safe distance of Farlingay Hall on the outskirts of Woodbridge. He continued to visit Crabbe regularly at Bredfield and his death in 1857 followed two years later by Browne's fatal riding accident cast a long shadow over Fitzgerald's life. At Boulge he had come to appreciate the subtle beauty of a countryside that had once seemed so dull, and its destruction became powerfully associated with personal loss:

My chief amusement in life is boating, on river and sea. The County about here is the Cemetery of so many of my oldest Friends: and the petty race of Squires who have succeeded only use the Earth for an Investment: cut down every old Tree; level every Violet Bank: and make the old Country of my Youth hideous to me in my Decline. There are fewer Birds to be heard, as fewer Trees for them to resort to. So I get to the Water; where friends are not buried nor parkways stopt up: but all is, as the Poets say, as Creation's Dawn beheld. I am happier going in my little Boat round the Coast to Aldbro' with some Bottled Porter and some Bread and Cheese, and some good rough soul who works the Boat and chews his Tobacco in peace.

The failure of Fitzgerald's marriage however caused him fewer regrets. On his deathbed Bernard Barton had extracted a promise from Fitzgerald to look after his daughter that amounted to a form of engagement. Lucy Barton, a

Edward Fitzgerald
(1809 - 93)

Fitzgerald's lodgings above Berry's gunshop on Market Hill.

Little Grange where Fitzgerald
entertained Tennyson in 1876.

Alfred Tennyson
(1809 - 92)

model of Victorian propriety, soon realised the impossibility of reforming
Fitzgerald's anti-social behaviour and bachelor habits. They separated after
just six months and with some relief Fitzgerald turned his attention to Cowell's
transcript of the ***Rubaiyat of Omar Khayyam***. Published anonymously by
Fitzgerald, it first appeared on the shelves of Bernard Quaritch's London
bookshop in 1859 where it attracted little interest until a copy came to the
attention of Rossetti and Swinburne. The freedom of Fitzgerald's translation,
'*better a live sparrow than a stuffed Eagle*' he argued, succeeded in distilling
the essence of Omar Khayyam's languid, sensuous rhetoric from the religious
overtones of the original manuscript. The beauty of the poetry with its
universal themes of love and suffering immediately appealed to the Pre-
Raphaelities and has captured the imagination of the reading public ever since.

In 1860 Fitzgerald moved into lodgings above Berry's gunsmith shop on
Market Hill where he remained for the next thirteen years. Despite the
speculation surrounding his failed marriage and the odd looks that
accompanied this strange, abstracted figure as he drifted through the streets
wrapped in a green and black plaid shawl, Fitzgerald enjoyed the bustle of
town life and was renowned as much for his kindness to local people as for his
eccentric appearance. Eventually he found a property in six acres of wooded
grounds on the edge of town and began drawing up plans to convert the cottage
into a chateau where he became known as 'The Laird of Little Grange'.

In September 1876 **Alfred Tennyson** called unexpectedly on 'Dear Old Fitz'
at the end of a touring holiday in Norfolk with his son Hallam, staying two
nights at The Bull on Market Hill. The meeting revived a friendship that had
fallen apart through prolonged estrangement and as Fitzgerald recalled: '*We fell
at once into the old humour .... as if we had parted only twenty days instead of
so many years*'. They took a boat trip down the Deben estuary to Harwich and

in the garden at Little Grange they *'went over the same old grounds of debate; told some of the old stories'*, but familiar differences resurfaced when Fitzgerald returned to the merits of Tennyson's later verse, repeating with perverse pleasure the criticisms that had always undermined their relationship.

The two men had first met forty years ago in the Lake District. Fitzgerald was already an admirer of 'Marianna' and 'The Lady of Shalott' but while boating on Lake Windermere he listened enraptured as Tennyson read from his 'Morte D'Arthur' manuscript. The visit had a profound effect on Fitzgerald who praised Tennyson's genius and provided generous financial support as the young poet struggled for recognition. Their friendship, nurtured in those early years by leisurely discussions at Fitzgerald's London flat, soon became tainted by resentment. Fitzgerald felt *'a sense of depression at times from the overshadowing of so much more lofty intellect than my own'* and Tennyson came to dislike the uncompromising and iconoclastic criticism of his benefactor. Although Fitzgerald still regarded his friend as the greatest living poet, he privately mourned what he regarded as the decay of his genius under the protective influence of his wife.

There is little doubt that Fitzgerald's 'old crochets', uninvited and often unwelcomed, put a strain on their friendship and after one visit to the Tennysons on the Isle of Wight in June 1854, Fitzgerald never felt disposed to accept further invitations on the pretext that they lived too grandly. Tennyson showed his displeasure by refusing to respond directly to Fitzgerald's letters, leaving such formalities to his wife, but the bond of friendship revived by Tennyson's detour to Little Grange, was never entirely exhausted and having seen him depart on the London train Fitzgerald reflected ruefully, *'I suppose I may never see him again'*. In the few remaining years Tennyson never even wrote again but, prompted by their final reunion, he wrote a prologue to **Tiresias,** an unpublished poem from the period Fitzgerald most admired:

> *Old Fitz, who from your suburb grange,*
> *Where once I tarried for a while,*
> *Glance at the wheeling Orb of change,*
> *And greet it with a kindly smile*

But even this affectionate dedication contained a passing reference to Fitzgerald's habitual criticism.

> *and welcome, as I know*
> *Less for its own that for the sake*
> *Of one recalling gracious times,*
> *When, in our younger London days,*
> *You found some merit in my rhymes*
> *And I more pleasure in your praise.*

Ironically Fitzgerald never read the lines that Tennyson completed only a few days before his friend's death, but on hearing *'The tolling of his funeral bell'*, the poet spoke for all whose lives had been enriched by knowing Old Fitz when he wrote: *'I had no truer friend: he was one of the kindliest of men, and I have never known one of so fine and delicate a wit'*.

8
Waterland
Suffolk Estuaries &
Essex Marshes

The Essex marshlands that stand north from Shoebury Ness to Clacton form still a strange terra incognita: .... The vast God-denying skies, the endless grey horizon, the icy north-easterlies, all these belong more to the Arctic tundra of Northern Norway. The whole area is set to the key of winter - it is for the dour, the taciturn, the obstinate, the solitary musselpicker, the wildfowler, the anachronisms in our age. .... It is not English .... but spiteful, anti-human .... a Beckett nightmare waiting for the world to grow desolate again, and ominously in harmony with the recent grey blocks of the nuclear reactor at Bradwell. One cannot think comedy for long here; nothing will turn out well.

From the ***Introduction*** to Mehalah by **John Fowles**

Orfordness

It is hard to imagine a more desolate or inaccessible spot on the whole coastline than this long, curving shingle spit. Known as the North Vere in **Richard Cobbold's** stirring tale ***The History of Margaret Catchpole*** (1845), it forms a dramatic backdrop to the desperate struggle between John Luff's notorious gang of smugglers and the preventative officers. Later Cobbold's heroine is captured here on the shore and her lover Will Laud shot dead as they wait for a boat to take them to Holland. The martello towers built during the Napoleonic Wars between Bawdsey and Shingle Street were still under construction in Margaret Catchpole's day and they remain as a stark reminder that the coast here has always been vulnerable to invasion.

After the Second World War the beaches were littered with tank traps, pill boxes and unexploded mines, and until recently Orfordness was owned by the Ministry of Defence. Meandering aimlessly behind this uneasy truce between land and sea, renegotiated with every storm, the river Ore is finally released into the sea some ten miles south of Aldeburgh at Shingle Street. The Ness remains a bleak and inhospitable place, the low horizon broken only by the lighthouse and a strange collection of abandoned bunkers once used to test components for nuclear warheads. Although the area is now in the hands of the National Trust these great pagoda-like structures seem unwilling to yield up their secrets in this surreal landscape, the ominous silence disturbed only by the dull, rhythmic thud of the waves and sea birds screeching overhead.

In November 1940 the young Anglo-Welsh poet **Alun Lewis** was stationed here in the South Wales Borderers. Before his transfer to the new battle school at Aldeburgh, one of his duties was to guard the RAF Station at Bawdsey: '*a queer isolated life among mists and frosts and flat marshes, wrecks and martello towers and German raiders and tall radio masts*'. Influenced by his fellow countryman Edward Thomas, Lewis's reputation as a poet was already established, but military service undoubtedly extended his range of experience. Several short stories emerged from his few months here as well as ***Dawn on the East Coast,*** published posthumously in 'Ha! Ha! Among the Trumpets' (1945) in which the dream of domestic simplicity recalling his recent marriage, fades with the dawn. The line '*And pours his ashes in a tiny urn*', anticipates with disturbing accuracy his own death in Burma at the end of the war.

From Orford Ness to Shingle Street
The grey disturbance spreads
Washing the icy seas on Deben Head.

Cock pheasants scratch the frozen fields
Gulls lift thin horny legs and step
Fastidiously among the rusted mines.

The soldier leaning on the sandbagged wall
Hears in the combers' curling rush and crash
His single self-centred monotonous wish;

And time is a froth of such transparency
His drowning eyes see what they wish to see;
A girl laying his table with a white cloth.

Dawn on the East Coast.

The light assails him from a flank,
Two carbons touching in his brain
Crumple the cellophane lanterns of his dream.

And then the day, grown feminine and kind,
Stoops with the gulfing motion of the tide
And pours his ashes in a tiny urn.

From Orford Ness to Shingle Street
The grey disturbance lifts its head
And one by one, reluctantly,
The living come back slowly from the dead.

Hollesley

For most writers the Suffolk coast evokes happy memories of childhood holidays on the beach or excursions from the weekend cottage, time taken freely and spent at leisure. But for **Brendan Behan**, playwright and ardent nationalist, his time at Hollesley was of a different kind. This was no writer's self-imposed exile, he would rather have been back in his native Dublin, but for three years of his youth he was detained at a bleak outpost on the edge of the marshes at His Majesty's pleasure. Recruited into the IRA at the age of 14 he was arrested two years later in Liverpool on suspicion of terrorist activities and held at Walton jail before being sentenced to borstal training.

Behan was fortunate, he could have been assigned to one of the country's more notorious institutions but the Hollesley Bay Colony was a new open borstal with a more tolerant regime and twenty years later he recalled his experiences there with something bordering on affection in his autobiographical novel ***Borstal Boy*** (1958). Instead of sewing mail bags inmates were put to work in the vegetable gardens or repairing sea defences or were assigned to one of the maintenance gangs. Despite the initial isolation, Behan soon found ways of coping with his new life. He was popular among fellow inmates and knew how to handle himself, the screws were not aggressive, there was always enough tobacco for smokes and he used the library to widen his knowledge of Irish literature. He particularly enjoyed the long summer evenings harvesting fruit in the orchards which, with the occasional swim in the river Ore, enabled him to see more countryside than he had ever known at home:

I was never in the country much, except an odd time training with the Webley and Thompson on the Dublin hills with the I.R.A., and had never slept a night in any countryside except this. It was flat and foreign, and I missed the mountains for you can see them any side of you, even from the middle of Dublin, but now, in the sun, this countryside was rich and fat and, walking down the road, I felt quite proud of it. The orchards were shining, and the corn, and there was an odd glint of the sea in the distance.

Towards the end of his detention as the weather deteriorated, the Hollesley Bay Colony began to take on the grim reality of a penal institution in wartime. Behan caught the mood exactly with his terse Irish prose:

The autumn got weaker and beaten, and the leaves all fell, and a bloody awful east wind that was up before us and we, on our way to work in the morning, sweeping down off the top of the North Sea, which in the distance looked like a bitter band of deadly blue steel out along the length of the horizon, around the freezing marshes, the dirty grey shore, the gunmetal sea, and over us the sky, lead coloured for a few hours, till the dark fell and the wind rose, and we went down the road from work at five o'clock in the perishing night.

Felixstowe

Burnstow, the setting for the **M R James** ghost story *Oh Whistle And I'll Come To You My Lad* is unmistakably Felixstowe, but not the Edwardian resort beloved by Betjeman. Written at the turn of the century just before the arrival of the large hotels and the pier, the town already had an elite golf club near the ferry where A J Balfour was club captain in 1889. The prospect of improving his game persuades Professor Parkins to vacate his Cambridge college (James' protagonists are always thinly disguised self portraits) and take rooms at The Globe Inn on the seafront.

Felixstowe Ferry, site of the Templars' Preceptory in M R James' ghost story.

The Alde valley at Sweffling. George Crabbe was rector here from 1796 to 1805 and drew on his experiences in *The Parish Register.* John Cowper's visit to his brother T F Powys resulted in *Sonnet Written in Sweffling Churchyard*.

The eerie emptiness of Orfordness where in ***Dawn on The East Coast*** by the war poet Alun Lewis
'the living come back slowly from the dead'.

The beautiful 16th century 'lookout tower' on the shores of the Orwell estuary is a familiar landmark in *Margaret Catchpole* and provided Richard Cobbold with the title for a subsequent novel, *Freston Tower*.

Angus Wilson lived on the edge of Bradfield Woods for many years and the wild garden became a major theme in his work, notably in *The Old Men at The Zoo*. The wood as a refuge reappears in Ian McEwan's novel *The Child in Time.*

Before leaving, Parkins is asked by a colleague to inspect the site of the Templar's Preceptory near the shore, to see whether a dig later in the year would be worth undertaking. James was himself a keen archaeologist and well acquainted with the region's antiquities. Even though his 'Suffolk and Norfolk' perambulations were not published until 1930, he would have known the whereabouts of Walton Castle, the Roman fort buried beneath the waves, as well as the site of the Benedictine Priory by Old Felixstowe church. Together they give his Preceptory, midway between the two, a certain credibility. Walking back from the golf course, Parkins stumbles across the foundations half hidden in the sand and, on closer inspection, unearths a small, cylindrical object that unwittingly sets in motion a calamitous sequence of events as he heads towards The Globe:

Bleak and solemn was the view on which he took a last look before starting homeward. A faint yellow light in the west showed the links on which a few figures moving towards the club-house where still visible; the squat martello tower, the lights of Aldsey (Bawdsey) village, the pale ribbon of sands intersected at intervals by black, wooden groynes, the dim and murmuring sea. The wind was bitter from the North but was at his back when he set out for The Globe .... one last look behind to measure the distance he had made since leaving the ruined Templar's Church, showed him a prospect of company on his walk in the shape of a rather indistinct personage who seemed to be making great efforts to catch up with him

One of James' earliest ghost stories, **Oh Whistle** appeared in 1904 in 'Ghost Stories of an Antiquary'. Having first been tried out on friends at King's College these tales helped establish his reputation amongst the very best story tellers.

*   *   *   *   *

Sometime during the early 1950s a steam train trundling across the flat peninsula between the Deben and Orwell estuaries carried John Betjeman towards the delights of another Edwardian seaside resort. The branch line from Ipswich had arrived rather late and then only because a certain Col. Tomline of Orwell Park saw the commercial potential of a terminus on this bleak stretch of the Suffolk coast. Gazing out of the window with boyish anticipation as the train pulled away from Trimley Halt, Betjeman first caught sight of St John's spire announcing his destination and the pleasures that awaited him within Sir Arthur Bloomfield's Gothic Revival building. Most holiday makers alighted at Beach Station, close to the boarding houses that stretched away along the front *'dominated by the great blue prayer wheel of Mr Butlin's Amusement Park'*, but Betjeman would have chosen Pier Station, making his way quickly down to the Promenade, and to one of the larger Edwardian hotels, perhaps the grandly Neo-Jacobean Felix Hotel or The Cliff.

Felixstowe was, in a sense, familiar territory to Betjeman. His 'Westgate on Sea' (1932) recalls the delights of childhood holidays and the seaside world of trams, bandstands and putting greens had already been celebrated in 'Margate 1940'. The full title of the poem prompted by his visit, **Felixstowe or The Last of Her Order,** suggests a more serious religious theme within the cavernous red brick interior of St John's.

Betjeman's visit to St Johns prompted the poem ***Felixstowe or The Last of Her Order.***

With one consuming roar along the shingle
The long wave claws and rakes the pebbles down
To where its backwash and the next wave mingle,
A mounting arch of water weedy-brown
Against the tide the off-shore breezes blow.
Oh wind and water, this is Felixstowe.

In winter when the sea winds chill and shriller
Than those of summer, all their cold unload
Full on the gimcrack attic of the villa
Where I am lodging off the Orwell Road,
I put my final shilling in the meter
And only make my loneliness completer.

In eighteen ninety-four when we were founded,
Counting our Reverend Mother we were six,
How full of hope we were and prayer-surrounded
"The Little Sisters of the Hanging Pyx".
We built our orphanage. We ran our school.
Now only I am left to keep the rule.

Here in the gardens of the Spa Pavilion
Warm in the whisper of a summer sea,
The cushioned scabious, a deep vermilion,
With white pins stuck in it, looks up at me
A sun lit kingdom touched by butterflies
And so my memory of winter dies.

Across the grass the poplar shades grow longer
And louder clang the waves along the coast.
The band packs up. The evening breeze is stronger
And all the world goes home to tea and toast.
I hurry past a cakeshop's tempting scones
Bound for the red brick twilight of St John's.

"Thou knowest my sitting and mine uprising"
Here where the white light burns with steady glow
Safe from vain world's silly sympathising,
Safe with the Love that I was born to know,
Safe from the surging of the lonely sea
My heart finds rest, my heart finds rest in Thee.

Rev Richard Cobbold
(1797 - 1877)

The Orwell

The History of Margaret Catchpole (1845) is the tale of a brave and virtuous country girl's love for the smuggler Will Laud and the disastrous repercussions of her blind attachment to this worthless rogue. Despite the tendency of its author **Richard Cobbold** to moralise, his lumbering prose and picturesque asides, the novel succeeds as an adventure story. A sequence of daring escapades before the heroine's character is finally redeemed, ensured its place among the popular classics of the late 19th century. The basis for Margaret Catchpole in historical fact, the use of surnames still common in this part of Suffolk and a landscape made more familiar by reference to topographical features and local place names, gives the story a stronger claim to the title of 'regional novel' than the works of more accomplished East Anglian writers.

Cobbold's tale is woven around the extraordinary life of Margaret Catchpole, a trusted servant employed by his parents in Ipswich at the turn of the century. The notorious episode in which the girl steals her master's horse and rides to London disguised as a stable boy, the manner of her escape from Ipswich gaol, her recapture and transportation to Australia, are all taken from Catchpole's signed confession and the newspaper reports of her trial. But the love for Will Laud that drives her to such reckless action is pure invention for the sake of a good story.

Earlier in the novel, events unfold across the flat landscape between Ipswich and the coast, scene of several desperate encounters between Laud's ruthless gang of smugglers and the preventative officers, but the story remains anchored in the sheltered reaches of the Orwell estuary. For Cobbold, whose family home overlooked the river, this painterly landscape of parkland and rich barley fields popular with Constable and eulogised by travellers in search of the picturesque, expressed all the achievements of civilised society. Writing nearly a century earlier, John Kirby had expressed the same sentiments:

one of the most beautiful Salt Rivers in the World. The Beauty of it arises chiefly from its being bounded with High-land on both Sides, almost the whole Way. These Hills on each side are enriched and adorned with almost every object that can make a Landscape agreeable; such as Churches, Mills, Gentlemen's Seats, Villages and other Buildings, Woods, noble Avenues, Parks whose Pales reach down to the Water's Edge, well stored with Deer and other Cattle, feeding in fine Lawns .... all these and more are so happily disposed and diversified, as if Nature and Art had jointly contrived how they might most agreeably entertain and delight the Eye.

This is the orderly countryside of Margaret Catchpole's childhood spent on the Nacton estate where her father was head horseman and a respected member of the community. The harvest supper at Priory Farm where Margaret is in service, is a symbol of well-earned prosperity, but Cobbold's tale bears little resemblance to the rural novels of Betham Edwards set a few miles away on the other side of Ipswich. This high point of the agricultural year is used as a backdrop to Margaret's moonlight assignation with Laud on the banks of the Orwell but his attempted abduction is thwarted by the intervention of John Barry, the industrious and worthy suitor rejected by Cobbold's heroine.

Although her family have their roots in Nacton, once Margaret Catchpole's restless search for Laud takes her beyond the safety of her native parish, she steps outside the law. Her willingness to suffer for his sake in the vain hope that she might save him from a life of crime, ignores the shame and grief brought upon her family. The illicit goods sent by Laud, but refused by Margaret, are sold by her brothers who either die of drink or are shot by gamekeepers. Her father's reputation becomes tainted and he is forced to live on the edge of the heath and find work as a jobbing labourer.

The heath is part of '*a large tract of extraparochial land*' that lay to the north of Nacton and stretched across the peninsular to the Deben estuary. This hostile waste of sheep warrens, the haunt of gypsies and the dispossessed, was where the gibbet stood as a stark reminder to all those who transgressed the laws of property. This is the underlying theme of Cobbold's novel at a time when, despite the death penalty for a wide range of offenses, poverty and hunger ensured that the more remote areas of countryside remained beyond the law. Smuggling, poaching and sheep rustling all carried savage penalties but nothing was guaranteed to incur the wrath of the gentry more than the crime of horse stealing and Margaret Catchpole's refusal to disclose the real reason for taking her master's horse for fear of implicating Laud, leaves her branded as a common horse thief.

The Orwell estuary and the wooded slopes of Nacton shore, scene of Margaret Catchpole's assignation with Will Laud, and where for Lalage Rush, time stood still.

Pin Mill

Having spent much of her childhood clambering out of leaky boats abandoned in remote creeks around the east coast when she would rather have been birdwatching on the mudflats, **E Arnot Robertson** grew passionately to loathe the sea. When later she began to write fiction she exacted her revenge in ***Ordinary Families*** (1933), a novel set at Pin Mill between the wars. In it the antics of her nautical family and their insufferable middle class friends are ridiculed through the eyes of her adolescent heroine, Lalage Rush. Preparations for the regatta and her birthday 'treat', another disastrous boat trip, are perceived with the relentless gaze of an animal tracking its prey. At one time Robertson's ambition was to become a naturalist and her subjects are scrutinised like specimens in a jar with all the irony of detached observation. As Polly Devlin suggested:

She was a cartographer of their territory, always working on an ordinance scale, closing in on her chosen terrain, stalking and observing the tribes therein with rapt interest as though from behind an invisible hide, and with such close and passionate attention .... that these accounts of thirties life in Suffolk have an anthropological exploratory quality.

Imbued with their sense of fair play and fearful of the 'robust humour' in which her family specialised, Lalage felt helpless to resist the prospect of another drenching on the river. She knew that only Time itself and her own growing awareness would eventually rescue her from what the remote and supercilious Mr Cottrell referred to as the 'mental squalor' of village gossip. More immediately her only means of escape was to slip away to some quiet spot on the wooded shores of the estuary where, in the company of Ted Mawley, son of a local fisherman, she could watch her beloved sea birds. There, perfectly still and completely absorbed, the short afternoons became transformed into *'those lustrous, immeasurable stretches of childhood's time'* where she experienced a *'breath-stopping newness'* and where *'unimaginably exciting or lovely things might come at any moment.'*

The yachting fraternity at Pin Mill ridiculed by E Arnot Robertson in *Ordinary Families* and celebrated by Arthur Ransome in *We Didn't Mean To Go To Sea.*

These moments of transcendent beauty sprang directly from the author's own childhood memories on the Orwell and her exquisite awareness of the natural world. Enraptured by the startled movements of a hare just yards from where they lay, Lalage thought '*how good and rather improbable a dispensation of Providence*' that creatures designed for speed '*should have latent in them such loveliness*' and '*How nice of Heaven .... to chuck in such a really unnecessary excellence with all the other benevolences about me at that moment.*' Later this same enchanted afternoon seemed almost to compensate for the wasted hours of her childhood when a heron, blind in one eye, is disturbed by the chattering of a nearby squirrel. As it takes flight the bird, starved of nourishment, becomes symbolic of the girl's predicament and her own approaching farewell:

Her flight seemed to add a touch of almost unbearable perfection to the water over which the violet shadow sailed, to the bright, pale sky that received the moment's imprint of all wild loneliness on the wing as this one living thing cried desolately in the warm silence, to the shimmering wall of trees which hid her suddenly as the currents of upper air caught her and swirled her, gleaming white in the sun as she banked, over them and beyond our sight, back into a secret existence of her own that we could not share. I wanted to cry out that I was not prepared for this royal extravagance of one afternoon. .... What queer, glowing discontent such trifles as a heron's flight could let loose in one's mind in the days before it had grown a little inured to joy, the days when despair lurked behind every sunset because of the mingling of a child's greed to treasure its glories for ever, with the adolescent's knowledge that in a few moments nothing would remain of them, nothing at all save a vague and priggish satisfaction in regretting them. The feeling seemed so shamefully inadequate to the dying splendours which might never, one felt, crowd into the sky in such profusion

* * * * *

Arthur Ransome
(1884 - 1967)

When at the age of fifty **Arthur Ransome** and his Russian wife Eugenia found Broke Farm, Levington on the north bank of the Orwell, it brought to an end their search for a place on the East Anglian coast. The sheltered estuarine waters here and in the Blackwater offered Ransome endless opportunities to indulge his lifelong passion for sailing. The couple spent five happy years in Suffolk until, at the outbreak of war, they returned to the Lake District where his reputation as a writer of children's stories had first been established with the publication of 'Swallows and Amazons' in 1930. The move to Suffolk was, in a sense, a home-coming. Ransome and Rapier, the Ipswich firm of agricultural engineers had been founded in the last century by a member of his family and the author always had a special affection for the area. Ransome was by now a successful writer with several books to his name including 'Coot Club' (1934) set on the Norfolk Broads. The sailing community at Pin Mill where his yacht 'Nancy Blackett' was moored, provided plenty of fresh material for the kind of nautical adventures that have delighted generations of children ever since, unless of course they were like E Arnot Robertson.

In the first of these, ***We Didn't Mean To Go To Sea*** (1937) the Walker children, otherwise known as the Swallows, are staying in lodgings with their mother awaiting the arrival of Commander Walker from a tour of duty abroad:

Everything on the river was new to them. Only the evening before they had come down the deep green lane that ended in the river itself, with its crowds of yachts, and its big brown-sailed barges and steamers going up to Ipswich or down to the sea. Last night they had slept for the first time at Alma Cottage and this morning had waked for the first time to look out through Miss Powell's climbing roses at this happy place where almost everybody wore sea-boots, and land, in comparison with water, seemed hardly to matter at all.

They spent the morning watching the tide come in round the barges on the hard, and envying the people who kept putting off to the anchored yachts and coming ashore from them .... (and later) .... it was getting on for low water .... on the hard men were walking round a barge that had been afloat in the middle of the day, and were busy with scrapers and tar-brushes. A clock chimed six from among the trees on the farther side of the river.

Here the children soon befriend Jim Brading and make themselves useful aboard his yacht 'Goblin'. On a trip downstream to Harwich the owner goes ashore to get petrol and is involved in an accident. Meanwhile the boat drags its anchor as the tide rises and is swept out to sea in a swirling fog past the Beach End buoy. Illustrated with Ransome's spidery sketches and annotated diagrams that enable readers to chart the course of the Swallows' adventure, the book is brimful with nautical jargon and all the enthusiasm of well-behaved middle class children. Every new discovery is greeted with 'Gosh' and 'Wizard' as the young crew grapple with the jib or *'make the foot of the stay sail fast'*. With growing confidence they manage to navigate the boat safely through a series of potential disasters before finding themselves off the Dutch coast.

Alma Cottage to the right of the Butt and Oyster, where the Walker family took lodgings.

King's boatyard at Pin Mill.

The children's landlady at Alma Cottage was based on the real Mrs Annie Powell who bought the old pub in 1918 and lived there until her death in the 1950s. The view from her window with water lapping the base of the Butt and Oyster at high tide and weekend sailors striding purposefully about the hard has changed remarkably little in the 60 years since Ransome wrote about the place. Harry King's boatyard where 'Selina King' was built as a replacement for 'Nancy Blackett' remains in business beyond the stream where children still re-enact scenes from their favourite Arthur Ransome adventures.

Hamford Water

Downstream from Pin Mill and out into open water at the mouth of the Orwell Estuary, it is a short distance along the coast to Hamford Water and the setting for *Secret Waters*, the **Arthur Ransome** sequel to 'We Didn't Mean To Go To Sea'. The story in which the children become marooned for a week on Swallow Island (Horsey Island) with tents and provisions, their dinghy 'Wizard' and a blank map of the area, arose out of a trip made in the company of the Busk family from Chelmondiston . Having established base camp on the largest island, the intrepid Swallows embark on their 'Great Archipelago Expedition' to survey the bewildering system of islands, creeks and mudflats

Here in the author's watery haven with only the sea birds and 'buffalos' (cattle) grazing on the marshes for company, the Swallows display all the resourcefulness of middle class children away from the protective gaze of the 'missionaries' (adults). In Ransome's world there is always 'tons of grub'. Rations are supplemented by blackberries and wild mushrooms gathered while foraging for driftwood and the children, mindful of the importance of regular meals, improvise a 'meal dial'. Armed with only their blank map and a tide table they set out each day after a hearty breakfast to chart the next stretch of Secret Water. Pushing on up another tidal creek, what appears at first to be a mere promontory is transformed into a whole new island as the Swallows complete another circumnavigation and, thanks to Titty's cartography, they conclude their exploration just before the reappearance of 'Goblin' signals the end of another adventure.

Set on a vulnerable stretch of the Essex coast at the outbreak of war, *Secret Waters* was published in 1939, the only dangers encountered by the Swallows are those invented by the author. They discover the Mastodon boy living in a wreck of a barge who is able to negotiate the treacherous mudflats with the aid of his 'splatchers'. But apart from the very real threat when three Swallows are caught by a rising tide halfway across the 'Red Sea' causeway, there is nothing more dangerous than their encounter with the 'Children of the Eel', a tribe of mud-daubed savages last seen at Pin Mill and looking remarkably like the Busk children, with whom both Swallows and Amazons do battle in time-honoured fashion before a final truce and celebratory feast around the campfire.

The causeway that connects Horsey Island to the mainland becomes the 'Red Sea' causeway in *Secret Waters*.

The Great Marsh

Since its publication in 1941 ***The Snow Goose*** has become a classic among readers of all ages. Set in wartime on the Essex marshes, *'One of the last wild places in England,'* **Paul Gallico**'s poignant tale of love and heroism is far removed from the safe world of 'Secret Waters.' Known only as 'The Great Marsh,' Gallico's impressionistic landscape of opalescent mudflats, leaden skies and infinite horizons is *'desolate, utterly lonely, and made lonelier by the calls and cries of the wild fowl,'* the liquid distance broken only by an abandoned lighthouse at the mouth of the river Aelder. Here a young artist, horribly disfigured, has withdrawn from the world, his heart filled with love for the wild geese that return in great flocks to his bird sanctuary each autumn.

Overcoming her fear one day Frith, a young girl from the oyster-village of Wickaeldroth, comes to Philip Rhayader carrying a snow goose that has been shot in the leg. She becomes a regular visitor to the lighthouse until her 'lost princess' is well enough to join the great spring migration. Frith returns each autumn to await the arrival of her snow goose and as she grows into an attractive young woman, so Rhayader's love for her grows stronger. Shortly after the outbreak of war as he prepares his boat to join the flotilla of craft heading for the Normandy beaches, Frith sees beyond the disfigured body to the beauty within Rhayader. *'Frith stood on the sea wall and watched the sail gliding down the swollen estuary. Suddenly from the darkness behind her there came a rush of wings and something swept passed her into the air '*

Following him to France, the snow goose becomes Rhayader's guardian angel. With its great wings outspread the bird is seen swooping over the beaches as though to engage the Stuka dive bombers while Rhayader sails repeatedly through enemy fire ferrying troops to safety. The following day, moments before it sinks, a small boat is reported drifting helplessly with the figure of a man face down in the bottom and a large white bird perched on the tail. Stories continued to circulate about the man's bravery under the bird's protection and out of them grew the 'legend of Dunkirk,' but *'long before the snow goose had come dropping out of a crimsoned eastern sky to circle the lighthouse in a last farewell, Fritha .... knew that Rhayader would not return'.* As she watches the bird it becomes *'the soul of Rhayader taking farewell of her before departing for ever.'* With a heavy heart she turns back to the empty lighthouse to find the portrait he had completed years before when she was a young girl.

East Mersea

Even by Victorian standards of eccentric endeavour, **Sabine Baring-Gould** must rank as one of the most extraodinary clergymen of his time, remembered not just for his splendidly archaic name and for writing 'Onward Christian Soldiers' but for his unsurpassed literary output of no less than 159 books reflecting a wide-ranging interest in folklore, travel, history and theology. John Betjeman acknowledged his own debt to the man: *'I know I am far more indebted to him for a romantic sense of place and local legend that I am to any other writer.'*

Sabine Baring-Gould
(1834 - 1924)

Spanning almost a century his life was prodigious in every sense. At Cambridge he developed a taste for the High Church Movement, took holy orders soon after graduating and married a mill girl he met while working in the Yorkshire Dales who eventually bore him fifteen children. By 1871 the family were living in rather cramped conditions in the village rectory at Dalton, but fortunately Gladstone, who had read his 'Origin and Development of Religious Belief', offered him the crown living at East Mersea and a way out of his predicament. The offer was gratefully received and Baring-Gould found himself on the Essex Marshes where, despite his despair of the place and its people, he remained for the next ten years.

Writing in his autobiography Baring-Gould came to the conclusion that: *'The Essex peasants were dull, sly, reserved and suspicious - my impression was that generations afflicted with these complaints* (ague and rheumatism) *had lowered the physique and the mental development of the islanders'*. His High Church manners and his Devon background of paternal feudalism did little to endear him to his flock, many of whom were Dissenters. Compounding his physical isolation from the mainland, with the Colchester road impassable for much of the year, he found the absence of any resident gentry a further deprivation. As if this were not enough, the surrounding fields were manured with a mixture of London muck and sprats during the winter months and *'the stench was horrible'*. They were in addition plagued with mosquitos and the piping of the wind in the bedroom, which to him sounded like *'the souls of drowned sailors .... sobbing all night long because of their inability to reach the fire.'*

The Jacobean pulpit in East Mersea church from where Baring-Gould preached in vain to his dwindling flock.

Baring-Gould's dogged persistence in this flat, windswept and ungodly landscape arose partly from his ability to become immersed in the hagiological research necessary for his latest scholarly work ***The Lives of the Saints***, a remarkable undertaking which ran to sixteen volumes and contained 3600 saintly biographies. This, his most ambitious project, was the work of an enthusiastic amateur and, like much of his antiquarian research, owed more to his imagination than to authenticated fact. During this time he maintained his interest in the West Country by writing a biography of the Rev Hawker of Morwenstow in Cornwall, an equally eccentric clergyman and poet with whom Baring-Gould had much in common.

Because of their inaccuracies and fabrications, these two works are of little more than antiquarian interest today, but Baring-Gould's lasting achievement at East Mersea was his novel ***Mehalah*** published in 1880, the year before he returned to Devon. Although the two main characters, Elijah Rebow the brutal landlord and Mehalah Sharland the defiant heroine, are vividly portrayed, the real force behind the story is the bleak marshy wasteland which conspires to warp their minds and seal their fate. As Baring-Gould's biographer observed, *'all the time the landscape and atmosphere of the sombre flats were working upon him,'* rather like the mudflats of the Alde estuary had worked on Crabbe's Peter Grimes a century earlier. The book's subtitle 'A Story of the Salt Marshes' is a reminder that the *'ever present sea, constantly creeping on reconnaissance up creeks and inlets, was in every way the real genius of the place, the chief actor in the one great story which Sabine ever wrote'*.

The novel opens on the Ray, a long low islet connected to Mersea island by a causeway, known locally as the Strood and separated from the mainland by a channel referred to as the Rhyn. Here in the only house on the island lives Mehalah and her mother, tenants of Elijah Rebow whose Red Hall lies to the south on reclaimed saltings between Salcot and Tollesbury Channels. The action takes place in the treacherous landscape '*of debatable ground contested by sea and land*' between these two desolate spots known only to smugglers and the few local inhabitants. In this ominous setting the story of Rebow's struggle to possess Mehalah - '*blind will against blind pride*' - is pursued with a relentless narrative vigour through a series of memorable set pieces; the firing of the farmhouse, the incident at Burnt Hill, the madman's escape and the blinding of Rebow, to the inevitable climax of the book. On its publication the author's style was favourably compared with that of Emily Bronte; Swinburne even thought it was '*as good as Wuthering Heights*'. John Fowles considers 'Margaret Catchpole' (1845) by another East Anglian clergyman to have been a possible source, especially for the brave and rather masculine heroine, Mehalah Sharland.

Many of the characters have surnames taken straight from the locality, especially those like Rebow and De Witt derived from French Hugenot settlers in the 17th century, and they were often modelled on people known to Baring-Gould. The character of Elijah Rebow was developed from a leading Dissenter in West Mersea, while Billy Baker's wife became the model for Mrs De Witt. The Bakers lived on an old barge at the eastern end of Mersea Island and Billy often rowed Baring-Gould across to Brightlingsea. Billy's daughter by a previous marriage was thought to be the inspiration for Mehalah.

The *debatable ground* of creeks and mudflats that is the real force at work in Baring-Gould's 'Story of the Salt Marshes'.

East Mersea church. Baring-Gould wrote ***Mehalah*** and ***The Lives of the Saints*** while rector here from 1871 to 1881.

In February 1881 the death of his uncle, the Rev Charles Baring-Gould, provided the rector of East Mersea with the long-awaited opportunity to return to his beloved Devon. He lost no time in presenting himself to his uncle's living at Lew Trenchard, and remained there until his death in 1924. The rectory at East Mersea was rebuilt following the Fingringhoe earthquake three years after his departure, and apart from the church which remains much as he knew it, the only reminder of his ten year stay is a group of suitably bleak council houses known as 'Baring-Gould Cottages'.

Sylvia Townsend Warner
(1893 - 1978)

Drinkwater St Lawrence

Having discovered the '*melancholy eerie beauty*' of the Essex Marshes while living in London in 1922, **Sylvia Townsend Warner** took her next rail excursion further north via Burnham-on-Crouch to Southminster at the end of the line. Alighting on the platform she set out with great determination towards the Blackwater estuary. Finding herself in the parish of Drinkwater St Lawrence late in the day with no accommodation she was directed to a Mrs May at Drinkwater Farm who gave her lodgings for the night. Next morning she was barely able to contain her excitement as she stared out of the bedroom window:

I could see nothing but an intense blue sky and a thick white mist, a mushroom mist, from which the thatched roof of the barn and some low tree tops emerged. This melting veil over my new landscape pleased me more than any clear sight could do. I watched it thin and become stained with the presence of a barn and some sheds, and the bean vines in the garden, and some apple trees, and the green of the marsh beyond. The next day she walked out again to the water's edge and spent all day reading perfectly content: *The nest of tall grass gave onto a little bank of shingle; the ripples clinked over it, the sun shone. I knew that mysterious sensation of being where I wanted to be and as I wanted to be, socketed into the universe and passionately quiescent.*

Intent originally on staying only a few days, Sylvia's new love affair with the Essex Marshes lasted a whole month. During this time she discovered her muse and a delicate sense of place as she busily stored away images which were to resurface in her third novel. According to her biographer:

The Essex marshes, a vast network of creeks and channels that became the setting for Sylvia Townsend Warner's novel **The True Heart**.

The visit to the marshes marked a change in Sylvia; she felt .... that she had become properly her own person .... Her first youth with its peculiar oppressions, was over, as were the most difficult and lonely years of her bereavement (the death of her father). *In Essex that hot August she drew breath, took stock and in her mood of "passionate quiescence" was surprised by "the discovery that it was possible to write poetry" .... Sylvia had discovered a new country - one whose maps she had been studying for years.*

The most enduring literary achievement born out of her rambles on the Essex marshes, came in the form of **The True Heart** published in 1929. There is no evidence that Sylvia had read or even heard of Baring-Gould's 'Mehalah' but it seems an odd coincidence that her novel is set in 1873, the year after he became rector of East Mersea. The story is a retelling of the love story of Cupid and Psyche. The main character, Sukey Bond, is sent from an orphanage to work at New Easter Farm on Derryman's Island. Here, like Sylvia, she soon discovers that special transient quality which is peculiar to the marshes:

Out here on the Saltings she was in a secret place between two worlds, and putting her hand to her face to wipe off the sweat, she discovered that she smelled of this ambiguous territory - a smell of salt, of rich mud, of the bitter aromatic breath of the wild southern wood.

Sukey falls in love with Eric Seaborn, the backward son of the local rector and their love is transported on the wind, stirring ancient memories in the marsh itself:

But on the way home they laughed and ran races, for the wind was getting up, blowing in moist from the sea, and it bunted against then like a friendly dog that wants to play. The marsh darkened about them; behind them the ilex-trees of the Dannie churchyard were rising and falling and roaring like a sombre steadfast wave; layers of thin grey cloud were hurrying over the sky, covering it from east to west, weaving a swift-coming darkness. The long taciturn autumn that had endured into the last week of November was suddenly at an end, and now, as through a breach in the sea wall, in the space of a couple of hours the winter had come flooding in over the marsh. With every gust of wind, with every increment of darkness, a nameless ecstasy and excitement seemed to be rising up all around. Even the water in the drains and land-locked pools, which ever since she had been in the marsh Sukey had seen mutely and sullenly swelling and diminishing, was now come to life, was moving against the banks with curt slapping sounds and ruffling up its surface against the wind.

A wisp of straw blew past them like a witch on a broomstick and crouched thorns clapped their skeleton hands. Sukey ran faster and faster; her skirts blew out and she thought that she could mount on the wind .... and yet she felt everywhere rising up and enveloping her, a raving welcome in which she too must join

9

Anglo Saxon Attitudes
Bury &
The Stour Valley

Through this country the Stour burrowed secretly, bearded with willows, stubby pollards or tall willows with silky tresses. In the fields were superstructures of broken locks, besides which we rested on our walks, and listened to water spouting through breached floodgates, which elsewhere was slow, silent and paved with lily pads. By July water-hens no longer swam the river; they walked it.

From *My Own Master* by **Adrian Bell**

Adrian Bell
(1901 - 80)

Stradishall

Before leaving school **Adrian Bell** had already begun to develop an aesthetic response to landscape that was to inform his literary talent. He read poetry, tramped the footpaths around Uppingham and experimented with watercolours, but it was a holiday in the Wye valley that first introduced him to life on the land. He found the sounds and smells of the countryside so evocative that his decision to abandon a career in journalism and become a farmer, a decision confirmed the following year when he saw Suffolk Punches at the county show, seemed entirely natural and was one he never regretted. His father was then news editor on The Observer and, despite his disappointment, it was with some relief that he agreed his son should learn the necessary skills and arranged for him to become apprenticed to a Mr Colville in west Suffolk. In the spring of 1920 Bell swung his motorcycle into the yard at Farley Hall in the parish of Stradishall and presented himself to his new boss. Colville and his men were convinced he would be back in London by the end of the year but Bell was determined to prove them wrong and ended up farming in the county for the rest of his life. Some years later while staying with his mother in Sudbury he began work on *Corduroy* (1930), the first part of his celebrated trilogy on farming life, at the suggestion of his friend the poet Edmund Blunden. In the opening paragraph Bell recalled his first impressions on arrival:

I was upon the fringe of Suffolk, a county rich in agricultural detail missed by my untutored eye. It was but scenery to me: nor had I an inkling of what it might become. Farming to my mind, was as yet the townsman's glib catalogue of creatures and a symbol of escape. The true friendliness of the scene before me lay beneath ardours of which I knew nothing.

233

Ploughing with Suffolk Punches
between the wars.

Fascinated by the seasonal round of farming life, the young pupil applied himself to each task with great enthusiasm and despite numerous mistakes he earned the grudging respect of the older farmhands. Deceptively clumsy in their appearance, Bell soon came to admire the way in which they worked with an economy of movement born out of years of experience that made his own efforts seem slow and awkward. He became deeply affected by the pace and rhythms of this new life; the relationships between farming people, their skills and knowledge of the countryside. His ear gradually became attuned to the Suffolk dialect which seemed always about to burst into song:

When the Suffolk men spoke they chanted. That is what is sounded like to me - the ring and rhythm having gone out of educated language. It was a new language and I did not at first understand a word of it. The same phrases flowed through the conversation of cottage and farmhouse; of the men at the muck-heap and the women in the drawing room.

Mr Colville emerges as the central character in **Corduroy,** a shrewd yeoman farmer of the old school with a love of hunting and horses who, but for his low church religion, could have been mistaken for a Victorian country squire.

Farley Hall, '*large Georgian-fronted, gentlemanly in front and slatted and dairy-like at the back*' was the centre of a 500 acre farm that employed twenty labourers and a dozen horses to work the land. Patient and straight forward in his dealings, Colville proved an excellent tutor teaching Bell not only the whole range of agricultural skills; how to plough, harrow, drill and harvest, but book keeping and the points to look for when purchasing livestock or selecting seed.

The following year Colville moved to Park Farm and Bell's father bought his son a thirty acre holding nearby with its own cottage, '*a table, a chair, a bed, a pot for porridge and a pot for stew*'. Colville continued to keep an eye on his neighbour and was always on hand with advice or the loan of machinery. *Silver Ley* (1931) is Bell's account of working his own 'two horse farm'; the elation of turning his first furrow with a wooden wheel-less plough, the experience of purchasing his first heifer at Sudbury market with Colville's help and, above all, the satisfaction that despite the arduous toil he was his own master at last. Bell recalled: '*It was the first real moment of my adult life*' and signalled the '*beginning of my education*'. When his parents decided to buy a large farmhouse in the next village he greeted the news without enthusiasm. His mother's attempts to become involved in the local community were quite often hilarious but his parents soon realised their mistake and left Bell alone to reflect on his narrow escape.

The Cherry Tree (1932) concludes Bell's autobiographical trilogy with a sobering picture of the Suffolk countryside transformed by a new scientific agriculture financed by industry and driven by business efficiency; a vision of the future now a common place reality across the prairie landscapes of East Anglia. The agricultural depression between the wars had a devastating effect, forcing many small farmers into bankruptcy from which they never recovered. As Bell observed, '*Heavy-land farms were going out of cultivation. A farm in Benfield* (Stradishall) *was abandoned altogether. Tramps dossed in the house; the fields grew waist deep with weeds.*'

A man called Rayner moved into the parish and began buying up land. Ditches were systematically filled in, hedges grubbed out and the land planted with rows of young fruit trees until nearly 1000 acres looked like an enormous orchard. He bought the old rectory and cut down the trees because they harboured fruit pest, he gassed the rabbits and erected barbed wire fences to keep out the hunt. The labour force, housed in neat new bungalows, rode around in land rovers and tractors, and the '*sons of the old rabbiters, thatchers and bell ringers grew up to become clerks, mechanics and truck drivers*'.

Bell's reaction to this ruthless destruction of a way of life that had persisted for centuries and with which he had become intimately involved was strangely muted. He deplored the loss of mature trees but as a farmer himself, he was sufficiently unsentimental about the countryside to recognise the need for change. Unlike Suffolk's other rural novelist Harold Freeman in 'Joseph and his Bretheren' (see p184), he felt no mystical attachment to a single patch of land and if circumstances demanded he faced the challenge of beginning again elsewhere with few regrets. It was the noise from the new military air base at

Stradishall which finally persuaded Bell and his wife to sell up and move to a new farm in Dedham Vale where the landscape had hardly changed since Constable was a boy.

The novels that followed were an elaboration of Bell's vision of the countryside as a workplace seen through the eyes of an ex-townsman. Although he was never a major novelist he remains unrivalled as a writer about country life. His work demands attention as much for his familiarity with the material that came from practical experience as for his gently ironic and expansive style. As one critic observed: '*Bell combines a steady, almost documentary, account of the social realities of country life with a deep aesthetic response to landscape; he has a personal involvement both physical and spiritual in the life he describes.*' The best of his work sprang from the tension between sensitive poet and practical farmer. His ability to convey the sense of continual renewal at work through the seasonal rhythms of the farming year has ensured him a distinguished place in the large body of rural literature that flourished between the wars.

Sudbury

Charles Dickens
(1812 - 70)

Although **Charles Dickens** went to some lengths to disguise the exact whereabouts of Eatanswill, the chaotic scenes that unfold in *Pickwick Papers* (1837) closely resemble the elections in Sudbury reported by the author two years earlier for the Morning Chronicle, and as a result the Suffolk market town became associated with electioneering malpractice. Mr Pickwick arrives on the London coach to find Eatanswill in a state of excited agitation as election day draws near. Every aspect of life in the town and every dispute, no matter how small, takes on a political significance. While the two local papers, the Eatanswill Gazette and the Independent, intensify a campaign which has already set new standards for scandalous accusation and scurrilous attacks , the battle lines between the two parties are being clearly drawn up on the streets. Every shop and pub, even the aisles in the church, are taken over by supporters of either the Blues from their headquarters in the Town Hall Arms or by the Buffs from their base at The Peacock.

These people are prepared to go to any lengths to secure extra votes. Supporters are plied with drink, then locked away to prevent them being 'got at' by their opponents and at the last election the barman at the Town Hall Arms had been bribed by the Buffs to slip a few drops of laudanum into the brandy of his regular customers. This revelation prompts Sam Weller to recall the occasion when his father accepted a bribe to contrive an accident while driving a coach load of 'supporters' from London, which left them stranded in a canal with no possibility of reaching the town in time.

The following morning the people of Eatanswill, many of them with sore heads, are awakened by '*the beating of drums, the blowing of horns and trumpets, the shouting of men, and the tramping of horses*' as last minute campaigning gets under way. Flag-waving crowds, nervous with anticipation, begin to gather in the streets; their festive mood occasionally disrupted by gangs of jostling, drunken supporters. As Horatio Fizkin, the official Buffs'

Sudbury Town Hall, scene of the Eatanswill election results in *Pickwick Papers.*

candidate, rises to address the crowd in front of the Town Hall, his words are drowned out by the band striking up to salute the arrival of his opponent. The Hon Samuel Slumkey, stopping only to bless a few babies and greet elderly supporters, steps onto the platform to be received by his followers and hear the mayor pronounce him the newly-elected MP for Eatanswill.

After the day's excitement the two Pickwickians, Mr Thompson and Mr Snodgrass, retire to their lodgings at The Peacock (The Swan, since demolished, near the Corn Exchange) where they are entertained by the Bagman's story in the faintly seedy atmosphere of its commercial rooms:

The walls were garnished with one or two large maps; and several weather beaten rough great coats, with complicated capes, dangled from a long row of pegs in one corner. The mantleshelf was ornamented with a wooden inkstand, containing one stump of a pen and half a wafer: a road book and a directory: a county history minus the cover: and the mortal remains of a trout in a glass coffin. The atmosphere was redolent of tobacco-smoke, the fumes of which had communicated a rather dingy hue to the whole room.

In the meantime Mr Pickwick's reputation has reached Mrs Leo Hunter, a hostess of formidable ambition whose rendition of her 'Ode to a Dying Frog' is the high spot of every literary breakfast or 'fetes-champetre'. Mr Pickwick and his companions arrive in fancy dress at 'The Den' the following morning for one of these illustrious gatherings, where, in addition to the local literatii there are London authors '*who had written whole books, and printed them afterwards*', and the splendid Court Smorltork who mistakes Mr Pickwick for BigVig, an eminent legal brain. Just as Mr Pickwick begins to find the conversation uncomfortable, he recognises the familiar face of Mr Alfred Jingle who, at that point, disappears into the crowd. On discovering his residence to be The Angel at Bury, Mr Pickwick and Sam set off in hot pursuit. (see p246)

Creams, in the Stour valley, was Adrian Bell's home in the 1930s.

The river Stour bearded with willows, stubby pollards or tall willows with silky tresses.

The Stour Valley

Forsaking the windswept uplands of High Suffolk for the rolling, bucolic landscape of the Stour valley, **Adrian Bell** purchased a farmhouse with thirty acres of rich water meadows running down to the river. 'Creams' was, after years of neglect, settling gently back into its natural surroundings. Making it habitable presented a daunting challenge:

The house had a roof of jumbled red brown tiles, like a mountain side in a sunset glow. It was nearly all roof, and fertile roof; a house leek thrived on it, and several sorts of mosses, not to mention a young ash tree rooted in a compost of plaster, and old birds' nests in a hole in the wall.

Bell immediately felt at home here among the *'fierce old shepherds'* and the same breed of small independent farmers he had grown to admire in Stradishall. There were in addition the struggling artists who had come in search of a landscape that had hardly changed since Constable and Gainsborough painted it a century or more ago, and who were happy enough to rent cottages too dilapidated even for farm labourers. Between the rigors of farming and house renovation, this working landscape provided Bell with the inspiration and the material for several more agricultural novels. But he came increasingly to prefer the more direct style of the essay, contributing 'The Suffolk Stour' to H J Massingham's 'English Country' in 1934, and to edit his own anthologies of country writing. ***The Open Air*** (1936) was quickly followed by ***Men of the Fields*** (1939) illustrated by his friend, the artist John Nash, who rented a thatch cottage in the same parish of Winston.

Bell sought the company of landscape painters rather than fellow writers and it was his friendship with Alfred Munnings that proved most fruitful. He would often drive through flooded lanes to visit the artist in his studio at Castle House, Dedham. Although by this time Munnings had abandoned the lyrical scenes of horse fairs and poppy fields that marked his early work in the Waveney valley for more formal and lucrative equestrian subjects, the two men shared an enthusiasm for the traditional Suffolk countryside and spent many hours together exploring its churches and country inns. Bell often saw the countryside with a painter's eyes and his writing was full of descriptive passages in which he tried to '*put a framework round a moment of life*' just as the French Impressionists had:

I remember looking out of my mullion window in Summer dawns which flushed the myriad small leaves of that tree which the first breeze made rustle. (a wych elm leaning over the roof of his house). *The valley floor stretched level, clouded blue with woods crowding the horizon. The river among its reeds revealed itself at a zigzag bend, like a flash of lightning where the sun struck.*

If Bell's response to the Stour valley was essentially romantic it never obscured a more practical response to changing circumstances. By the outbreak of war his young family was fast outgrowing 'Creams' and they decided to move to a larger house with electricity and more land on the edge of the Waveney valley. (see p141)

Cockfield

To a man destined to become one of the great Romantics of his age, the prospect of a summer with his cousin deep in the Suffolk countryside held little appeal for **Robert Louis Stevenson** but at the age of twenty two his travels were only just beginning. His parents were already resigned to their son becoming a writer in preference to entering the family firm but, having brought him under '*the heavy cloak of Presbyterian conformity*' they were profoundly shocked when Louis announced his agnosticism. The atmosphere in the Stevenson's Edinburgh household became unbearable and, hopeful that a 'safely religious' environment elsewhere might rescue their wayward son, his parents arranged for him to travel to Cockfield. Resigned to an uneventful stay, Stephenson found himself walking up the rectory drive in July 1872 quite unprepared for the encounter that was to change his life.

Robert Louis Stevenson
(1850 - 94)

With St Peter's church visible across fields at the other end of the village, the rectory remains hidden in its own wooded grounds, an elegant late Georgian house built from local Woolpit brick where Stevenson's cousin Maud had gone to live with her new husband the Rev Churchill Babington. A young man of delicate health, Louis found Suffolk cold even in summer and admitted being '*afraid of the clay soil*' but his heart warmed immediately to the beautiful woman staying at the rectory as his cousin's guest. Mrs Fanny Sitwell was twelve years older than Stevenson and although already separated from her husband, had many admirers including Sidney Colvin whom she later married. This did not stop Louis falling hopelessly in love with the woman he referred to as 'madonna' and the 'mother of my soul' in a deluge of love letters she received on his return to Edinburgh. At Cockfield they spent their time exploring the grounds and a mutual interest in literature while Stevenson poured out his feelings.

As his letters in the National Library of Scotland suggest, Stevenson regarded Fanny Sitwell more as a surrogate mother than a lover, while she was clearly impressed by his knowledge and enjoyed his company. Their time together at Cockfield began a lifelong friendship which included Colvin and on his arrival in London, Colvin proposed Stevenson for membership of the Saville Club. Here among the many literary figures he became friends with Edmund Gosse and his career as a writer began to take shape.

Cockfield rectory where R L Stevenson met his *madonna*.

Bradfield Woods

A few miles south east of Bury St Edmunds in the parish of Bradfield St George is one of the largest surviving remnants of the primeval forest that lies scattered across the boulder clay uplands of Suffolk . Originally owned by the abbey of Bury St Edmunds, part of Bradfield Woods had been a medieval deer park but the remaining area has been continuously managed since the 13th century with the underwood of hazel, ash and willow coppiced at regular intervals leaving the standard trees, mainly of oak, to reach maturity. The rotational clearing allows daylight into every part of the wood and, as a result, Bradfield Woods is one of the richest habitats in Britain with over 350 flowering plants including the Wild Service tree, Small Leaf Lime, Herb Paris and the equally rare Oxlip; species restricted to a few woodland sites.

At the northern edge of the wood near the main entrance stands Felsham Woodside, an old woodman's cottage that for many years was the home of the novelist **Angus Wilson** and his partner Tony Garrett. During his time at the British Museum library, Wilson had begun to establish his reputation as a writer with two volumes of short stories and his first novel 'Hemlock and After' (1953), when in 1955 he decided to move out of London and begin a new life as a full time novelist. Owned by a friend, the cottage was by chance available at just the right time and what began as a temporary refuge from city life, grew into a long and creative association with the region at a time of great importance for East Anglian literature. As Wilson explained:

It happened to be in a part of England untouched by any memories for me, it happened to be that undulating yet hardly hilly country which I most love; it happened to be not too near the seaside. It happened to fulfil all my requirements. It also happened to be on the edge of a wood with a much neglected garden. Even if I were not to stay, I must do something, if not to drive the nettles back, at least not to allow them further invasion .... It was a role for which neither my London manners and outlook nor my total lack of physical co-ordination nor my innate clumsiness fitted me. Yet I have got on with it, civilising the house, eventually turning a clearing in the wild into a carefully artificial wild garden. The symbols underlying my novels have been realised in practice, or more or less realised.

Angus Wilson in the wild garden at Felsham Woodside that became a recurrent theme in his writing.

Wilson's unconscious search for roots in the English countryside can be seen as a direct response to his own itinerant childhood on the south coast where he was brought up in a series of boarding houses by middle class parents of 'reduced circumstances'. Reflecting on the major themes in his fiction in *The Wild Garden* (1963), Wilson identified the creation of atmosphere through a series of recurring images, notably flowers and gardens; images not deliberately constructed but which sprang from his parents' own childhood experiences. He makes the distinction between the garden as a clearing in the wild associated with his mother's upbringing in South Africa and the English 'wild garden' of his father's boyhood on the edge of a wood in the Dumfrieshire hills:

If the wild garden seems tame or effete, then the garden in the wild steps in to provide a rough reality; if the garden in the wild seems all colonial pioneer greed and insensitivity, then the wild garden steps in with its elegance, its English absurdity.

The two symbols have become so powerful for me and, as I shall suggest, lie behind the major themes of my work. They lie in the very earliest conception I ever received of happiness, not even my own infant happiness, but in the childhood happiness of my mother and father, unhappy people both, who looked back from lives of broken-down, failed urbanism to real childhood paradises.

Although he had been enticed by the visual delights of the Suffolk countryside, the wild garden as a source of nourishment had still not completely formed in his mind. Only later in *The Old Men at the Zoo* (1961) did it become a central part of his work in the form of the wildlife reserve, but as he acknowledged, his subconscious was fully aware of its vulnerability as a symbolic union of the wild and the cultivated. The narrator, Simon Carter, as administrator of the London Zoo and an authority on badgers, represents the moral ambiguity between city and country, artificial protection and natural habitat. As the story unfolds, the idea to create a National Park on the Welsh borders is abandoned at the outbreak of war and Carter, travelling through a beleaguered countryside in search of a safe haven for the animals, arrives at a cottage on the edge of a wood. Here on the point of starvation, he is forced to kill and eat his beloved badger, the gentlest of nocturnal creatures whose only enemy is man. This act of perverted totemism ensures not only his own survival but that of the people in the cottage. Wilson later admitted: '*the catastrophic and horrible climax turned out to be at the very centre of my symbolic paradise*'.

Even before the move Wilson had begun planning his second novel but *Anglo Saxon Attitudes* was written in the garden at Felsham Woodside . In this most ambitious work his enthusiasm for archaeological discovery is mixed with a taste for academic scandal acquired during his years at the British Museum. He was already aware of East Anglia's reputation for spectacular finds, notably the Romano-British treasure from Mildenhall and the Snettisham torcs discovered the year before his arrival at Felsham. While at the museum he had taken a keen interest in the Sutton Hoo excavation near Woodbridge and the character of his protagonist Gerald Middleton owes much to Thomas

Hendrick who uncovered the ship burial and who later became director of the British Museum. The proximity of Bradfield to St.Edmund's shrine in Bury gave Wilson a particular satisfaction and he took the name for the deceased Canon Portway from a tomb in the Abbey precincts, but he only later came to realise the true significance of the place he had chosen deep in the Suffolk countryside.

Felsham Woodside was Angus Wilson's home for many years. Most of his novels including *Anglo Saxon Attitudes* were written here.

Over the next twenty five years Wilson produced a series of novels and works of literary criticism. In the 1960s he became Professor of English at the University of East Anglia and here in 1970, with the help of Malcolm Bradbury, he established the course in creative writing that saw the emergence of a new generation of young novelists including Rose Tremain and **Ian McEwan**. In *The Child in Time* (1987) McEwan acknowledges Wilson's influence when in a sequence reminiscent of Simon Carter's journey to the cottage nearly thirty years earlier, Stephen Lewis, the novel's central character, travels to Suffolk and the wood '*set in a pocket of land visited by commercial photographers and film makers because of its resemblance to what was generally accepted as the English countryside,*' to visit his friend. No longer able to cope with the mounting pressures of his post as a junior minister in the Tory government, Charles Darke has resigned his seat and retreated with his wife to their weekend cottage that with its collection of stuffed birds, closely resembles Felsham Woodside. Here for a time he rediscovers an inner peace. On arrival Lewis plunges into a world of sensory delight among the wood's luxuriant vegetation in search of his friend:

Where the path crossed a brook, a slab of rock, the remains of an old wall, was host to a miniature Amazon, a jungle of moss, florescent litchen and microscopic trees. And overhead were creepers, thick as a rope, filtering the light. Down on the ground there were giant cabbages and rhubarbs, palm fronds, grasses bent double by the weight of their heads. In one place open to the sky there was an extravagant crop of purple flowers, in another, darker spot, the whiff of garlic .... The wood, this spider rotating on its thread, this beetle lumbering over blades of grass, would be all, the moment would be everything.

Emerging into a clearing Lewis recognises to his astonishment that the boyish figure dressed in grey shorts and a flannel shirt that steps from behind a dead tree is Charles Darke. Ignoring his questions and full of childish excitement, Darke leads him to an enormous beech where, after an alarming climb he proudly reveals his very own tree house, his sanctuary from an adult world where licensed beggars roam the streets of Thatcherite Britain and the land is poisoned by chemicals. Taking a catapult from his back pocket, Darke places a stone in the pouch, draws back the thongs as far as they will stretch and, pausing momentarily like a Zen archer, lets go launching the pebble in a great arc over the trees and out of sight.

Safe in the hands of the Suffolk Wildlife Trust, Bradfield Woods remains every bit as enchanting as Charles Darke's timeless paradise. In late spring the ground is covered with drifts of bluebells and wood anemones, nightingales sing in the coppiced glades, butterflies dance in the sunlit rides and the giant, twisted stools of coppiced hornbeams sprouting mysterious fungi are home to doormice and rare insects. Angus Wilson came to recognise that this ancient wood, this expression of man's harmonious relationship with nature, had drawn him to the cottage as *'a refuge from* (his) *fears'* where the creation of a wild garden became his absorbing passion as *'a sort of therapy'* and an inspirational source for his writing.

Bury St Edmunds

Since the eighteenth century the itinerary of every respectable traveller through East Anglia in search of the picturesque has included Bury St Edmunds with its streets of dignified Georgian buildings and the remains of its Benedictine Abbey on the banks of the river Lark, among the richest and most powerful religious foundations in medieval Europe. One of the earliest travel writers to record her impressions was **Celia Fiennes** who rode into town in 1698 towards the end of her Tour round England. In her journal she singled out Cupola House in the Traverse, recently completed for the wealthy apothecary Thomas Macro, for the *'pleasing prospect of the whole town'* to be had from its rooftop belvedere.

Arriving a few years later on the East Anglian leg of his ***Tour through England and Wales*** (1724), **Daniel Defoe** found to his annoyance *'a town of which other writers have talked very largely, and perhaps a little too much'*. He did manage a few polite if unoriginal, remarks: *'it is a town fam'd for its pleasant situation and wholesome air, the montpelier of Suffolk and perhaps of*

England', and again, perhaps conscious of his role as apologist for the aspiring middle classes he praised the town *'thronged with gentry, people of the best fashion and the most polite conversation'*. Finding little else remarkable about the place and aware that its wealth resided in the large country estates like Hengrave, Euston and *'the most delicious seat of Rushbrook'*, Defoe launched himself into a vigorous defence of an *'abundance of the finest ladies'* who converged on the town to attend the social gatherings held during Bury Fair. A recent writer had insinuated that *'the daughters of all the gentry of the three counties come hither to be picked up'* and that *'most of them are whores'*, but Defoe goes to such lengths to refute these scandalous allegations that the reader is left wondering whether they might not have contained a grain of truth.

By the time the young Charles Dickens came to Suffolk over a century later to cover local elections for the Morning Chronicle, Bury had been transformed into the elegant provincial town it remains today, a social centre for the whole region. It was here in 1819 that Edward Fitzgerald met his lifelong friend James Spedding while a pupil at King Edward VI's school. Streets of timber frame houses were by then hidden behind Georgian facades of silvery grey Woolpit brick and a series of impressive new cultural buildings designed to entertain the gentry, adorned the centre. The Market Cross on the Cornhill by Robert Adam became the town's first theatre until William Wilkin's delightful, balconied Theatre Royal (1819) opened in Westgate Street. Francis Sandys, architect of Ickworth Hall and many Regency buildings in Bury, lived on Angel Hill when designing the Atheneum's beautiful stucco interior that soon echoed to the sound of society gatherings at the turn of the century.

Angel Hill, the large theatrical space sweeping down to the monastery gates is where throughout the middle ages, the town confronted the enclosed and powerful world of the Abbey. Flanked by some of the town's most impressive secular and religious buildings, it has since 1779 been dominated by the imposing facade of the Angel Hotel where **Charles Dickens** first stayed in 1834. Commissioned to write a series of sporting articles for a monthly magazine that resulted in the creation of **The Posthumous Papers of the Pickwick Club** (1837), Dickens used his political assignment in East Anglia to gather material for further adventures of the Club. From Eatanswill (Sudbury), Mr Pickwick and Sam Weller pursue the fraudulent Alfred Jingle to Bury where *'the coach rattled through the well-paved streets of a handsome little town of thriving and cleanly appearance, and stopped before a large inn'*. The following morning in the yard at the Angel:

Mr Weller was dispelling all the feverish remains of the previous evening's conviviality, through the instrumentality of a half penny showerbath .... when he was attracted by the appearance of a young fellow in mulberry-coloured livery who was sitting on a bench in the yard; reading what appeared to be a hymn book, with an air of deep abstraction

The young man is none other than Job Trotter, Mr Jingle's artful accomplice who proceeds to reveal his master's intention to elope that very night with a rich heiress from Westgate House boarding school in the town. The trap is sprung and Dickens, aware perhaps from his reading of Defoe's 'Tour' of the slur cast upon the reputation of those fair ladies of Bury, sends a gallant but gullible Mr Pickwick in hot pursuit with hilarious results. Disentangling himself from a rose tree and several gooseberry bushes, having been rather too enthusiastically helped over the wall by his man servant, Mr Pickwick settles himself in the school grounds to await the appointed hour in a thunderous downpour. Soaked to the skin he stumbles into the building where, confronted by a startled headmistress, he discovers he has been the victim of an outrageous conspiracy. Jingle and Trotter have meanwhile fled the town and a dejected Mr Pickwick returns to the Angel where he is confined to bed with an attack of rheumatism.

An exhausting programme of public appearances brought Dickens back to Bury and the Angel Hotel in 1859 and again in 1861 when he read extracts from his work. On both occasions he received an enthusiastic reception from a packed Atheneum and was soon writing to Wilkie Collins: *'Last night I read "Copperfield" at Bury St Edmunds to a very fine audience. I don't think a word - not to say an idea - was lost!'*

Cupola House   Two of Bury's most distinguished literary landmarks.   The Angel hotel

The Norman gateway is the most impressive building to survive from the town's great Romanesque Abbey.

Just after Dickens' initial visit to Bury, the first translation of the ***Chronicle of the Abbey of Bury St Edmunds*** was published in 1840. Written near the end of the twelfth century by Abbot Samson's personal chaplain, **Jocelyn of Brakeland**, it remains a '*unique insight into the anatomy of medieval society*' and a biographical portrait of its autocratic ruler. Its publication prompted **Thomas Carlyle** to write ***Past and Present*** (1843) and provoked a debate on the nature of craftsmanship among advocates of a return to medieval scholarship and democratic principles that included Ruskin and William Morris. Unlike them, Carlyle was more attracted to the principles of feudalism enshrined in the harsh justice dispensed by Abbot Samson, but these notions of authority contributed to a decline in his reputation as political events in Europe began to unfold.

As head of the richest Benedictine monastery in England with huge estates in East Anglia, Abbot Samson was answerable only to king and pope and ruled with absolute power over the life of the town and much of the region. Jocelyn's ***Chronicle*** is full of the Abbot's fierce struggles over property and disputed allegiance to the Archbishop of Canterbury and his rival, the Abbot of Ely. His constant battle with the prosperous Jewish community in Bury led eventually to their expulsion from the town following the Palm Sunday riots in 1190. Events in the outside world often impinged on the contemplative life of the monastery, and from Jocelyn's graphic account of the fire which partially destroyed St Edmund's shrine and its glorious refurbishment by Samson, we have a picture of this most venerated object of pilgrimage. But he reserved his most sensitive observations for the conflicts that arose within the enclosed community between the monks and their abbot, despite the rule of obedience.

Today, wandering among the shapeless fragments of flint rubble in the municipal gardens, it is hard to imagine the grandeur of one of the country's most magnificent Romanesque churches, the nearest comparisons being Ely cathedral completed about the same time, and the west front of Peterborough cathedral. The most impressive survival known to Jocelyn is the beautifully proportioned Norman gateway, its surface covered with geometric patterning and '*one of the most moving sights in all England*'.

Bibliography

Ackland, Valentine, *For Sylvia*, Metheun, 1986.

Ackroyd, Peter, *Dickens*, Minerva.

Addison, Richard, *In the Steps of Charles Dickens*, Richard Cowan, 1955.

Barber, R., *The Pastons: The Letters of a Family in the Wars of the Roses*, Penguin, 1984.

Barbera, Jack, & McBrien, William, *Stevie: A Biography of Stevie Smith*, Heinemann, 1985.

Baring-Gould, Sabine, *Further Reminscences 1864-9*, John, 1925.

    Mehalah, The Boydell Press, 1983.

Barker, Christopher, & Barker, Sebastian, *Portraits of Poets*, The Folio Society, 1986.

Barker, George, *At Thurgarton Church*, Thigrame Press, 1969.

    To Aylsham Fair, Faber, 1971.

    Selected Poems, Faber, 1995.

Barker, Pat, *Regeneration*, Penguin, 1992.

Barker, Raffaella, *Come and Tell Me Some Lies*, Penguin, 1995.

Batty Shaw, A., *Sir Thomas Browne of Norwich*, Jarrolds, 1992.

Beauman, Nicola, *Morgan: A Biography of E.M. Forster*, Hodder and Stoughton, 1993.

Behan, Brendan, *Borstal Boy*, Hutchinson, 1958.

Bell, Adrian, *Apple Acre*, The Bodley Head, 1942.

    Corduroy, The Bodley Head, 1948.

    Men of The Fields, Alan, 1984.

    My Own Master, Faber, 1961.

    Silver Ley, The Bodley Head, 1948.

    The Cherry Tree, The Country Book Club, 1951.

Belloc, Hilaire, *The Hills and The Sea*, London, 1906.

Beresford, J., *The Diary of a Country Parson 1758-1802*, O.U.P. Paperback, 1978.

Betham Edwards, Matilda, *Lord of The Harvest*, Boydell Press, 1983.

Betjeman, John, *Collected Poems*, John Murray, 1980.

Blackburne, Neville, *The Restless Ocean: The Story of George Crabbe*, Terence Dalton,1972.

Blythe, Ronald (ed), *Aldeburgh Anthology*, Snape, 1972.

    Akenfield, London, 1969.

    Divine Landscapes, Viking, 1986.

    From The Headland, Chatto & Windus, 1982.

    Places: An Anthology of Britain, O.U.P., 1981.

Borrow, George, *Lavengro*, Mellifont Press.

    Romany Rye, Routledge and Sons.

Brooks, Peter, *Salthouse*, Poppyland Publishing, 1990.

Burke, E., *Musical Landscapes*, Webb and Bowyer, 1983.

Carpenter, Humphrey, *Benjamin Britten: A Biography*, Faber, 1992.

Cavaliero, Glen, *The Rural Tradition In The English Novel*, Macmillan, 1977.

Clarke, William, M., *The Secret Life of Wilkie Collins*, 1988.

Cobbold, Richard, *The History of Margaret Catchpole*, Boydell Press, 1979.

Collins, Wilkie, *Armadale*, Penguin, 1995.

    No Name, Oxford, The World's Classics, 1990.

Comfort, Nicholas, *The Lost City of Dunwich*, Terence Dalton, 1994.

Contemporary Novelists, 5th Edition, St James Press, 1991.

Contemporary Poets, 5th Edition, St James Press, 1991.

Cook, Olive, *Suffolk :* Vision of England Series, Paul Elek, 1948.

Cox, Michael, *M. R. James: An Informal Portrait*, O.U.P., 1983.

Crabbe, George, *The Life of George Crabbe By His Son*, The Cresset Press, 1947.

Crabbe, George, *Tales 1812*, ed. by H.Mills, C.U.P., 1967.

Crosby, Alan, *A History of Thetford*, Phillimore, 1988.

Crick, Bernard, *George Orwell - A Life*, Secker and Warburg, 1980.

Daiches, David and Flower,John , *Literary Landscapes:A Narrative Atlas*, Paddington, 1979.

David, Hugh, *Stephen Spender*, Heinemann, 1992.

Defoe, Daniel, *A Tour Through England And Wales Vol.1*, Everyman, J M Dent, 1928.

Dickens, Charles, *David Copperfield*, Nelson.

    The Pickwick Papers, Penguin Popular Classics, 1994.

Drabble, Margaret and Stringer, Jenny (eds), *The Concise Oxford Companion To English Literature*, O.U.P.,1990.

Drabble, Margaret, *A Writer's Britain*, Thames and Hudson, 1979.

Angus Wilson: A Biography, Secker and Warburg, 1995.

Dunwich Museum, *Dunwich: Time, Wind And Sea Poems 1173-1981*, Dunwich, 1983.

Dymond, David, *The Norfolk Landscape*, The Alistair Press, 1990.

Eagle, Dorothy, and Stephens, Meic, *The Oxford Literary Guide To Great Britain And Ireland* O.U.P.,1993.

Ellis, Peter, Beresford, *Rider Haggard: A Voice From The Infinite*, Routledge and Kegan Paul, 1978.

Evans, George, Ewart, *Ask The Fellows Who Cut The Hay*, Faber, 1956.

Horse In The Furrow, Faber, 1960.

Spoken History, Faber, 1987.

The Pattern Under The Plough, Faber, 1966.

The Strength of The Hills, Faber, 1983.

Farson, Daniel, *Henry Williamson: A Portrait*, Robinson Publishing, 1986.

Fitzgerald, Edward, *Letters of Edward Fitzgerald*, ed by J. M. Cohen, Centaur Press, 1960.

Fitzgerald, Penelope, *The Bookshop*, Flamingo, 1989.

Frazer, J.G., (ed), *Letters of William Cowper Vol II*, Macmillan, 1912.

Freeman, H.W., *Joseph And His Bretheren*, Boydell Press, 1983.

Gittings, Robert, *The Older Hardy*, Penguin, 1980.

Goodwyn, E.A.,& Baxter, J.C., *East Anglian Short Stories*, Boydell Press, 1977.

East Anglian Verse, Boydell Press, 1984.

Goodwyn, E.A., *East Anglian Literature*, Boydell Press, 1982.

Greene Graham (ed), *The Old School*, London, 1934.

Grigson, Geoffrey (ed) *The Faber Book of Poems And Places,* Faber and Faber, 1980.

Hadfield, John, (ed), *The Shell Guide To England*, Michael Joseph, 1970.

Haggard, Lilias, Rider, *The Cloak That I Left*, Boydell Press, 1976.

Haggard, Rider, *A Farmer's Year*, Longmans, 1906.

The Private Diaries of Sir Henry Rider Haggard, ed. by D.S.Higgins, London, 1980.

Hardwick, Michael, *A Literary Atlas of The British Isles*, David and Charles, 1973.

Harman, Claire, *Sylvia Townsend Warner: A Biography*, Chatto and Windus, 1989.

Harrod, Wilhelmine and Linnell, C.L.S., *Norfolk: A Shell Guide*, Faber 1969.

Hartley, L.P., *Eustace And Hilda: A Trilogy*, Faber Paperback, 1979.

The Go-Between, Penguin, 1958.

Higgins, Jack, *The Eagle Has Landed*, Pan, 1976.

Hill, Susan (ed) *The Spirit of Britain*, Headline, 1994.

Hillier, Bevis, *John Betjeman: A Life In Pictures*, John Murray, 1984.

Young Betjeman, John Murray, 1988.

Holroyd, Michael, *Lytton Strachey*, Vintage, 1995.

Home, Michael, *Autumn Fields*, Methuen, 1944.

Spring Sowing, Methuen, 1945.

Winter Harvest, Methuen, 1967.

Hudson, W.H., *Adventures Among Birds*, Hutchinson, 1913.

Afoot In England, The Wayfarer's Library, J.M.Dent.

James, Henry, *English Hours*, O.U.P. 1981.

James, M. R., *Collected Ghost Stories*, Wordsworth Classics, 1992.

James, P.D., *Devices And Desires*, Faber Paperback, 1990.

Unnatural Causes, Penguin, 1989.

Jasen, D.P.G., *Wodehouse: A Portrait of A Master*, Garnstone Press, 1975.

Jebb, Miles, *Suffolk,* Pimlico County History Guide, 1995.

East Anglia: An Anthology, Barrie and Jenkins, 1990.

Jerome, K. Jerome, *My Life And Times*, Hodder and Stoughton, 1926

Jocelyn of Brakeland, *Chronicle of The Abbey of Bury St Edmunds*, O.U.P., 1989.

King, James, *William Cowper: A Biography*, Duke University Press, 1986.

Kingsley, Charles, *Hereward The Wake*, Nelson.

Bibliography

Lancaster, Osbert, *All Done From Memory*, Haughton Mifflin Co, 1953.
Lea, F.A., *The Life of John Middleton Murray*, Methuen, 1959.
Lee, Hermione, (ed), *Stevie Smith: A Selection*, Faber 1983.
Long, Maureen, *The Kessingland Connection: Rider Haggard*, The Kessingland Times, 1990.
Mabey, Richard, *Food For Free*, Fontana, 1975.
    Home Country, Century, 1990.
Macbeth, George, *Poems From Oby*, Secker and Warburg, 1982.
Mann, Mary, *Tales of Victorian Norfolk*, Morrow and Co., 1992.
    The Fields of Dulditch, Boydell Press, 1976.
Mantel, Hilary, *A Change of Climate*, Penguin, 1995.
Marsh, Jan, *Edward Thomas*, Elek Books, 1978.
Martin, R.B., *With Friends Possessed: A Life of Edward Fitzgerald*, Faber, 1985.
McEwan, Ian, *The Child In Time,* Picador, 1988.
Mitchell, J.Laurence, *One Foot In The Furrow: T F. Powys In East Anglia*, The Powys
    Review No.23, 1989.
Moorman, Mary, *William Wordsworth: A Biography, The Early Years 1770-1803*, OUP 1957
Morley, Frank, *Literary Britain,* Hutchinson, 1980.
Murphy, Norman, T.P., *In Search of Blandings* , Secker and Warburg, 1986.
O'Sullivan, Timothy, *Thomas Hardy: An Illustrated Biography*, Macmillan, 1977.
Orwell, George, *Collected Essays, Journalism and Letters, Four Vols.*, ed. by Sonia Orwell
    & Ian Angus, Secker & Warburg, 1968.
    The Clergyman's Daughter, Penguin, 1990.
Osbourne, Charles, *W.H.Auden: The Life of a Poet*, Eye Methuen, 1980.
Pestell, Ronald, and Stannard, David, *Eccles-Juxta-Mare: A Lost Village Rediscovered*,
    Steeple Publishing, 1995.
Peters, Catherine, *Wilkie Collins, The King of Inventors*, Secker and Warburg, 1991.
Pevsner, Nikolaus and Racliffe Enid, *Suffolk*, Penguin, 1974.
Pevsner, Nikolaus, *North East Norfolk and Norwich*, Penguin, 1962.
    North West and South Norfolk, Penguin, 1962.
Pikoulis, J., *Alun Lewis: A Life*, Seran Books, 1985.
Plumbridge, Andrew, *The Folly of P. G. Wodehouse*, Journal of the Folly Fellowship, Vol 5,
    No.5, 1994.
Pocock, Tom, *Norfolk*, Pimlico County History Guide, 1995.
    Rider Haggard and The Lost Empire: A Biography, Weidenfeld and Nicolson, 1993.
Porter, Peter, *Collected Poems*, O.U.P. 1984.
Powell, David, *Tom Paine: The Greatest Exile*, Groom Helm, 1985.
Powys, John, Cowper, *Autobiography*, Macdonald, 1967.
    A Glastonbury Romance, Macdonald, 1955.
Price, Bernard, *Creative Landscapes*, Ebury Press, 1983.
Pudney, John, *Home and Away*, London, 1960.
Purcell, William, *Onward Christain Soldier: A Life of Sabine Baring-Gould*; Longmans,1957
Rackham, Oliver, *Trees and Woodland in the British Landscape*, J. M. Dent, 1976.
Ransome, Arthur, *Coot Club*, Jonathan Cape, 1934.
    Secret Waters, Jonathan Cape, 1939.
    We Didn't Mean to Go to Sea, Jonathan Cape, 1937.
Robertson, E. Arnot, *Ordinary Families*, Virago, 1982.
Rose, Martial, *George Borrow: A Vignette*, Dereham, 1987.
    William Cowper: A Vignette, Dereham, 1987.
Sager, Peter, *East Anglia*: Pallas Guides, Pallas Athene, 1994.
St. Aubin de Teran, Lisa, *Off The Rails : Memoirs of a Train Addict,* Sphere, 1990.
Scarfe, Norman, *Suffolk: A Shell Guide*, Faber 1965.
    The Suffolk Landscape, Hodder and Stoughton, 1972.
Selincourt, E.de, *Dorothy Wordsworth: A Biography,* Oxford Clarendon Press, 1933.
    The Letters of William and Dorothy Wordsworth: The Early Years 1787-1804, OUP 1967.
Simpson, R., *Literary Walks In Norwich.*
    Who Was Julian?, Norwich, 1994.

Shelden, Michael, *Orwell: The Authorised Biography,* Heinemann, 1991.

Smart, Elizabeth, *Necessary Secrets, Journals Vol 1*, ed. by Alice Van Wart, Toronto, 1986.

 On The Side of The Angels, Journals Vol 2, Harper Collins, 1994.

Smith, Stevie, *Collected Poems*, Penguin, 1985.

Spalding, Frances, *Vanessa Bell*, Weidenfeld and Nicolson, 1983.

Spender, Stephen, *Collected Poems 1928-85*, Faber, 1985.

 World Within World, Faber, 1977.

Stibbons, P. and Cleveland, D, *Poppyland*, Poppyland Publishing, 1990.

Srachey, Lytton, *Lytton Strachey by Himself*, ed. by M.Holroyd, Heinemann, 1971.

Style Associates Ltd., *Anna Sewell Country*, Norwich, 1990.

Sullivan, Rosemary, *By Heart: The Life of Elizabeth Smart*, Flamingo, 1992.

Theroux, Paul, *The Kingdom by the Sea*, Penguin, 1984.

Thomas, Edward, *A Literary Pilgrim in England*, O.U.P., 1980.

Thomas, Edward, *Letters from Edward Thomas to Gordon Bottomley*, ed by R G Thomas, O.U.P., 1968.

Thorn, Michael, *Tennyson*, Little Brown and Co., 1992.

Thwaite, Anthony, *Poems 1953-1988*, Hutchinson, 1989.

 The Dust of The World, Sinclair-Stevenson, 1994.

Tolhurst, Peter, *Thetford in Ruins*, 1990.

Tomalin, Ruth, *W. H. Hudson: A Biography*, O.U.P. 1984,

Trehune, Alfred Mckinley, *The Life of Edward Fitzgerald*, O.U.P., 1947.

Warner, Oliver, *Captain Marryat: A Resdiscovery*, Constable, 1953.

Warner, Sylvia Townsend, *Collected Poems*, ed. by Claire Harman, Carcanet New Press,1982

 Diaries, ed. by Claire Harman, Chatto and Windus, 1994.

 Letters, ed. by William Maxwell, Chatto and Windus, 1982.

 The Cat's Cradle Book, Chatto and Windus, 1960.

 The Corner That Held Them, Virago, 1993.

 The Flint Anchor, Chatto and Windus, 1954.

 The True Heart, Virago, 1981.

Waters, W.G., *Norfolk in Literature*, Jarrolds, 1923.

Wesker, Arnold, *As Much as I Dare*, Century, 1994.

 The Wesker Trilogy, Penguin Books, 1979.

Wickett, William, & Duval, Nicholas, *The Farmer's Boy*, Terence Dalton , 1971.

Williams, Gareth, *Writers of Wales: George Ewart Evans,* University of Wales Press, 1991.

Williamson, Anne, *Henry Williamson , Tarka and The Last Romantic*, Alan Sutton, 1995.

Williamson, Henry, *The Story of a Norfolk Farm,* Faber, 1941.

Williamson, Audrey, *Thomas Paine: His Life, Work and Times,* Allen and Unwin, 1973.

Wilson, Angus, (ed), *East Anglia in Verse*, Penguin Books, 1982.

 Writers of East Anglia, Secker and Warburg, 1977.

 The Wild Garden, Secker and Warburg, 1963.

Wodehouse, P.G., *Very Good Jeeves*, Penguin, 1983.

Woodforde, James, *A Country Parson, James Woodforde's Diaries 1759-1802*: Tiger Books, 1991.

Woolf Virginia, *The Question of Things Happening: The Letters of Virginia Woolf, Vol 2, 1912 -1922,* ed. by N. Nicholson, Hogarth Press, 1976.

 A Passionate Apprentice: The Early Journals, Hogarth Press, 1990.

 The Captain's Death Bed, The Hogarth Press, 1950.

 The Common Reader, Hogarth Press, 1925.

 The Complete Shorter Fiction of Virginia Woolf, ed by S. Dick, Hogarth Press, 1985.

 The Flight of the Mind: The Letters of Virginia Woolf: Vol 1, 1882-1912, ed. by N.Nicholson, Hogarth Press, 1975.